STUDIO ANYWHERE 2
HARD LIGHT

A Photographer's Guide
to Shaping Hard Light

NICK FANCHER

STUDIO ANYWHERE 2: HARD LIGHT
A Photographer's Guide to Shaping Hard Light
Nick Fancher
nickfancher.com

Project editor: Ted Waitt
Project manager: Lisa Brazieal
Marketing manager: Jessica Tiernan
Editor: Linda Laflamme
Layout and type, original edition: Holly Beal Malone
Layout and type, updated edition: Kim Scott, Bumpy Design
Cover design: Kim Scott, Bumpy Design
Proofreader: Aaron Taylor

ISBN: 978-1-68198-226-7
1st Edition (1st printing, January 2017)
© 2017 Nick Fancher
All images © Nick Fancher unless otherwise noted

Rocky Nook Inc.
1010 B Street, Suite 350
San Rafael, CA 94901
USA

www.rockynook.com

Distributed in the U.S. by Ingram Publisher Services
Distributed in the UK and Europe by Publishers Group UK

Library of Congress Control Number: 2016950965

This book is printed on acid-free paper.
Printed in China

This book is dedicated to those who won't let obstacles stand in the way of their dreams. Keep pushing and fighting, ignoring the haters. Don't look back, and never stop learning.

ACKNOWLEDGEMENTS

I'd like to begin by acknowledging Valerie Witte and the folks at Peachpit Press who green-lit this project from the beginning. Sadly, due to layoffs at Pearson, of which whom Peachpit is a subsidiary, the project was nixed. I'd like to thank Ted Waitt at Rocky Nook for seamlessly transitioning the project from draft to print.

I couldn't have done it without the support of my wife Beth. I also need to call out Linda Laflamme, my editor, Holly Beal Malone, my designer, and Aaron Taylor, my proofreader, for helping me on this book, as well as Kim Scott at Bumpy Design and Lisa Brazieal, the Project Manager at Rocky Nook. You added a wonderful polish to this project.

Finally, thank you to all the readers of *Studio Anywhere*. Your enthusiasm around the book has exceeded my expectations. Continue to tag your images #studioanywhere so I can see what you're up to. It really makes all of this worthwhile.

—Nick

CONTENTS

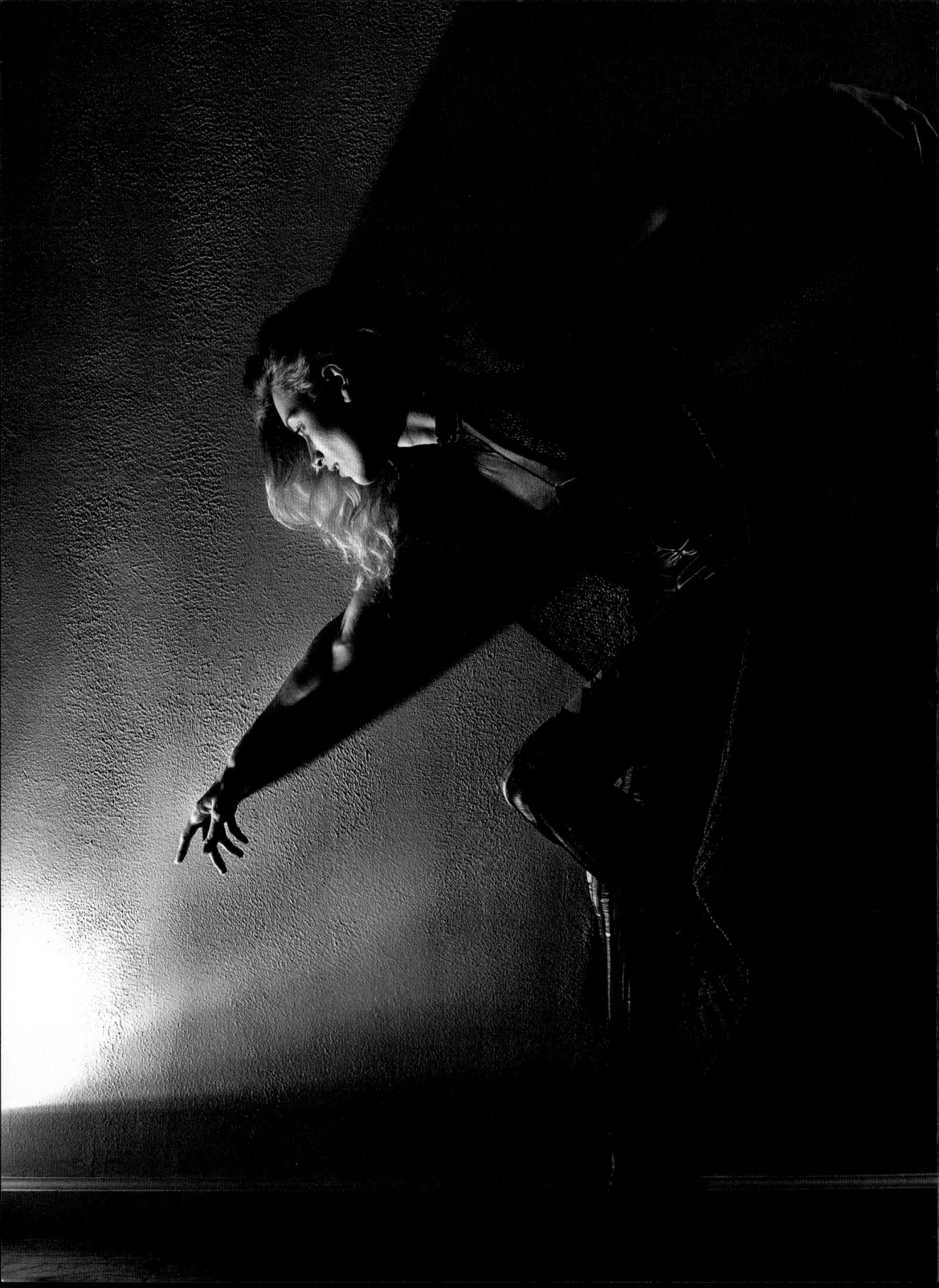

INTRODUCTION

WHY HARD LIGHT?

First off, let me preface by stating what this book is *not*. This book is not strictly hard light scenarios. Though it is mainly focused on scenarios using hard light, this book does include a few scenarios that involve mixing in a soft light source or softening an otherwise hard light source, so don't email to inform me of this "oversight." Secondly, this book isn't a manual. As a matter of fact, I rarely even read manuals. Even Ikea instruction manuals, which are chock full of helpful illustrations, barely get a glance from me. I'd rather dive right in and figure it out as I go. What this book is, however, is a compilation of techniques, hacks, and tips that I've figured out or picked up over the years that build upon the techniques discussed in my previous book.

The main reason I rarely read manuals is that I am extremely impatient. Whenever I am buying a new piece of gear, it's because I have thought about it and worked up to it for a while, so by the time the package arrives in the mail, the last thing I want to do is sit and read about it. I tear open the packaging, load up the batteries, and start shooting. Many times this results in my failure; I miss some important feature or do things out of order and have to backtrack. This haphazard manner of working isn't for everyone, but it allows me to figure things out in my own way and to discover some wonderful, unconventional ways of doing things.

Nor is this book a glorified list of a bunch of gear you need to buy, which you may not be able to afford anyway, and it's not meant to be an exhaustive guide to hard light, either.

Instead, I envision *Studio Anywhere 2* to be what I would have wanted to be included in the packaging when I bought my first flashgun: part manual, part compilation of ideas and techniques that has taken years to develop and perfect. The techniques in this book are predominantly for hard-light scenarios—i.e., scenarios lit with harsh, unmodified light. But this book is about more than that. It's also about how to manipulate, soften, and all-around shape light from an unmodified flashgun. Think about it: If all you needed to light any given scenario was one or two flashguns with few to no modifiers, you wouldn't need a team of assistants and thousands of dollars worth of lights and light modifiers to make the shot. Sound good? Keep reading.

HARD VERSUS SOFT

Preferences are subjective. Especially when it comes to the needs of a client. One client loves candid, on-the-fly shots while another prefers more polished, composed images. One Creative Director prefers natural light while their predecessor was only pleased with studio lighting. What I've learned to do is not get too comfortable in one particular niche of the industry and not take it personal if a client changes their mind after seeing my images mid-shoot. Maybe at first they thought that they wanted hard light, but after the shoot begins, they start asking for me to minimize shadows, and by the end of the shoot, I may end up firing a softbox through a scrim (FYI, that means extra, extra, extra soft light).

One of my regular clients is Jeni's Splendid Ice Creams, a high-end ice cream boutique that started in Columbus, Ohio, over 10 years ago but has expanded across the country. They brought me on to help elevate their brand through photography. They showed me images of what they've been producing—which was really solid, beautiful work—but expressed a desire to start pushing in a new direction. They really liked my vibrant colors and hard shadows and thought we'd make a great team. They were right. But every shoot doesn't consist of me just winging it, lighting according to the mood I'm in that day. I've learned that sometimes they still do want beautiful, soft light. So for the sake of time, money, and ice cream, I've learned to sometimes give them both soft and hard options for the same setup.

In **Figure I.1** you can see my setup. I have an unmodified flash on a stand to the left, giving me hard light. I am also using the Jeni's studio Paul C. Buff Einstein light, seen on the right, modified with a softbox to give me soft light. **Figure I.2** is the hard light image. Note the presence of the hard, black shadows and how they take up space between the products, leaving less blue space. The shadows actually become a style element in the image. In contrast, the soft light image in **Figure I.3** is almost shadowless. This results in more of the blue backdrop occupying real estate in the final image. I actually prefer the hard light image. How about you?

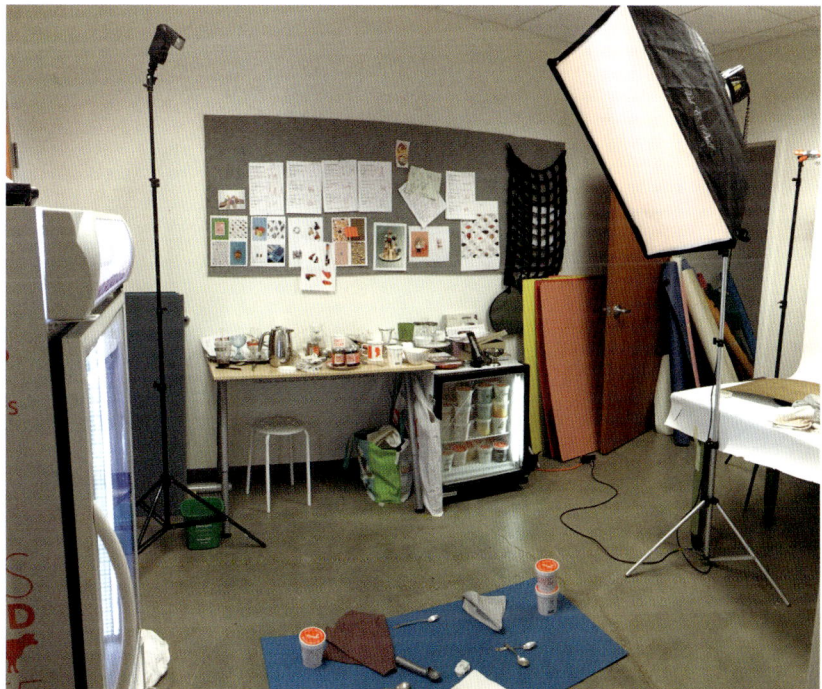

Figure I.1 This setup was for a Jeni's Ice Cream product shoot. I was providing them with both a hard light (light on the left) and a soft light (light on the right) option for each image.

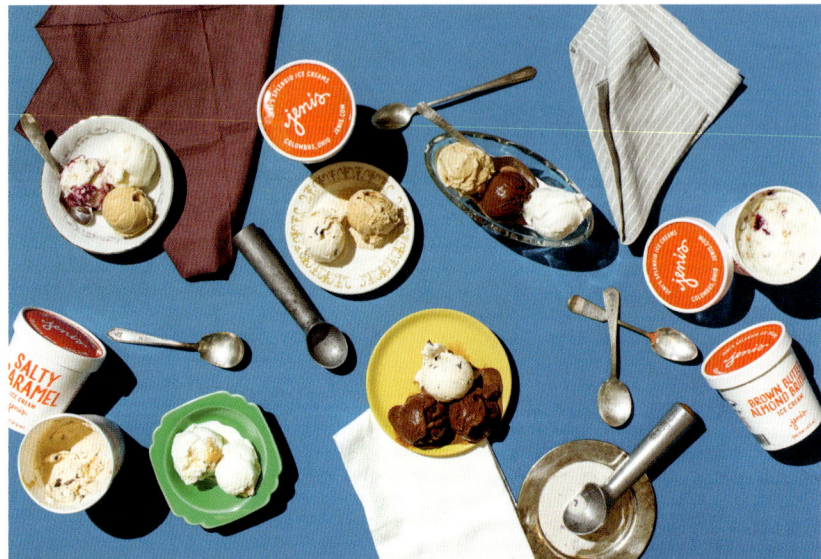

Figure I.2 The hard light shot. The presence of hard shadows adds another element to the image, lessening the blue space between objects and creating a fuller image.

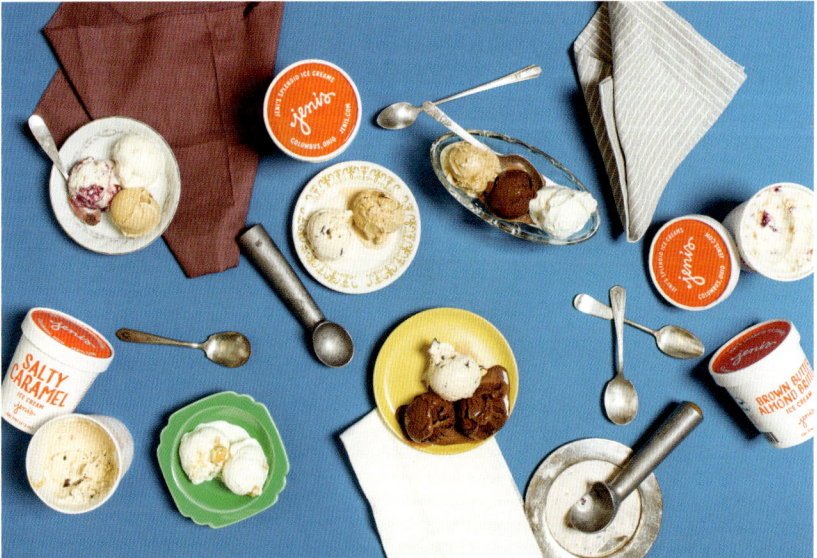

Figure I.3 The soft light shot. The shadows are softer and even non-existent in some spots, leaving more space for the blue background.

THE GREAT LIGHT HYPE

Broncolor or Profoto? Fender or Gibson? Lamborghini or Ferrari? Which toy/software/high-end piece of gear is the best so that I can do exactly what my favorite photographer is able to do?

This is a mentality that many photographers, musicians, and hobbyists share. Yes, high-end gear is nice. Both Profoto and Broncolor lights will provide you with quality light at a high output with which to light agency-represented models in couture clothing. But how often is that caliber of gear actually needed? The question should not be, "Which expensive, high-end lighting rig should I buy?" Rather, it should be, "Have I yet reached the limitations of my current gear?"

I've been asked why I opt for such a minimal or even anti-gear approach to photography, while other photographers laud gear upgrades. Well, it's not a choice made by moral reasons or even necessity; it's one of preference. I like traveling light and working alone. A big gear kit requires help to haul it, room to store it, and money to fund it. No thank you. This was not a decision that I came to overnight, but one that was forged through years of working with the only gear I could afford.

When I first launched my business in 2007, all I had in terms of gear was a Canon 20D, one 430 EX flashgun (which didn't have a port for a transmitter, so I couldn't use it off-camera), a piece of junk 18–55mm f/3.5–5.6 kit lens, and a Sigma 70–200mm f/2.8 lens (without image stabilization). Let's say, for example, that I wanted to get an off-camera flash shot. I would put my camera on a tripod and do a long exposure, walking over to the subject and manually popping the flash (think light painting). It was far from ideal, but I sure learned the limitations of my gear. It also gave me plenty of time to think about what piece of gear I needed next.

If your eyes don't work well, everything that you look at will appear out of focus or hazy. So it goes with camera lenses. Upgrading my glass, I decided, would need to come first. I shelved my kit lens in favor of a (used) 24–70L. Now I was in business. My image quality improved considerably. The next step was getting a couple (affordable) flashes with triggers, so I wasn't running around, flash in hand, hoping it would be dark enough for me to do a long exposure. I opted for the LumoPro LP160 flash unit, purchasing two, along with three PocketWizard wireless remote triggers. The whole transaction set me back $600, which was a big number for me at the time.

Getting reliable light and a quality image enabled me to realize that my camera sensor—a cropped 8-megapixel sensor—just wasn't giving me what I needed. Even with good light and good glass, my camera wasn't up to snuff with other, more current bodies on the market. However, I still couldn't afford the Canon 5DII, which had just hit the scene. I got a 40D instead. Although the sensor was still cropped, the quality was a bit better, and because I was taking on more paid photo gigs, I needed more reliable gear—not to mention a second camera body, so I'd have a backup if one failed.

Seven years later, I now have the ideal gear setup, but it's not identical to the setup of any other photographer. It's completely mine, unique to my needs. If I had simply used a $10,000 credit line when I first launched my business and bought a bunch of gear that other people said were "must haves," I would've cheated myself out of the learning process. My shooting and lighting process is now different than any other photographer's because it had time to evolve and grow. Through this learning process, I have found that I need only two (prime) lenses and I prefer to use flashguns to studio strobes. On the rare occasion that I am shooting tight interiors, I'll rent a 16–35mm lens, or if I am shooting small product, such as jewelry, I'll rent a 100mm macro lens, and add the rental costs to the client's bill.

Don't get me wrong. Studio strobe systems, such as Profoto, are fantastic—a luxury but not, I dare say, a necessity. They provide a consistent (high) output and color temperature. If I were strictly shooting in the studio, a Profoto system would be perfect—I even owned one for about a year. Once I was making enough money in my business to afford one, I bought a used Acute2 pack with two heads, excited about the increase in power I would have. I was excited to shoot portraits in full daylight, eclipsing the sun with my output. The problem was not only did I need a 10-pound battery pack to accompany the already 25-pound light kit, but my lights were also tethered to the pack. The farthest each light could be moved from the pack was about 10 feet on either side, without getting power cord extensions, which would mean more money and more weight. Additionally, there were cords running everywhere and I needed an assistant to help lug the massive gear kit which, with light stands and sand bags, was well over 100 pounds (before adding in the weight of my camera and lenses). This meant booking an assistant, which meant even more money and planning and less spontaneity—no more running and gunning, which is how I prefer to roll.

After realizing this large light system was actually handicapping me, I sold the gear and bought some used Canon 430EX Speedlites with RadioPopper wireless triggers, which allowed me to use high-speed sync (HSS). This was the mobile answer to eclipsing full sunlight, and now I was running and gunning again. Having flashguns rather than studio strobes allowed me to place them anywhere and easily reposition them so I could quickly dial in the lighting for a shot.

In the time that's passed since I last owned a Profoto system, the company has released the more portable B1 and B2 systems. The B1, a 500-watt head, has the battery right in the head, while the B2, a 250-watt light, has a smaller, flash-sized head with a battery pack attached by a cord. For the sake of better knowing my options when it comes to portable light, I did a comparison between the Profoto B1 and the Cactus RF60 flash (**Figure I.4**).

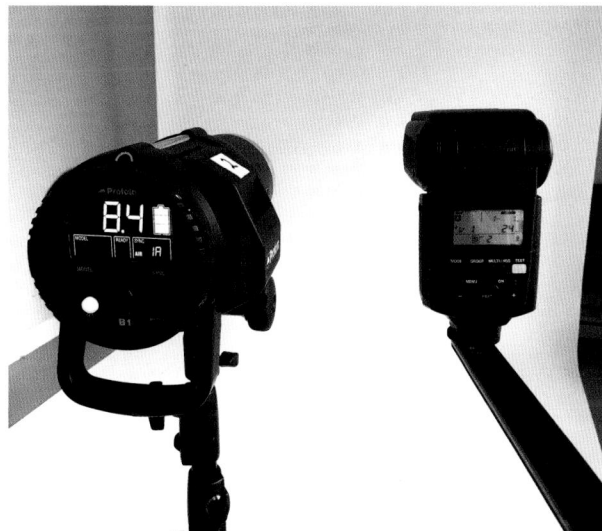

Figure I.4 I wanted to know my options when it came to portable lights, so I tested the Profoto B1 against a Cactus RF60.

Although the Profoto lights have a higher output and a longer lasting battery, I still prefer the Cactus flashes, for several reasons. First, the size. For every B1 I put in a camera case, I could take four Cactus flashes. Second, the light and shadow quality. In **Figure I.5** you can see the straight out of the camera (SOOC) file from the Profoto—nice light but soft shadows. Compare it with the cold, crisp shadows in **Figure I.6**, which was lit with the Cactus flashes. If hard light is what I'm going for, the victor is clear.

The one thing I'll point out is that the light spread of the Cactus flashes isn't as broad as the Profoto—even at 24mm. Also, when the Cactus is at full power, it's equivalent to the Profoto firing at 8.4, approximately. As you can likely guess, especially if you've shot with flashes much, you can't shoot with them at full power much at all without getting a ton of misfires. I prefer to keep my output at 1/4 power or lower to keep a fast refresh time. This isn't usually a big deal, especially when shooting indoors, because I can bump up my ISO a bit to allow for a smaller aperture without losing image quality. It only becomes an issue when you have a lot of ambient light that you need to overpower. That's when having the more powerful Profotos woud make your job much easier.

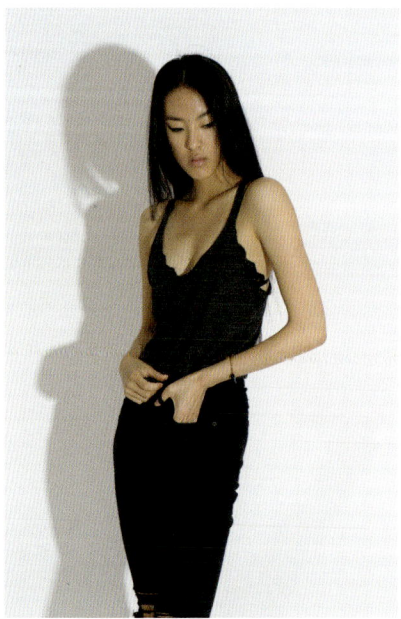 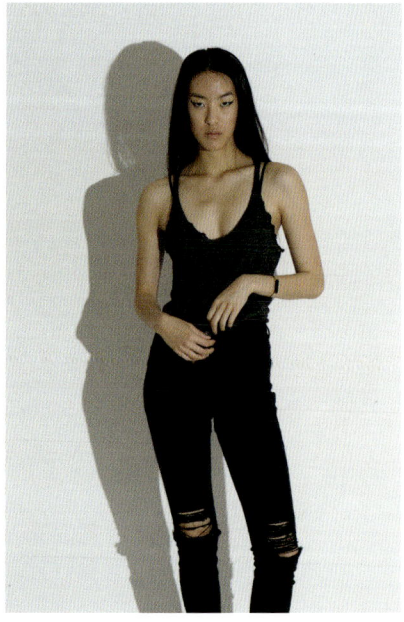

Figure I.5 This is the SOOC file that was lit with the Profoto. The light is nice but the shadows are soft.

Figure I.6 This is the SOOC file that was lit with the Cactus. Cold, crisp shadows.

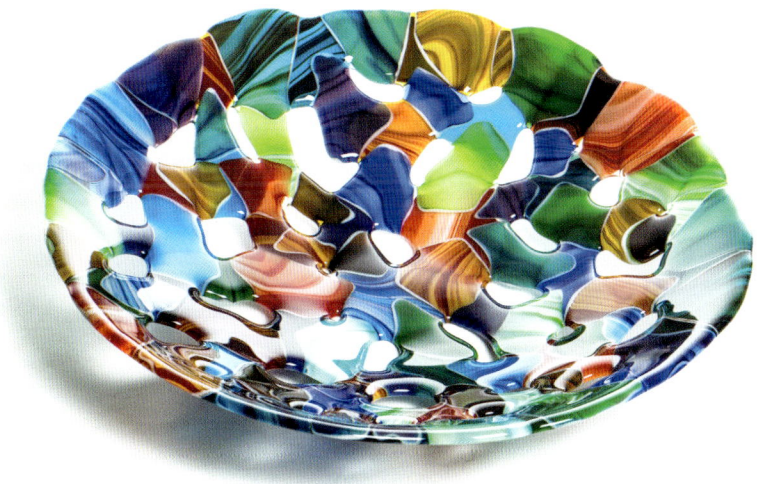

Figure I.7 This product shot was lit with three flashguns at 1/4 power, rather than studio strobes. By using a slightly higher ISO of 320, I was able to shoot at f/13, getting a sharp image.

Let's imagine that you are doing a shoot indoors with flashes and need a good amount of depth of field, meaning you need a smaller aperture. For example, I was recently shooting glass products on a white sweep, as you can see in **Figure I.7**. I had three flashes (two on the background and one into an umbrella on the product) all set to 1/4 power. By bumping up my ISO to 320 I was able to set my aperture at f/13, which allowed a deep depth of field. If I had needed an even smaller aperture, I would have felt comfortable going up to ISO 640 or even 800 with the 5DIII without losing image quality.

More often than needing more power when shooting product, I find myself needing smaller outputs, such as when I'm shooting with a large aperture in order to have a shallow depth of field in my shot. With flashes, I can easily dial down the power to 1/64 or even 1/128 in order to shoot at f/1.8, for example. If I were using studio strobes and wanted that large of an aperture, it'd be far more difficult. Even with the power pack dialed all the way down, I'd need to use a bleed light, which means plugging in an extra, unused light into my pack in order to pull additional power away from my light. My only other option would be to use a neutral density filter, which can result in a loss of image quality.

SMOKE AND MIRRORS

Occasionally, using this minimal setup on larger shoots has bit me in the ass. Earlier this year I was doing a two-day commercial shoot for a national ad campaign for a big client. It was one of those situations where the client knew just enough to be dangerous but not enough to trust me. My contact looked at my minimal rig and said, "The last photographer had more lights. Tomorrow can you bring more lights?" I should've said, "But mine go up to 11."

The problem was not sufficient firepower, but rather proper client-photographer communication. I was shooting based on my typical workflow, which the client was unfamiliar with. Part of my workflow was to supply straight-out-of-the-camera, small-resolution proofs immediately following the shoot, in order for the client to make selections for retouching. My contact for the client at the shoot was extremely happy with the images at the end of the first day, but when he forwarded the proofs to his boss late that evening, the response was less enthusiastic. The complaint was that the images were far too small and dark for print.

This was when my contact asked me to bring more lights to the second day of the shoot, as the previous photographer had done. He went on to explain that the previous photographer shot everything for $1000 and just gave them the raw files to edit. I did my best to not balk at this idea. I attempted to explain that I could light the images any way they liked and that they were looking at the preliminary, unedited proofs. They still weren't convinced. Finally, I color graded one image from each scenario and sent them over, side by side with the original, to show how the final image would look. After seeing that the polished, final images weren't, in fact, 800 pixels long and really dark, they relaxed a bit. Needless to say, at the end of day two, I made sure to throw a quick preset on all the proofs to brighten them up, before sending them over to the client.

After that interaction, the industry stories I'd been hearing started to make sense: photographers bringing a whole van full of lighting gear on high-budget shoots, knowing full well that they wouldn't use most of it. Appearance, the theory goes, is everything. If the client is paying you big bucks, the client expects to see a big production.

I find this charade to be as cumbersome as it is deceptive, but I suppose that some people aren't yet ready for change. Times are changing, nonetheless, whether the dinosaurs like it or not. It won't be long before whole campaigns are shot with nothing more than a smartphone. But until then, on larger-budget shoots, I now play the part, renting out a large studio with large strobes to more effectively cater to clients' large expectations.

DEMYSTIFYING LIGHT

This fixation on gear isn't limited to just clients. Whenever I look at images in the small flash, or strobist, communities, whether on Flickr, 500px, or elsewhere, I get frustrated. Why? Because I see a parade of similar images all rationalized by the same faulty explanations. Thus-and-such gear, the photographers argue, was used and needed to produce this image (which is often of an amateur model, looking more uncomfortable than beautifully lit). I see images created with the discussion focused on how many lights and modifiers were used—images that were lit with five or even seven strobes, when only two or three were needed—which I attribute to photographers not fully understanding the limitations of their gear (the more-is-more mentality), which I illustrated in **Figure I.8**. I often see poorly placed lights that create an unflattering or harsh look, even with a softening modifier like a softbox or umbrella. I see images taken by photographers who seem to be accepting "good enough" images and lighting rather than pushing themselves toward "great." My hope is that after reading this book, you can tell me why you used two lights instead of one or why you shot from an elevated perspective instead of from head-on. I want you to be able to separate yourself from the shoot to see the image objectively.

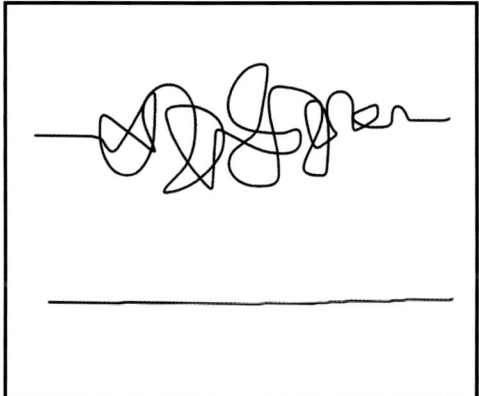

Figure I.8 This illustration depicts how I see many photographers overcomplicating their lighting setups (top) as opposed to how simple they could be (bottom).

I often tell my students that if tweaking the lighting is getting in the way of a shoot, it's time to turn off the lights and shoot with available light. Can't figure out why your new strobe is misfiring? Troubleshoot it later. Turn off the transmitter, change your exposure, and go ambient, shooting with what you know.

Don't fuss with your lights. Focus on putting your subject at ease. Talk to her. Ask her what she's been up to earlier that day or what she's doing later on, after the shoot. Casually snap some frames as you talk. Tell her that you're just getting your exposure and lighting worked out. Often, you get some nice candid shots during this time. Once you're ready to start, shoot for 30 to 60 seconds and review a few images (don't bounce around checking things like a chimp after each frame). Is the lighting looking good or does it need to be adjusted? Make the changes and then shoot for 30 to 60 more seconds. Once you get the lighting nailed down, flip through and find a good shot to show her. It'll help put her at ease and give her a little boost of confidence. Or maybe she'll see that she wants to change her posture or expression. Either way, it's helpful to do this before proceeding, and can save you the need for a re-shoot.

Once you're dialed in, turn off the technical side of your brain. Focus solely on watching her move and directing her accordingly. Try shooting with both of your eyes open, rather than squinting through the viewfinder. Stay in the moment with her. It helps to have music on that matches the vibe of the shoot, quietly in the background. Don't rush through it, if possible. You'll be able to tell when your window has closed and she is ready to be done with the shoot.

That said, If you're just getting started, start by doing a trade shoot, working with an equally inexperienced subject, so you can take the time to figure out your new gear in a low-pressure situation. By the time you're working with paying clients, your lighting knowledge needs to be second nature, so your attention can be on them.

One thing I've learned recently is to shoot for one or two more minutes than I think I need. When I was first getting my lighting skills worked out, if I got the light anywhere close to decent, I would be thrilled and move on. But I was forgetting to look at the poses and subject expressions. I was only looking at my lighting and was missing out on possibly getting better moments out of my subject.

TRAVELING LIGHT

Ditching extraneous gear pays dividends when you're traveling, as well—and not only the ones you might expect. Suppose you're booked for a photo shoot in a foreign country. Because you're not allowed to be in a foreign country to conduct work without a work permit, you have two options. You can get a work permit, which takes time and money, or you can do what I do: travel with a minimal gear kit to avoid suspicion. Not only is it easier and cheaper to do it on the sly, but traveling light (pun mildly intended) also helps you avoid checking bags. I've shot in Brazil, Japan, Tanzania, Jordan, and Iceland, and not once needed to check a bag. By knowing the full potential of my gear, I can enter any scenario with confidence that I can get the shot. In **Figure I.9**, for example, by zooming in my flash to 105mm and powering it up to 1/1, I had enough light output to back the light off the bride and groom. Doing so allowed the light to spread and illuminate them from head to toe, while I was still able to shoot at f/8, bringing back detail in the sky, thus adding a bit more drama to the already dramatic Icelandic landscape.

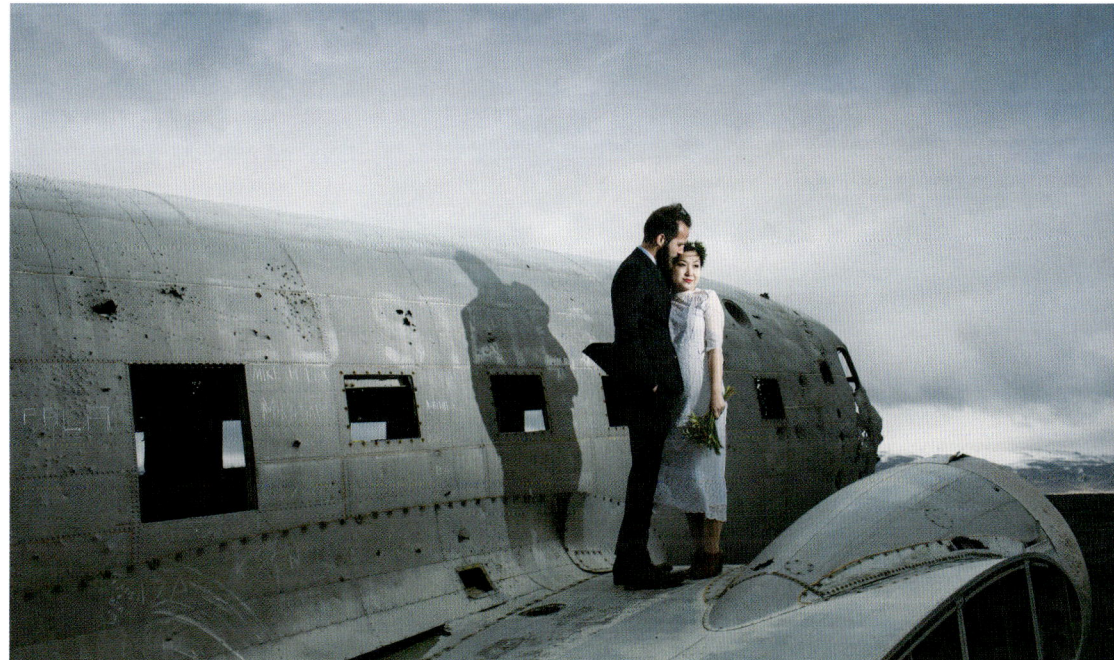

Figure I.9 I lit this Icelandic wedding portrait with one unmodified flashgun. By traveling with minimal gear, I am able to avoid checking bags or raising eyebrows.

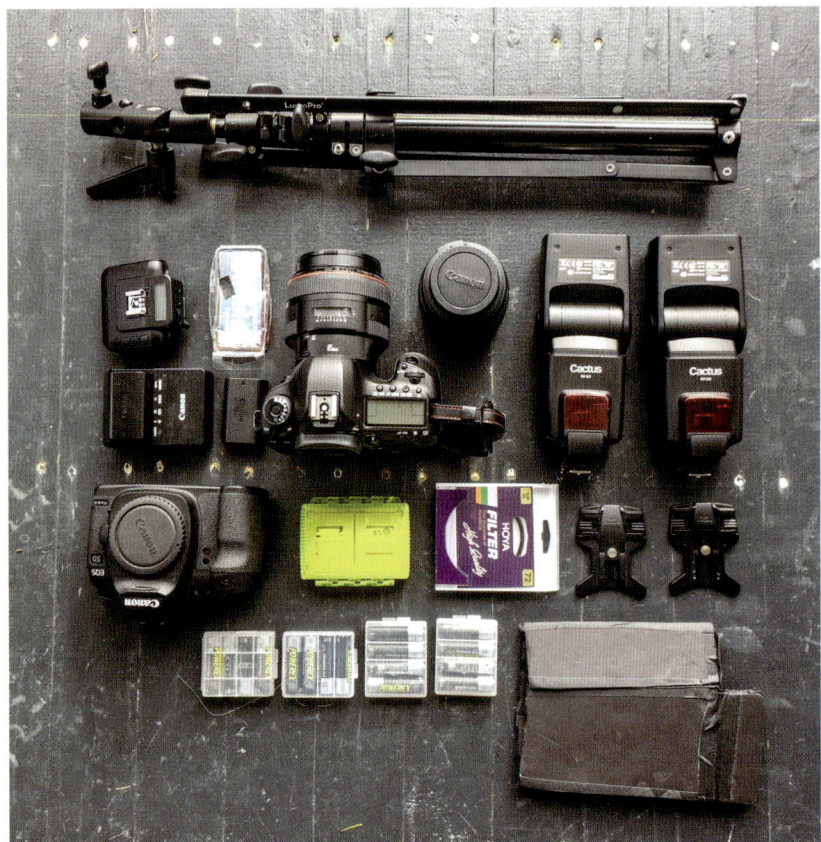

Figure I.10 This is my travel kit. It includes a Canon 5DIII body, a backup 5DII body, Canon 85 f/1.2LII and 35 f/1.4L lenses, two Cactus RF60 flashes and transmitter, several packs of Powerex AA batteries, memory cards, a gel kit, DIY barn doors, a star filter, and light stand. I can even squeeze my 13-inch MacBook Pro in there.

Airlines allow you to have one carry-on and one personal item, like a computer bag—which means essentially two bags. All the gear I need fits neatly into my Lowepro Flipside 300 bag (**Figures I.10** through **I.12**). Typically, I pack two camera bodies, two prime lenses, two flashes, memory cards, several sets of AA batteries, and my 13-inch MacBook Pro. For all intents and purposes, the Flipside is my computer bag. Then I fit in a compact light stand (I use a LumoPro LP605, which is 19 inches long but expands to 7.5 feet) and sometimes an umbrella, along with my clothing and toiletries, into a duffle bag.

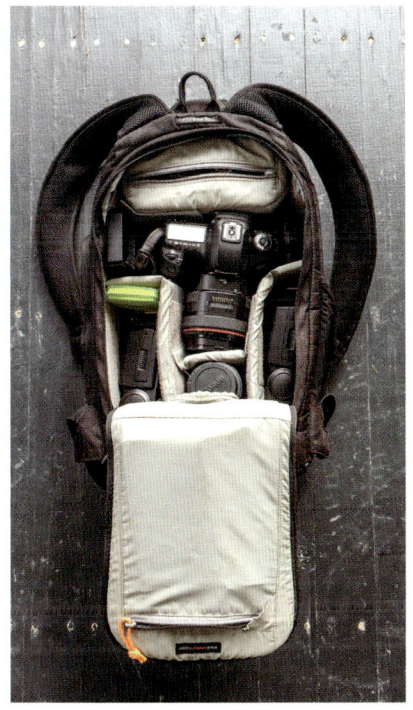

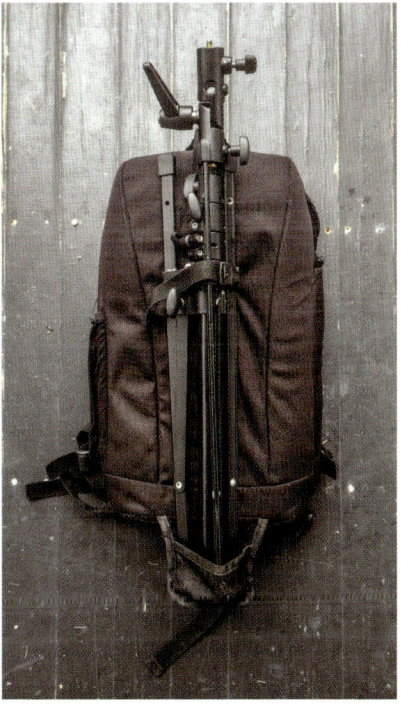

Figure I.11 All my gear fits neatly into a Lowepro Flipside 300 bag, which easily stows in any airline overhead compartment.

Figure I.12 My pack is locked and loaded for run-and-gun photography.

For my trip to Tanzania, I needed one more piece of gear. During my time there, I conducted two half-day Help-Portrait events. At these charitable events, photographers donate their time and often work with makeup and hair stylists to provide free, quality portraits for those who couldn't otherwise afford or even have access to these services. This time, I was working alone with no team to help me nor any local print labs to accommodate my needs. I needed to print on location, so I brought a Canon Selphy printer, which prints borderless, archival 4x6-inch prints in one minute, along with enough ink, paper, and envelopes for 300 portraits. (I still didn't need to check a bag.)

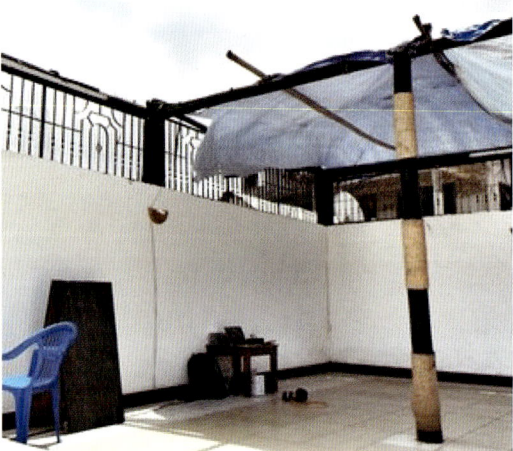

Figure I.13 During my time in Tanzania, I put on two Help-Portrait events. This was my setup on the first day.

My first session was held in a roofless church near an abandoned rock quarry, where the poorest of the region lived and worked (**Figures I.13** and **I.14**). The church's thatched roof had recently burned in a lightning storm, and the only shelter from the scorching sun that we had was under a tattered tarp that covered about ten feet of the corner of the space. That's exactly where I set up my laptop and printer and where I conducted the shoot. I didn't even need to light it, because light was so soft under the tarp. Plus, the bright sun was bouncing off the tile floor about five feet from the subjects, which made for a fantastic catch light in their eyes.

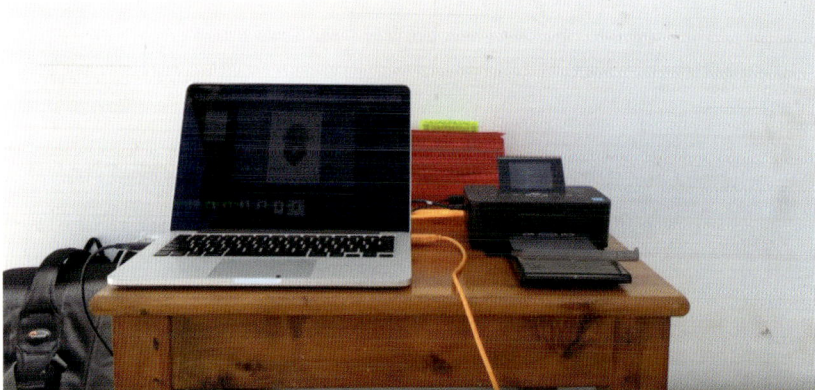

Figure I.14 All I needed was a power source. I shot tethered to Adobe Lightroom, applying a custom preset to each image as it imported. I printed borderless 4x6-inch prints, using a Canon Selphy printer.

I brought a 15-foot TetherPro cable with me and shot tethered to Adobe Lightroom. (I've since switched to using CaptureOne when shooting tethered—less crashing.) Lightroom was set up so that it would apply a custom preset, color grading each image, before printing it out. I had an eight-year-old assistant tearing the tabs off the prints and putting them in an envelope for the waiting subjects. We didn't even need to advertise what we were doing, because after we photographed the first wave of curious bystanders, they went home with their prints in hand and quickly returned with their friends and family who wanted ones of their own. See **Figures I.15** and **I.16**.

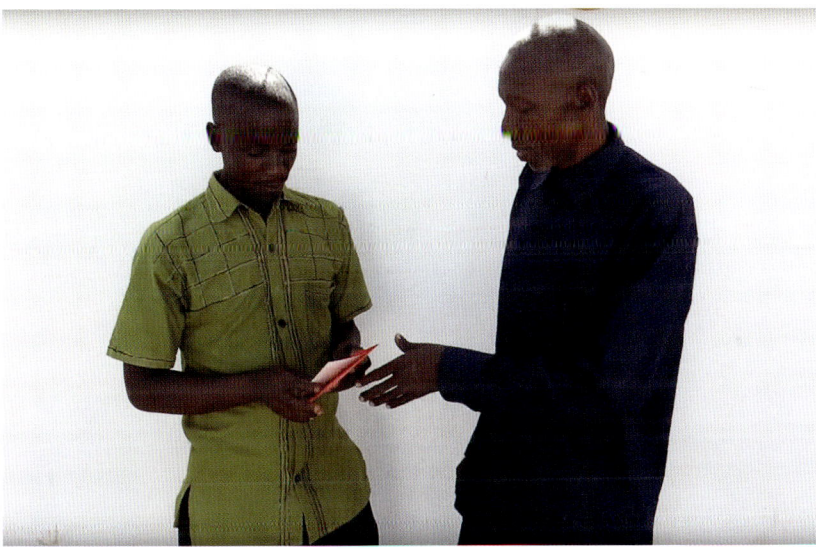

Figure I.15 I'm not sure who got more out of the portraits—the subjects or me.

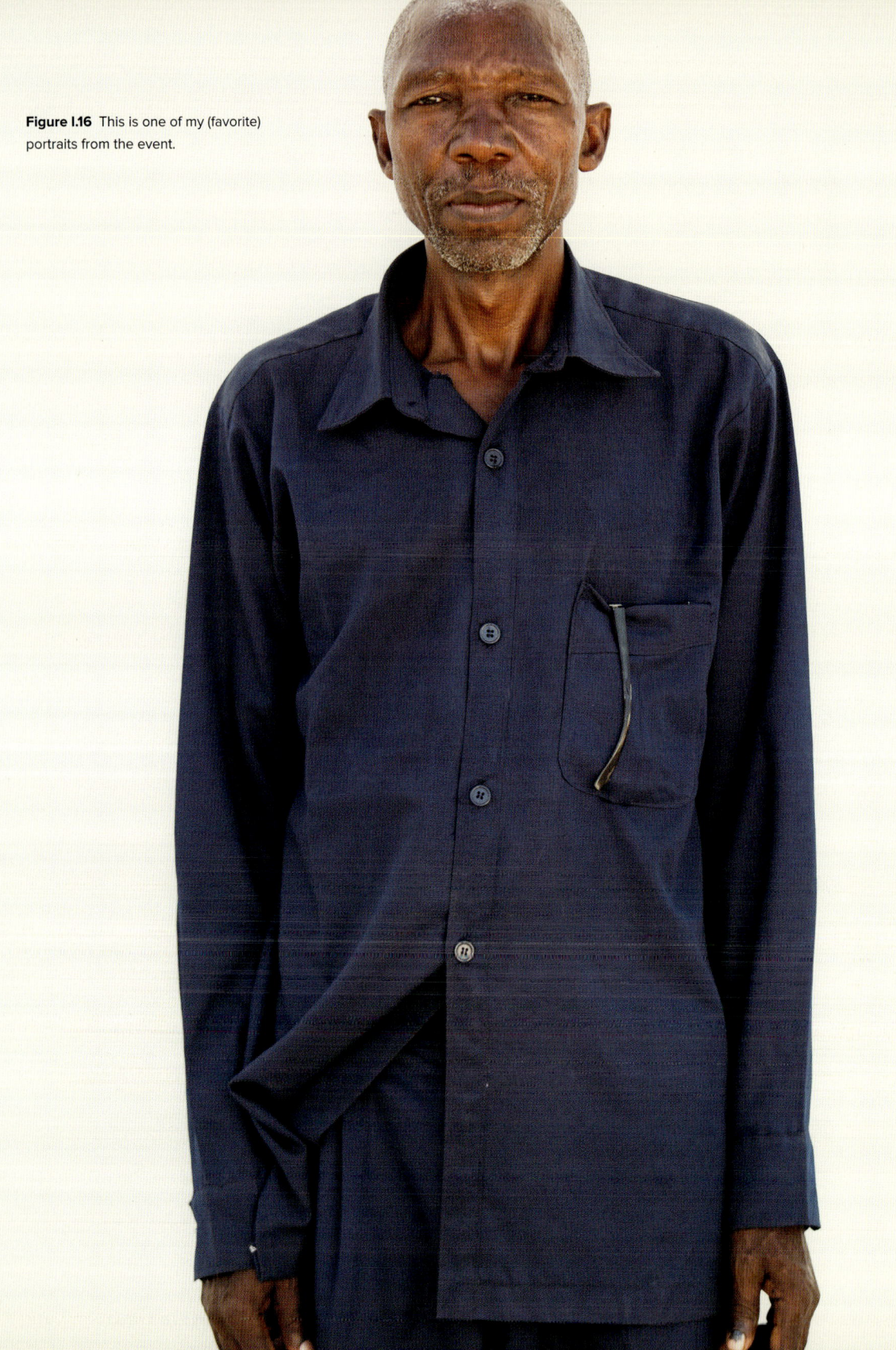

Figure I.16 This is one of my (favorite) portraits from the event.

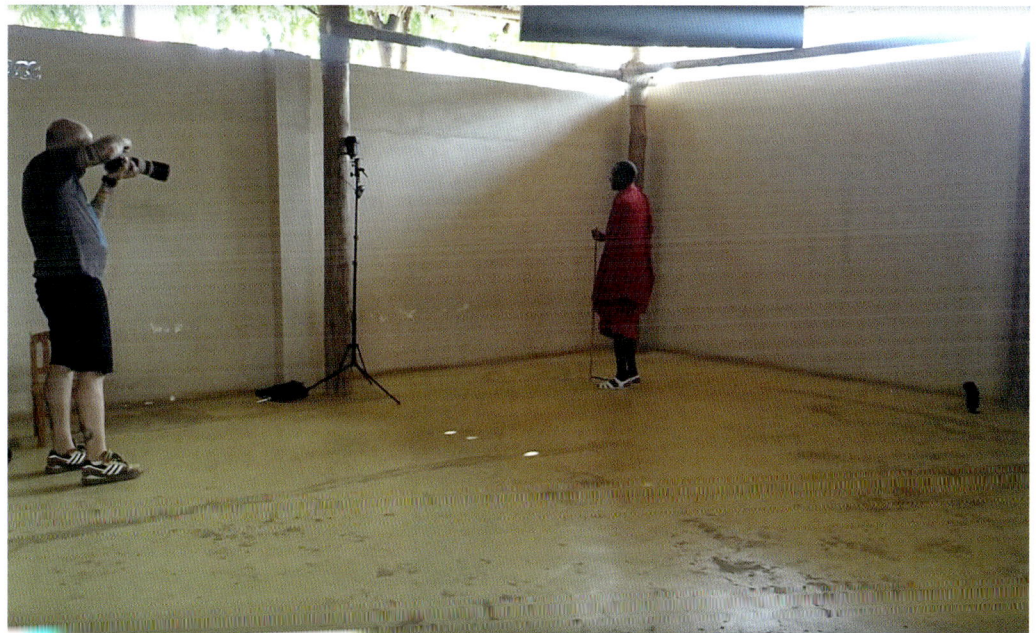

Figure I.17 The second Help-Portrait event was held a few days later in a school. The room was much darker, so I used my two flashes to light these portraits. The main light was bounced off the wall to the left of the subjects, and the background light was bounced off the back wall to the right of them.

The second Help-Portrait session was held a few days later in a school. This allowed me to work with a totally different group of people than those from the quarry. It was in a darker room, so I needed to light it this time. Even though I had traveled with an umbrella, I didn't even need it. As you can see in **Figure I.17**, I bounced the main light off of a cream-colored wall, which made for a larger light source than an umbrella could produce. I also had a background light, flanked into the back wall. **Figure I.18** is considerably more dramatic than the soft-light portraits of the first day, but feels just as polished. As you can see in **Figure I.19**, the Maasai guard, who had never before been photographed, was pleased with the result.

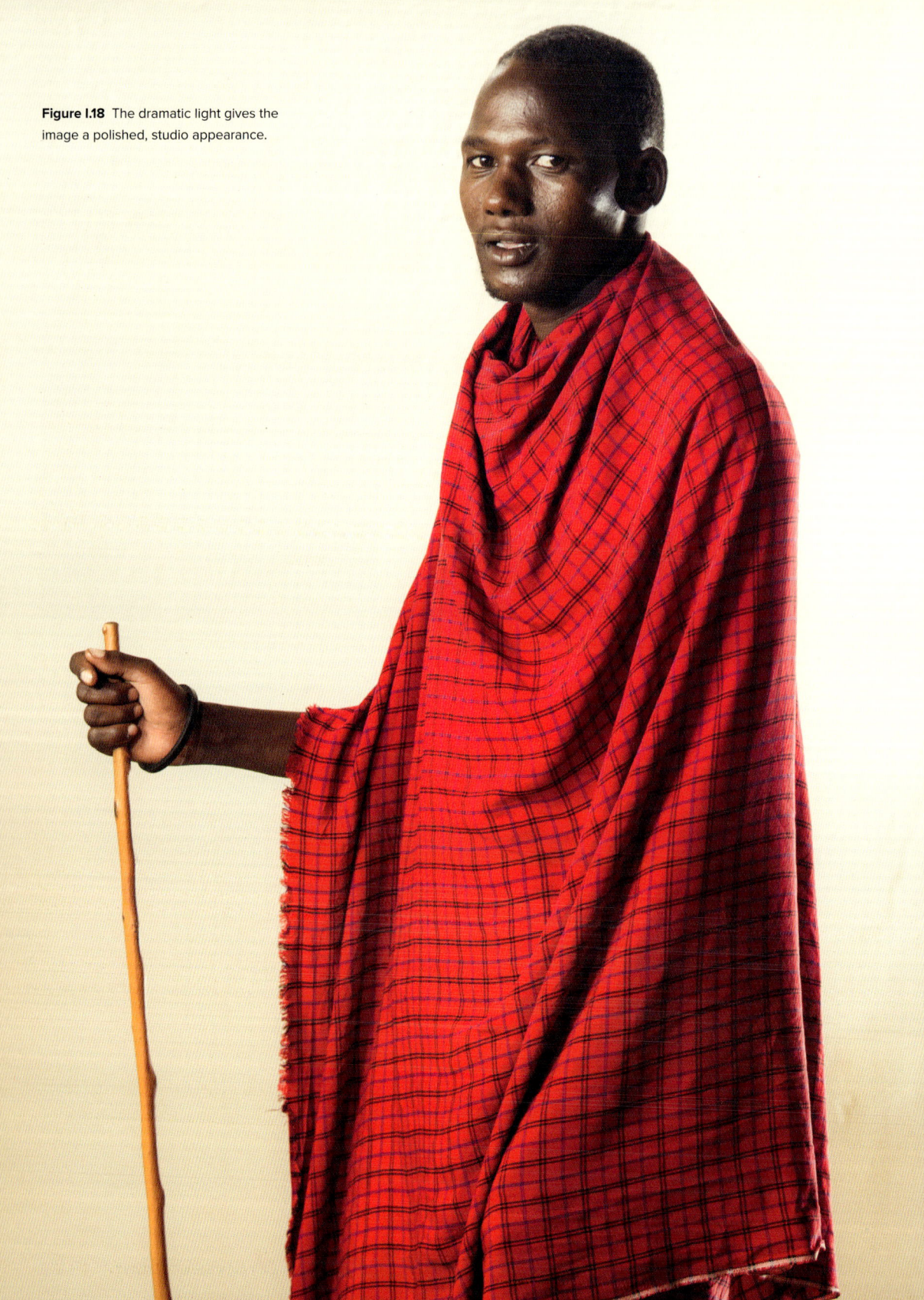

Figure I.18 The dramatic light gives the image a polished, studio appearance.

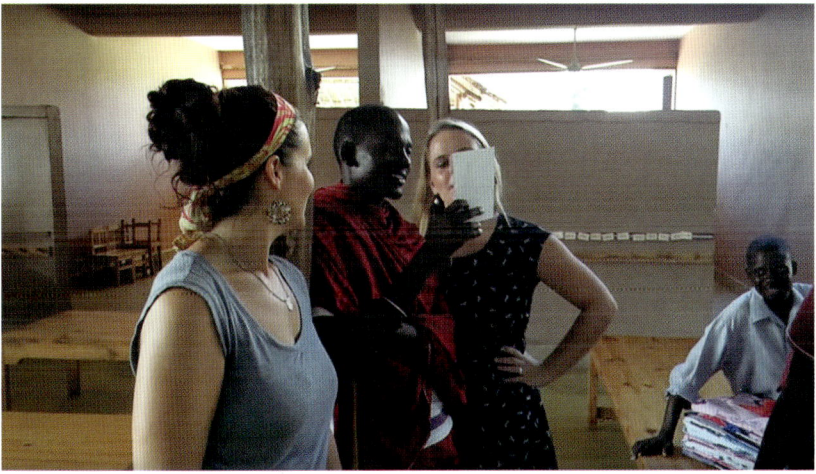

Figure I.19 The Maasai guard, who had never before been photographed, was fascinated by his image.

INTENTIONAL LIGHT

One of the only light modifiers that I travel with is an umbrella, which I rarely use. I avoid modifiers as much as possible because I am often shooting outdoors, which means wind, which means the light stand with an umbrella is now a sail boat. I don't carry a sandbag around with me (they're big and heavy), and I often don't have an assistant or travel companion to help hold the light in place. This means that unless I am shooting inside, I am shooting without a modifier. Even if I'm shooting indoors, I have learned to shape, bounce, balance, and all-around manipulate my unmodified flash into nice-looking light, meaning I also rarely use an umbrella inside. Beats the hell out of lugging sandbags all around town.

Achieving flattering light—especially if it's hard, unmodified light—generally boils down to two things: proper placement and ambient balance. As a rule of thumb, you should avoid lighting from a low angle, also known as monster lighting. Start with one light and place it at a three-quarter angle to your subject, slightly above the person's eye level (**Figure I.20**).

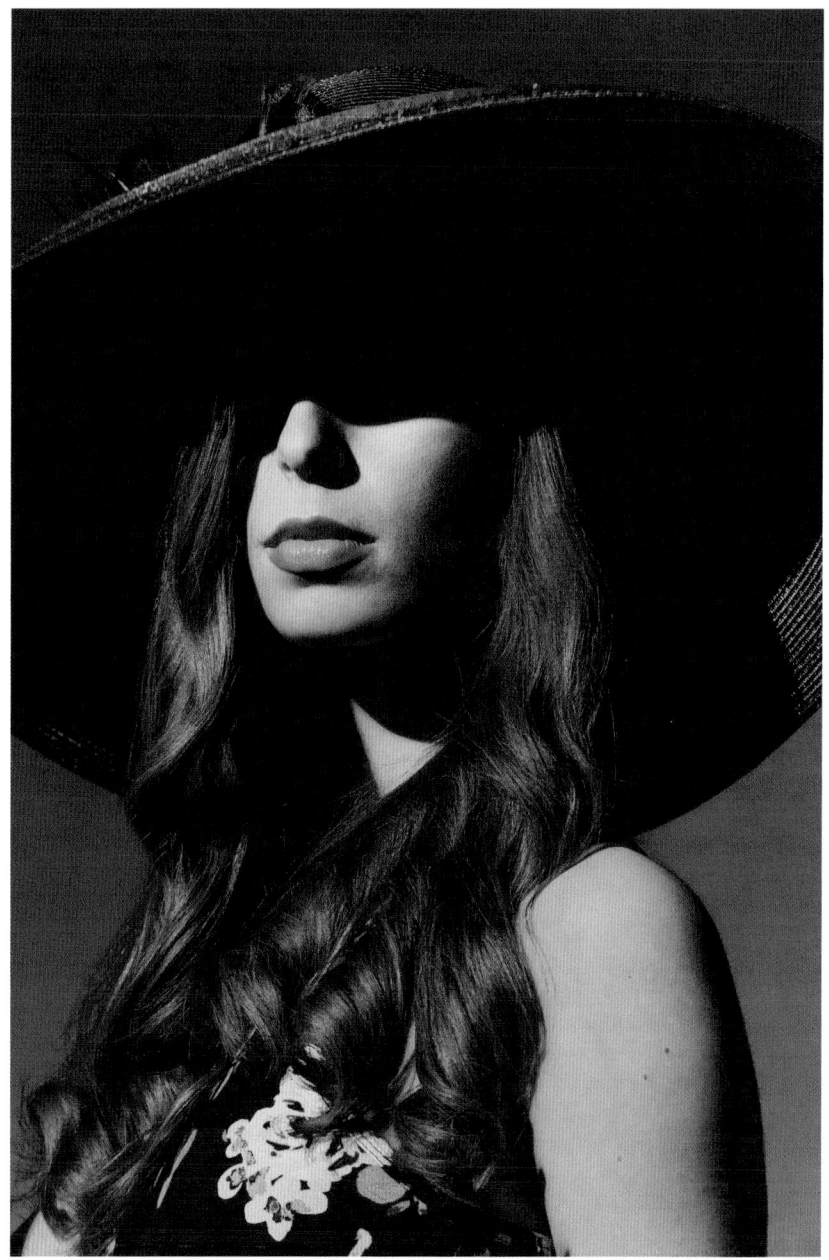

Figure I.20 When working with hard light, the most important thing to keep in mind is light placement. Start off with the light slightly higher than the subject, and off-center to the right or left, which is also known as a three-quarter angle.

Try to avoid shooting your subject from the same side that your light is coming from. This makes flat, uninteresting light. You want dramatic light. Even intentional light. Consider if there is a specific part of your subject that you want to highlight, such as Buzz Osborne's iconic hair, which I chose to backlight, as seen in **Figure I.21**. Try placing a light behind the person, aiming back toward the camera. This allows you to achieve a glowing silhouette, a la the *Nebraska* movie poster (**Figure I.22**).

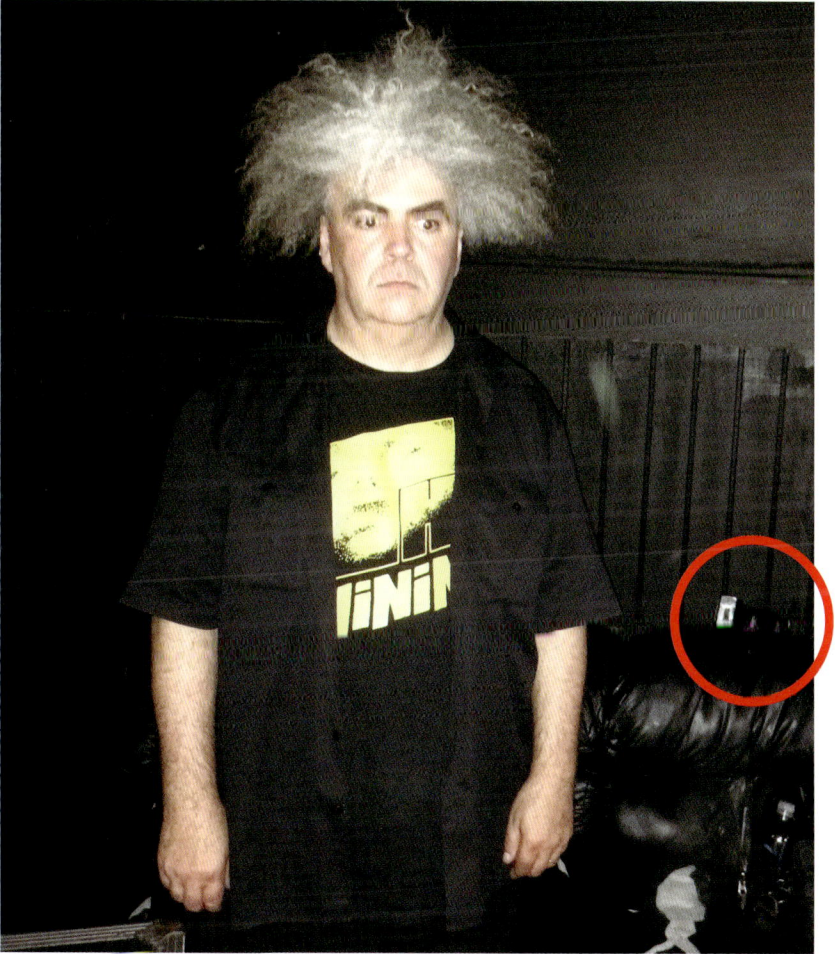

Figure I.21 When photographing the Melvins' lead Buzz Osborne, I knew I wanted to accentuate his iconic, fuzzy hair, so I opted to go for a dramatic silhouette by placing the flash behind him, aiming back toward the camera.

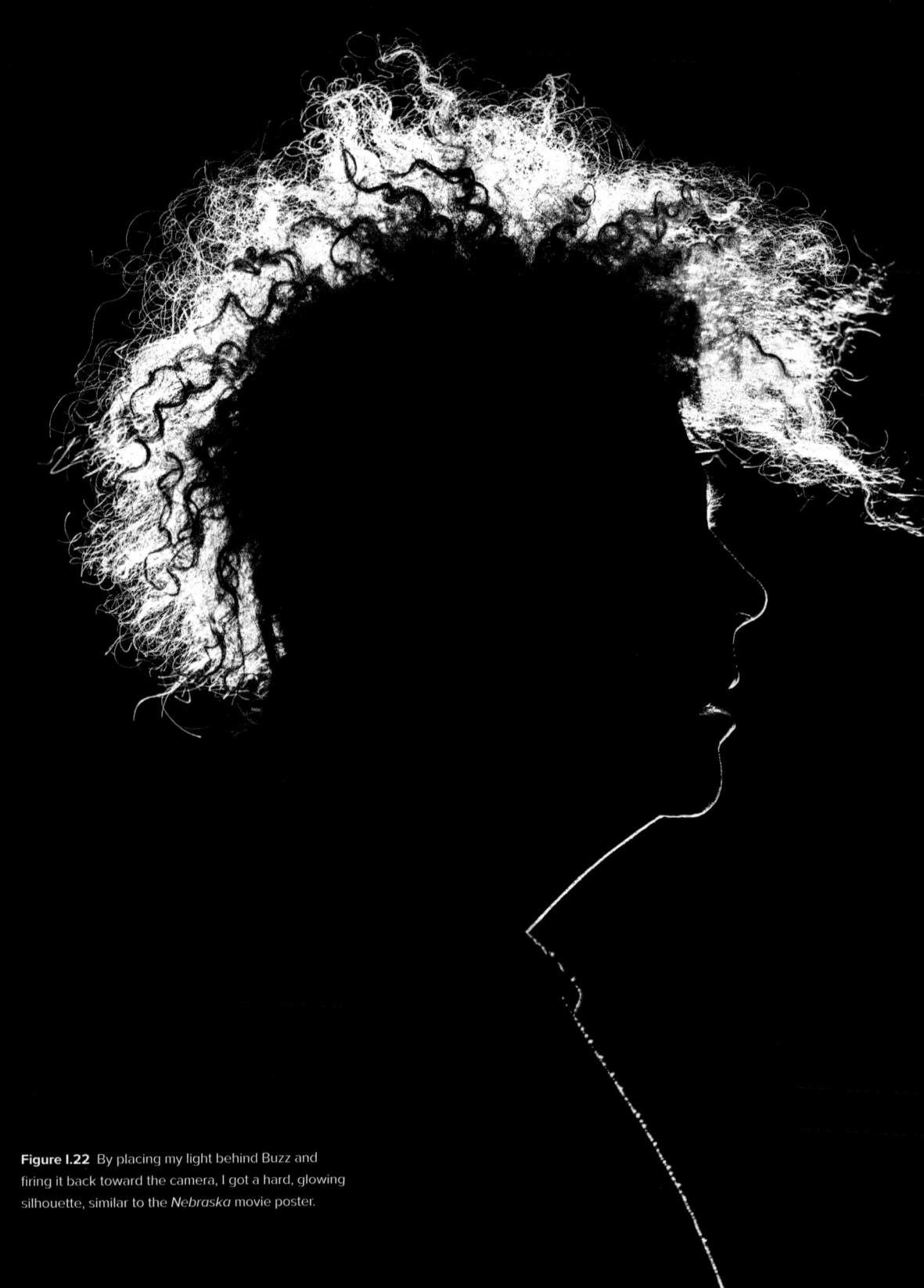

Figure I.22 By placing my light behind Buzz and firing it back toward the camera, I got a hard, glowing silhouette, similar to the *Nebraska* movie poster.

Or maybe you're photographing a fecal-focused writer, whose blog is aptly named Help Me Poop, and you want to have him sitting on a glowing toilet. Yeah, it happened (**Figures I.23** and **I.24**).

My hope is that you'll learn from the techniques in this book, build upon them, and come up with your own. Think strategically when lighting your subject. Take advantage of the fact that your light is small, which allows for strategic placement. Be intentional. Get inventive. Have fun.

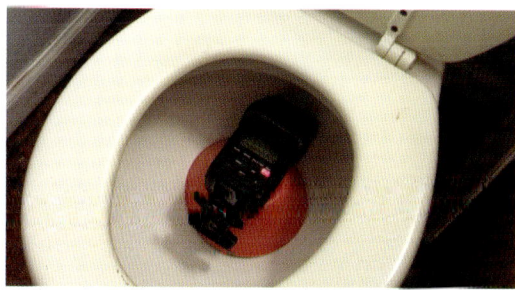

Figure I.23 By draining the toilet and placing my strobe in the bowl, I was able to create a glowing throne for this fecal-focused blogger.

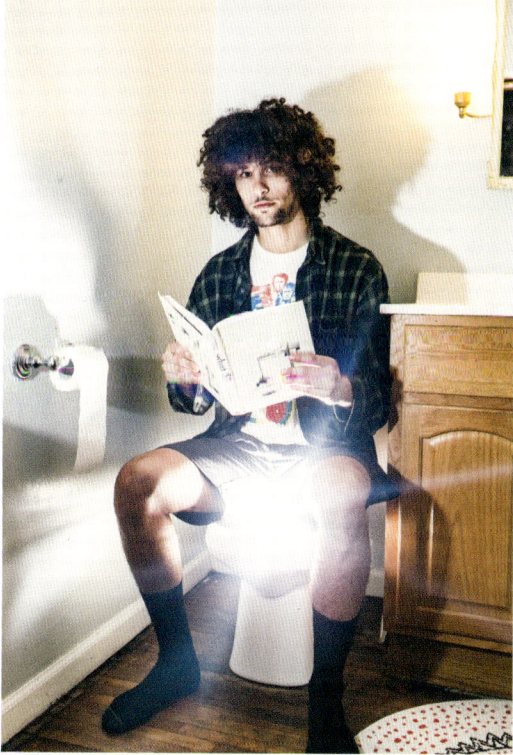

Figure I.24 This character writes a blog called Help Me Poop, which features things like tips to shorten your toilet time, so I was playing with the idea of poop enlightenment in the image.

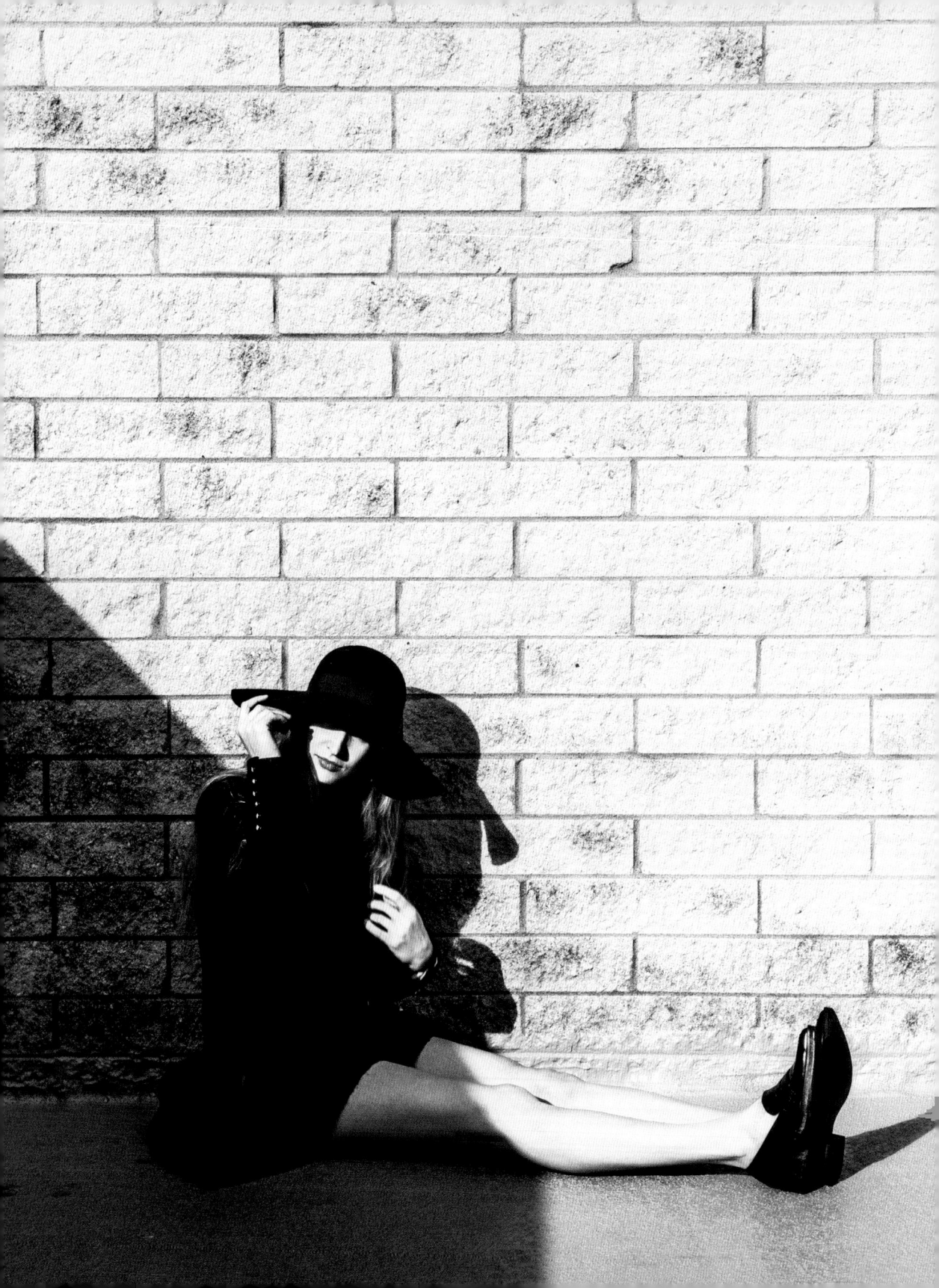

CHAPTER 1

SHAPING AVAILABLE

We photographers love our soft light. We are constantly on the lookout for shade, overcast days, and north-facing windows. But what if it isn't available? What if all you have to work with is harsh, mid-day sunlight? What if the room you're shooting in doesn't have a window with indirect light but only bright sun pouring in? Being able to make lemonade from the lemons that the ambient light often serves you is an invaluable skill. Though available light can be a bitch, it is also fairly compliant. It's a lot like a loyal dog: while it's often bouncing around the room, as if chasing an invisible squirrel, it will also willingly go wherever you lead it.

Figure 1.1 If you see cool shadows, take advantage of them.

LOOKING FOR LIGHT
IN ALL THE PLACES

Wherever I go, I look at the light. I especially love reflected light and complex shadows (**Figure 1.1**). You can easily find both in abundance in dense urban areas, such as the downtown area of a decent-sized city. When more than a couple skyscrapers are in close proximity to each other, light starts bouncing off the windows of one building and onto another as the sun makes its way across the sky. The season may affect the light and reflections you see, too. In the fall, for example, the sun is lower in the sky, so it hits different windows than it does in the spring, creating amazing reflected light and shadows where they wouldn't have occurred earlier in the year (**Figure 1.2**).

If this kind of light play isn't something you already notice, start paying attention. Watching light and shadows and how they interact has helped me learn

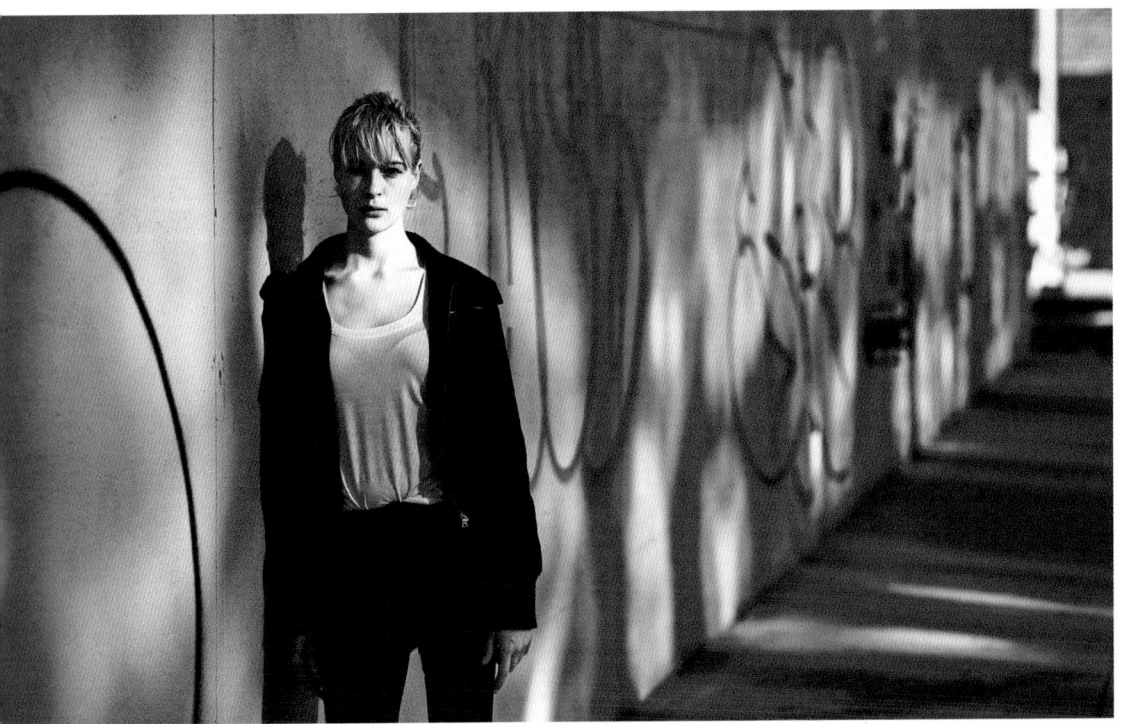

Figure 1.2 Keep an eye out for naturally occurring light and shadow play. Depending not only on the time of day but also the time of year, light will reach places where it previously hadn't.

more about off-camera lighting than anything else. Think of the sun as the ultimate studio head, far off in space. Because of the inverse square law, the sun's light, which is coming from far, far away, is even by the time it reaches us. The next time you're walking around on a sunny day, take note of your shadow. It's defined, but a bit soft around the edges. However, if you place your hand several inches from the ground, the shadow created will be especially crisp and defined.

All light works the same way. When you place a light on a light stand and turn it on, you are effectively recreating the sun and telling it where to go. After studying naturally occurring light scenarios around town, you now know that your light needs to be far enough away from your subject that the spread is even by the time it reaches them. If you want a crisp shadow on your background, place the subject close to it. If you want a softer or even zero shadow, move the subject further away from the background.

Fences are a fantastic resource for shadows and more (**Figure 1.3**). Depending on the style of fence and the height and strength of the sun, you can get

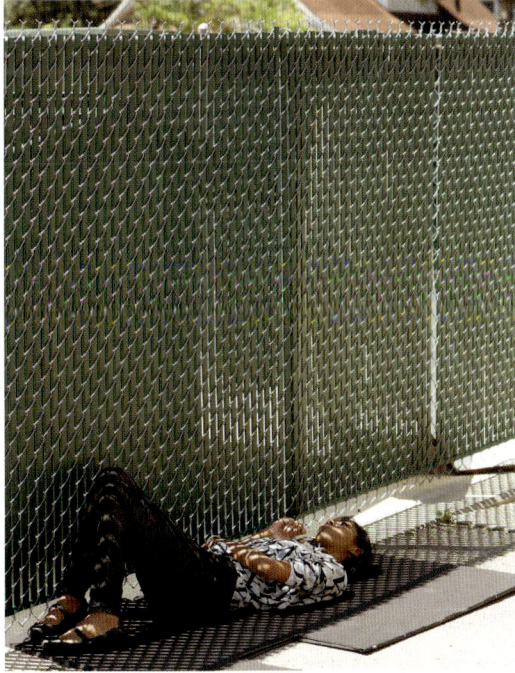

Figure 1.3 The setup. I have walked by this fence a hundred times, but one day I noticed the sun coming through it at just the right angle to create a fantastic shadow. So that's where I placed my subject.

dramatically different light and results, like those in **Figure 1.4**. I know the shot is quite busy, especially with the addition of the pattern on her shirt and her jewelry, but sometimes busy works. Once you start seeing the potential in the light that naturally surrounds you, you'll realize that you don't need much gear at all to create a compelling image.

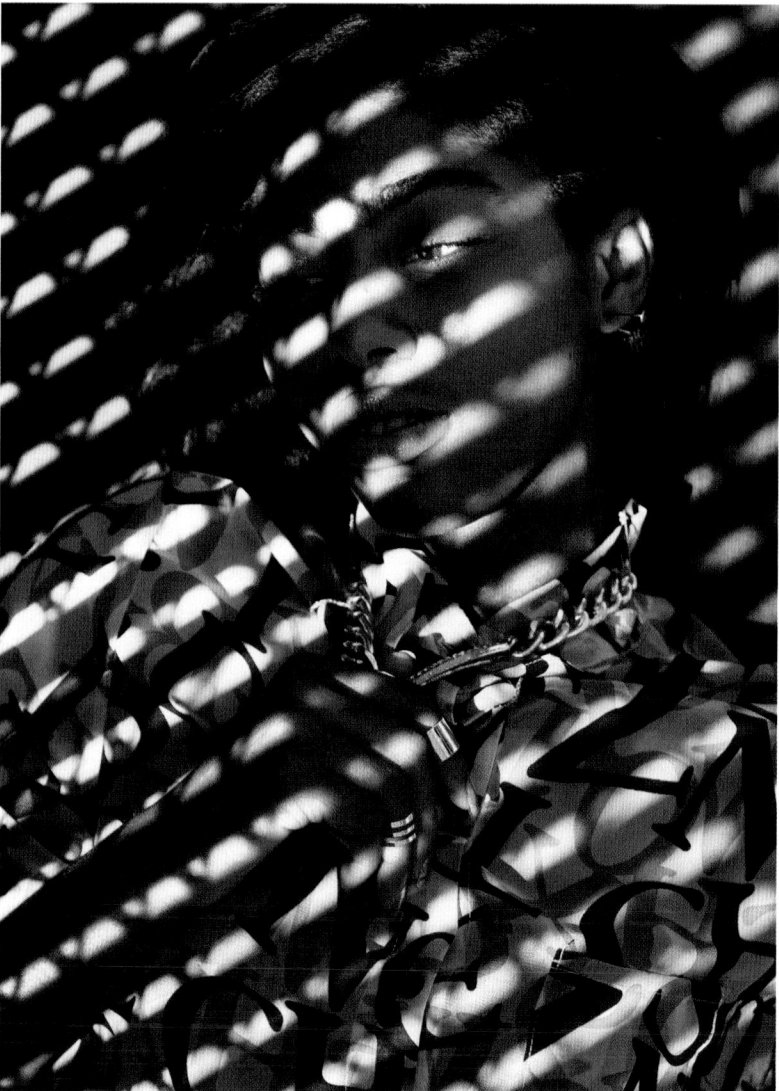

Figure 1.4 The final shot. It's a busy shot, but I like it.

DON'T GO ALL SOFT ON ME

For this shoot, I was photographing Mona at her home on a sunny day. The house was a bit small, and the dining room was the most spacious spot for the shoot. The available light was abundant, due to the large window by the table, but the sun pouring in was harsh. Although I had lights with me, the light was so bright in there that I thought it'd be easier to see if I could shape it into something useful rather than fighting to eliminate it with a high strobe output.

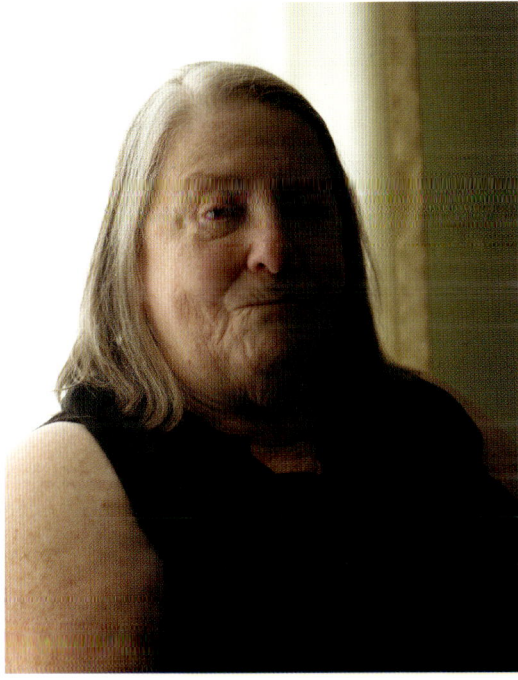

Figure 1.5 Here is the subject sitting in front of drawn curtains on a sunny day. The light, although soft, is boring and unflattering.

I first placed Mona by the window and closed the curtains. Even with the curtains drawn, there was plenty of light coming from the window. But as you can see in **Figure 1.5**, although the lighting is soft and even, the image is rather boring. After seeing the first shots, I decided a more visually interesting and flattering lighting for Mona would be a hard, narrow light source that created deep shadows. Think of the chiaroscuro light in old Rembrandt and Caravaggio paintings (if you are unfamiliar with these Renaissance masters, check out their work for plenty of lighting inspiration and ideas).

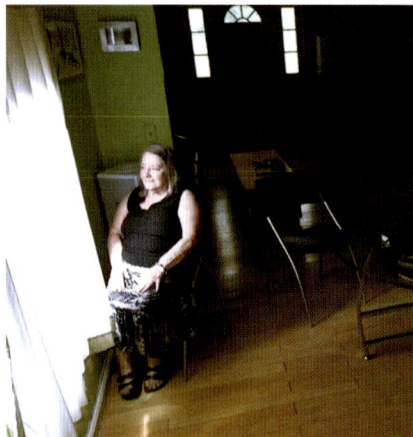

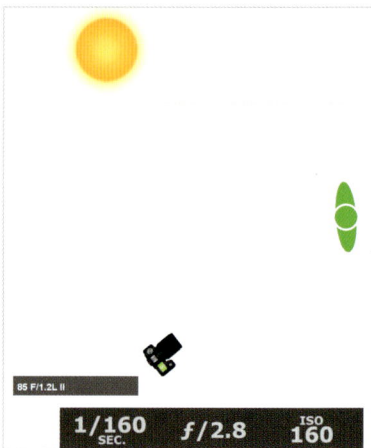

Figure 1.6 The setup. The harsh sun was pouring in the dining room window, but it was the best spot in the house for a portrait, so I pulled the curtains mostly closed to change the light. *Photo by Doral Chenoweth*

Figure 1.7 The lighting diagram. I shot at a wider aperture in order to have some separation between Mona and the wall behind her.

I rearranged Mona, placing her beside the window (**Figure 1.6**), and opened the curtain about three inches. Now, a sliver of hard sunlight was coming through the window and illuminating the narrow side of Mona, which created a slimming effect to the camera side of her. As you can see in the lighting diagram (**Figure 1.7**), I shot at a wider aperture in order to have a bit of separation between Mona and the wall behind her. Also, take note of how the vibrant color of the walls comes through in the hard-light image (**Figure 1.8**), which is the other reason why hard light is my favorite. Hard light punches out the characteristics in a thing. I think about the effect like this: Soft light covers and wraps like a blanket, while hard light penetrates like a nail.

Although the file looked good in the camera, I knew there were a couple of things I was going to need to clean up in Adobe Lightroom. In **Figure 1.9** you can see that I made a radial adjustment over her right arm by lowering the Highlights slider; the sun on her arm was a bit too harsh and distracting. By lowering the brightness in the bottom half of the frame, I was able to bring the attention to her face. Other than that, I increased the contrast, popping the colors, and I shifted the hue of the Yellow and Green channels to a warmer color. I like the dramatic light in **Figure 1.10** much better than the initial, soft light.

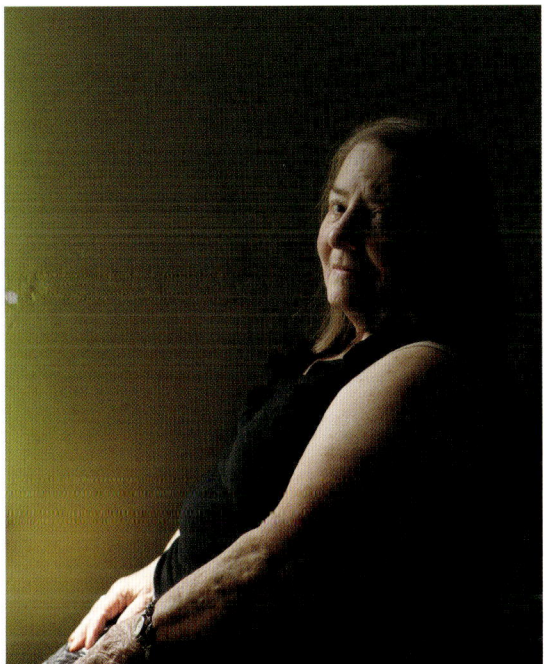

Figure 1.8 The raw file. The narrow sliver of hard light gave the portrait a flattering, beautiful quality, similar to Renaissance paintings.

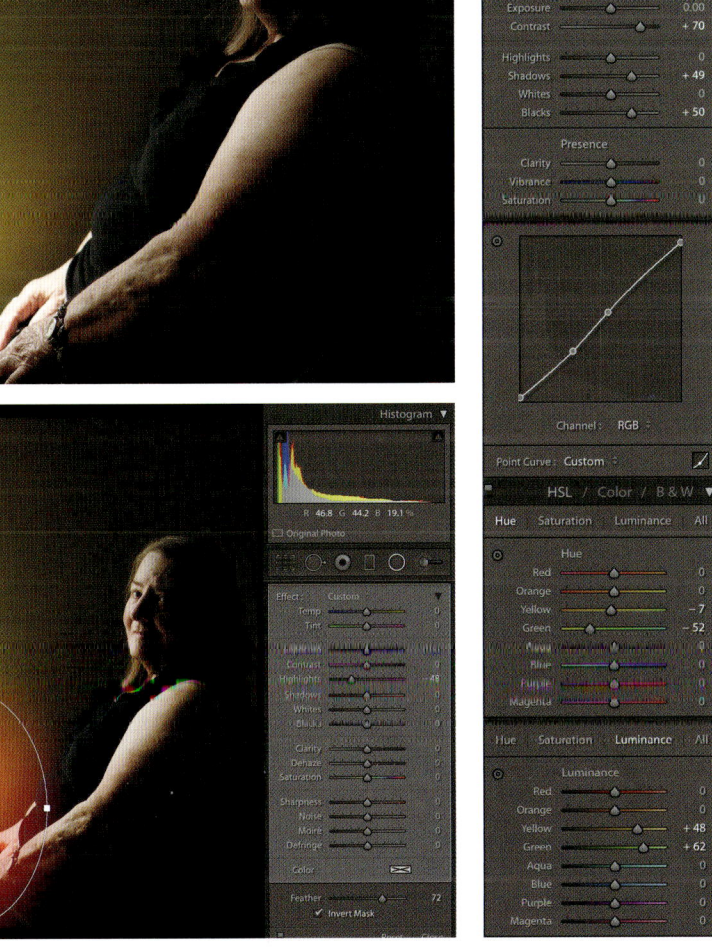

Figure 1.9 The Lightroom settings. I made a radial adjustment lowering the highlights on her arm, as well as shifted the yellow and green channels to a warmer color.

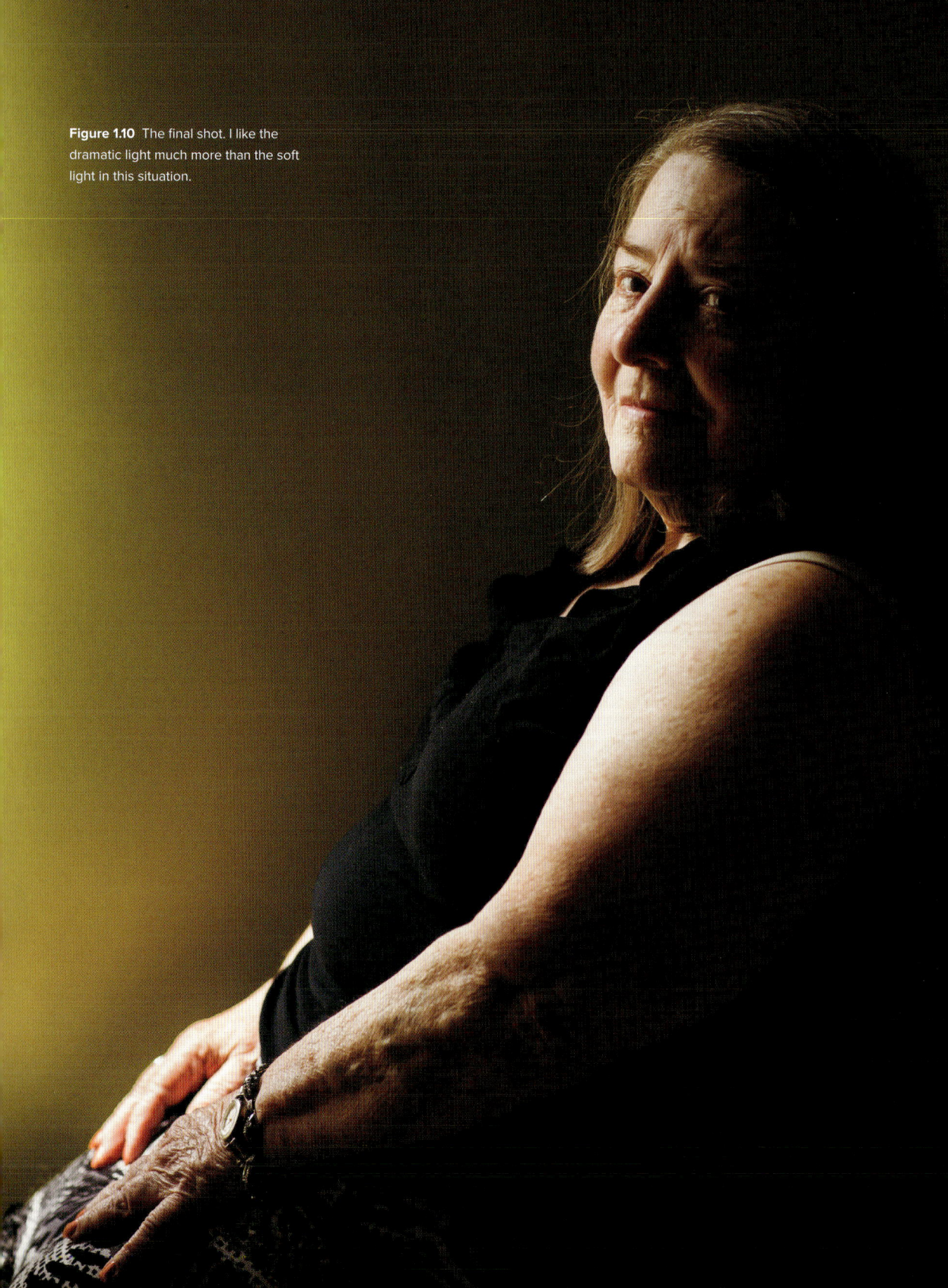

Figure 1.10 The final shot. I like the dramatic light much more than the soft light in this situation.

GOING BLIND(S)

Does your window have blinds instead of curtains? Draw them shut to create a natural light *gobo*. (A gobo is anything that "goes between" your light source and subject to modify the quality of the light. More on this in Chapter 2 and Chapter 8.) You can then place your subject under the pattern created by the closed blinds, as shown in **Figure 1.11**.

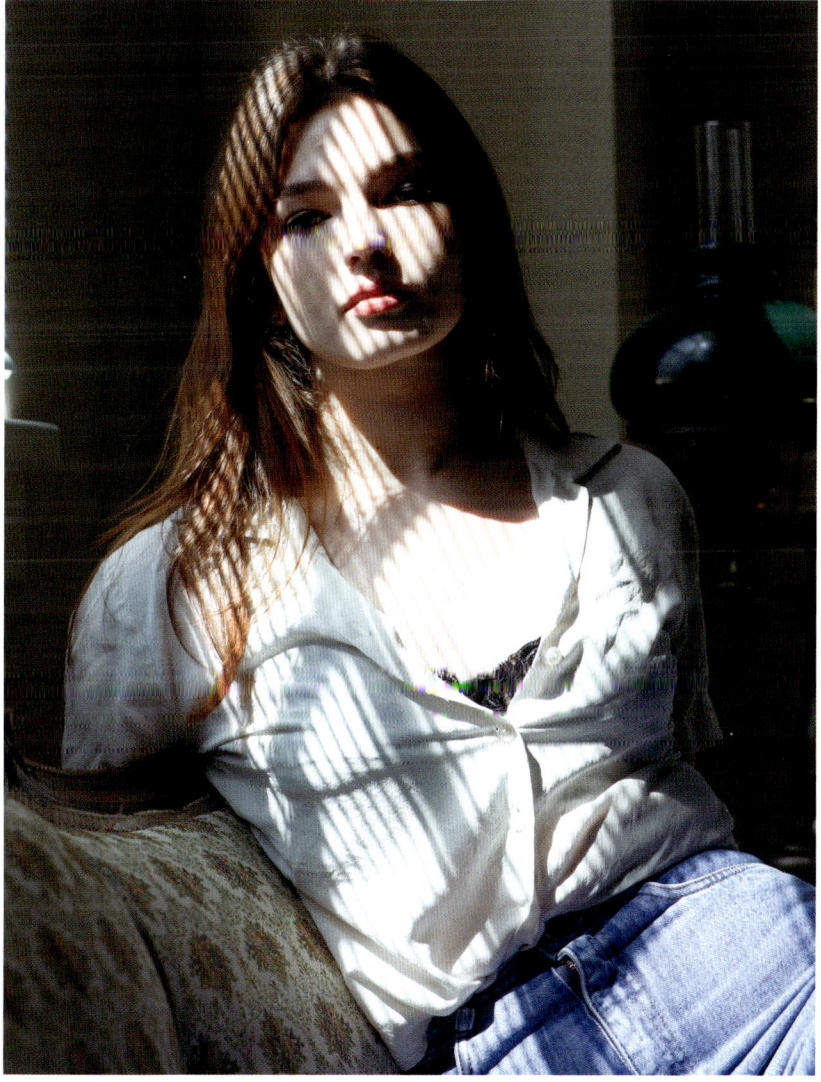

Figure 1.11 Although this image is properly exposed, it's rather boring.

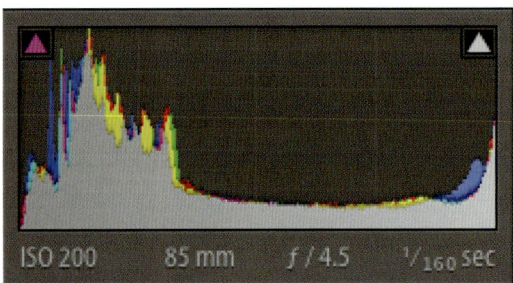

Figure 1.12 This is the histogram from the boring exposure.

When using this technique, however, be aware of your exposure. As you can see in **Figure 1.12**, the histogram for **Figure 1.11** contains information in both the shadows and the highlights. Technically, the shot is a properly exposed image, but the drama is lost—it's a boring image. By exposing for the highlights on the subject's face, you get a much darker exposure. Although **Figure 1.14** is technically a bit underexposed according to its histogram (**Figure 1.13**), I think you will agree that it is a more dramatic and emotive image. A successful portrait emotes, while an unsuccessful photo draws little to nothing from its viewer. Takeaway lesson: let your images be dark, when appropriate.

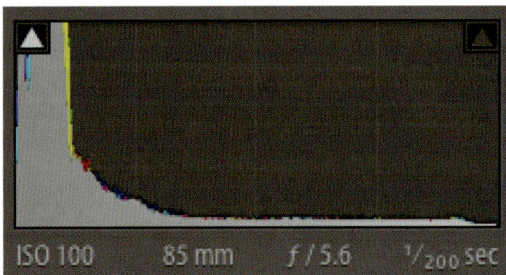

Figure 1.13 This is the histogram for the darker exposure.

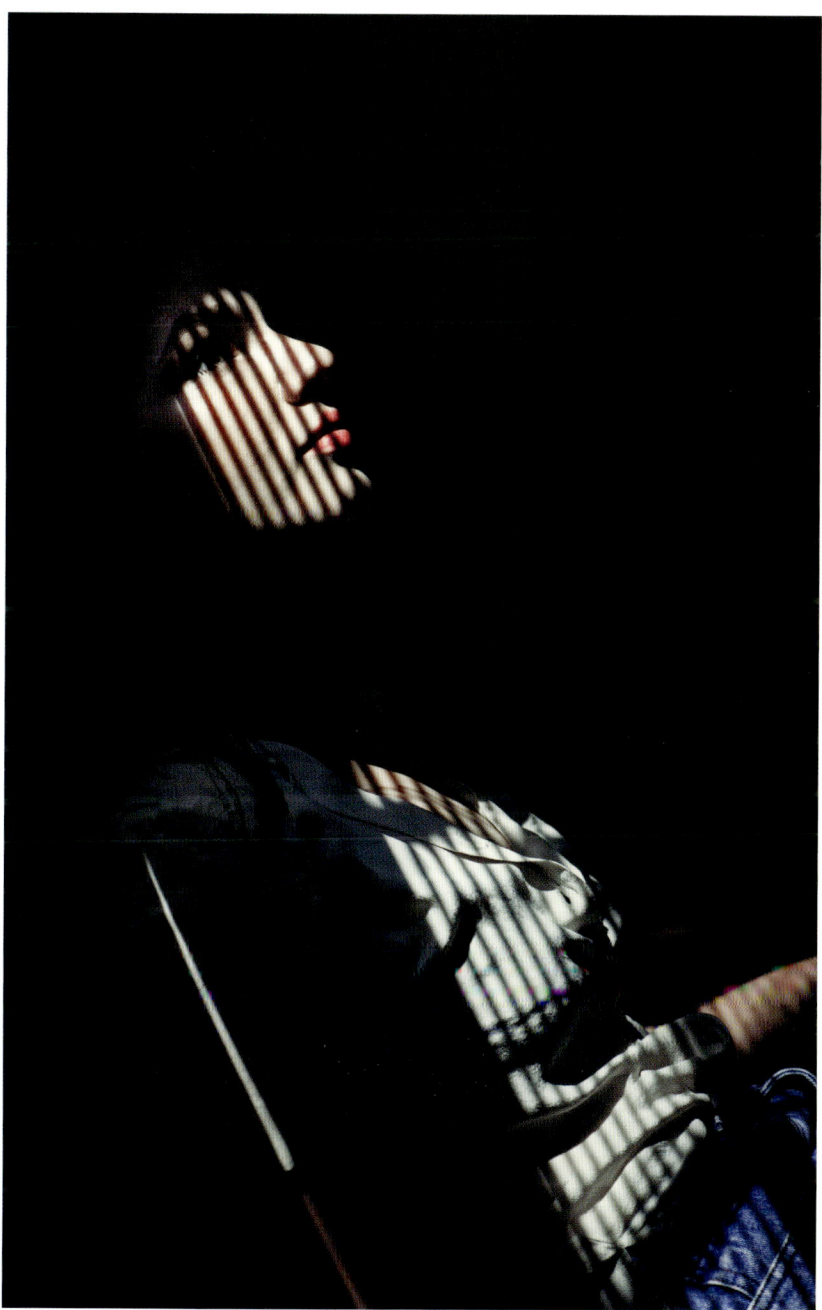

Figure 1.14 By exposing for the highlights, I created a more dramatic, successful image.

HACK YOUR REFLECTOR

This is the cheapest yet most effective photography hack I can think of. Step one: get disc reflector. Step two: cut lens-sized hole in said reflector (**Figure 1.15**). Step three: profit.

Seriously, though, there is almost no reason not to do this hack. First of all, the reflector's fabric is really tough, which means the hole will not spread. Secondly, the reflector can still be used traditionally, even with a hole in it. The only issue that ever arises is if I am using the reflector to block the sun—now there is a spot of hard sunlight poking through.

But...but...what about the Westcott Omega Reflector??? Well, since you asked, not only is the Omega around $100, it also requires the use of an assistant or reflector stand to use. I can operate a hacked reflector by myself. The camera lens holds the reflector in place, allowing me to use my non-camera hand to angle the reflector to the desired position.

By gaining the ability to shoot through the reflector instead of bouncing light from below or beside the camera, the reflected light is now acting like a ring light—lighting the subject evenly from the front, creating shadow-less light.

In **Figure 1.16** I was shooting in a room that had two large windows with about two feet of space between them. The model's close proximity to the windows on either side of her created a soft, rim light effect (**Figure 1.17**).

You can see in the lighting diagram (**Figure 1.18**) that even though I was standing very close to the model, because of the indirect window light, the reflector didn't provide a ton of light. This meant that I needed to use a slightly higher ISO and wider aperture. In Lightroom, I brought up the shadows and midtones in the RGB and Blue channels of the Tone Curve (**Figure 1.19**) to give the image a vintage feel. My client for this shoot, a hair salon, requested that I outsource the image to a retoucher to fine-tune the final shot, which you can see in **Figure 1.20**.

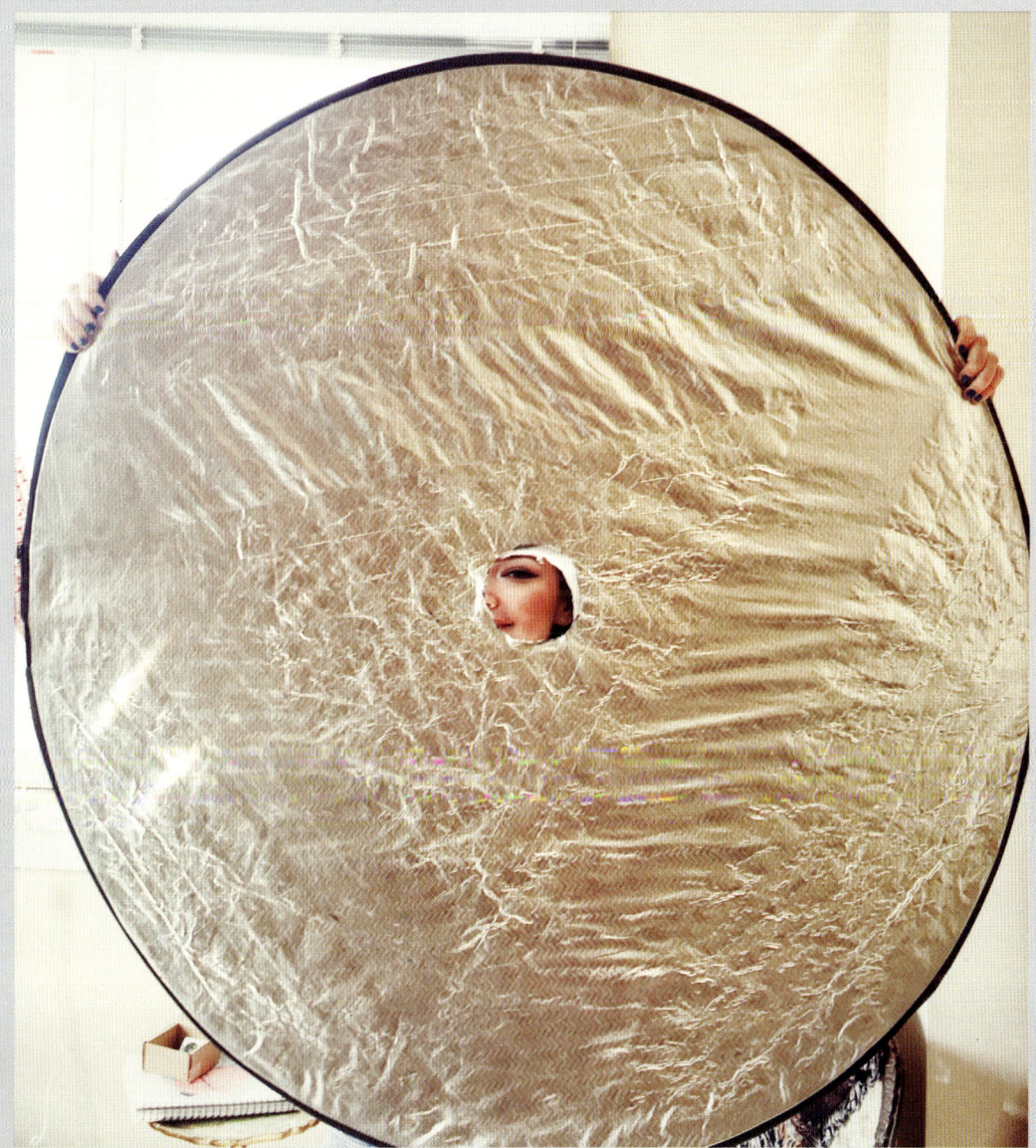

Figure 1.15 The hacked reflector. The hole is just larger than the size of my lens.

Now I have a soft, natural ring light, and I didn't even need to drop $100 on Ghionis's Omega Reflector (which still requires an assistant or stand to operate). Take note that using and angling your hacked reflector may feel a bit awkward at first, but you'll quickly get used to it. If you are using a larger reflector and your arm can't easily reach to your reflector's edge, try modifying a smaller diameter reflector so it better fits your arm span.

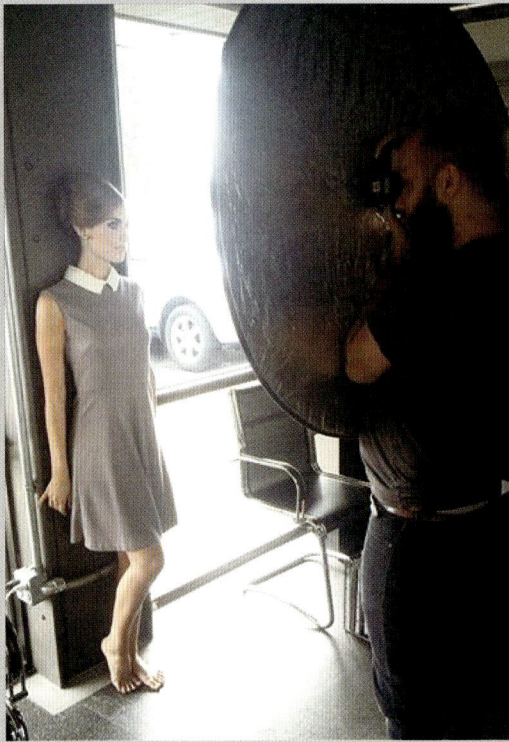

Figure 1.16 The setup. The subject is placed between two windows, which create a rim light. A hacked reflector acts as a natural-light ring fill.

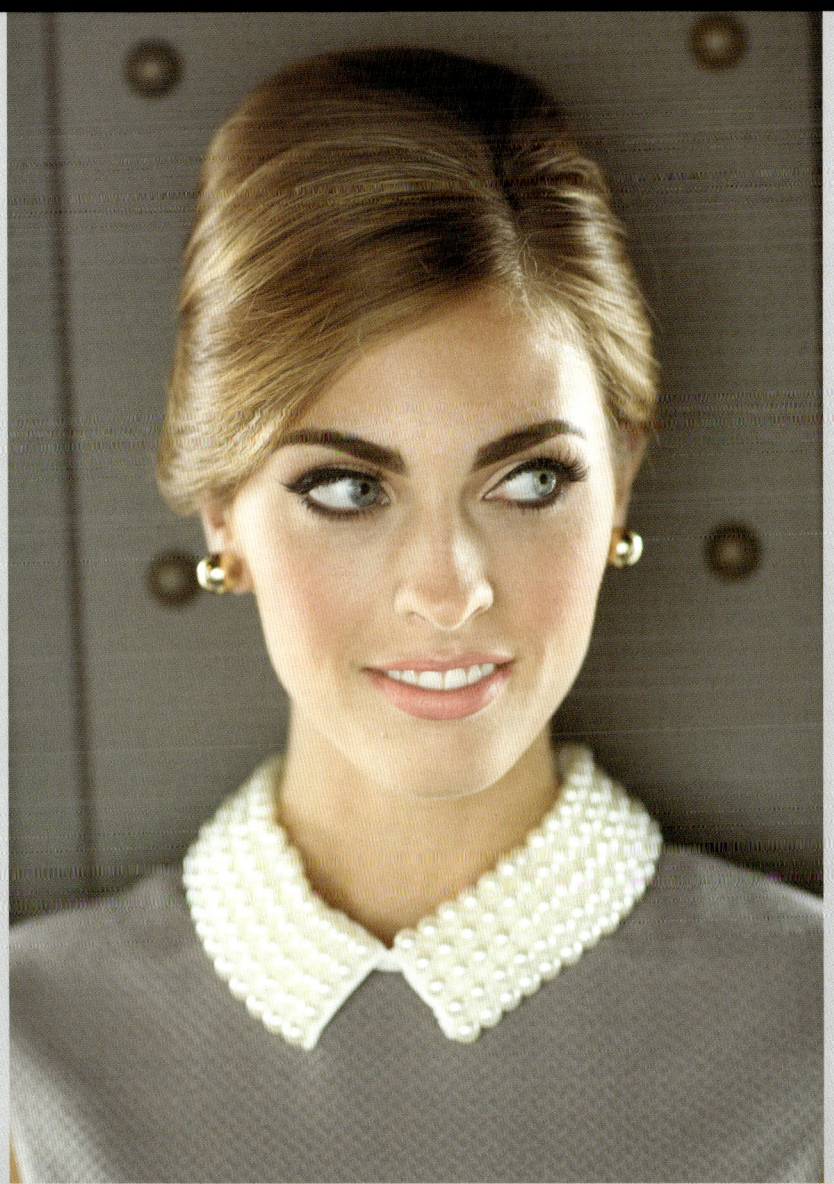

Figure 1.17 The raw file. The model's close proximity to the two windows on either side of her resulted in a soft, rim light effect.

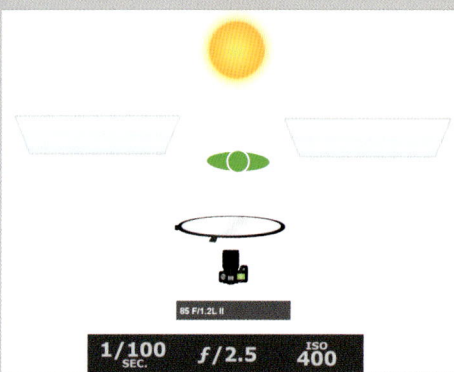

Figure 1.18 The lighting diagram. Even with the close proximity of the reflector to the model, my ISO was a bit elevated and my aperture was fairly wide in order to get a decent exposure.

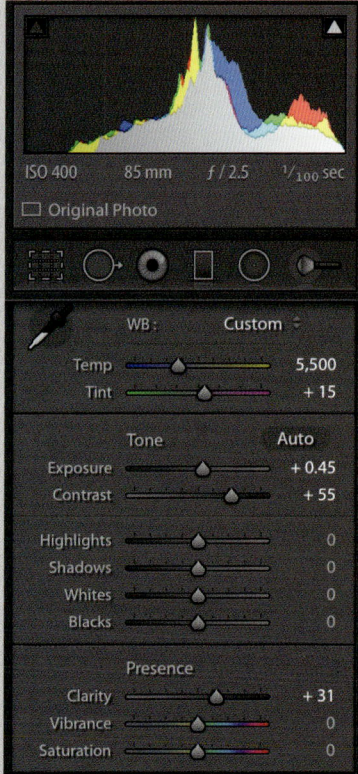

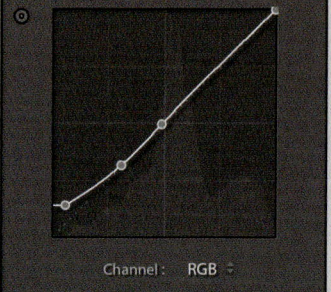

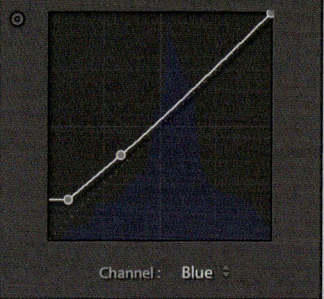

Figure 1.19 The Lightroom settings. After increasing the contrast, I brought up the shadows and midtones in the RGB and Blue channels of the Tone Curve to give the image a vintage feel.

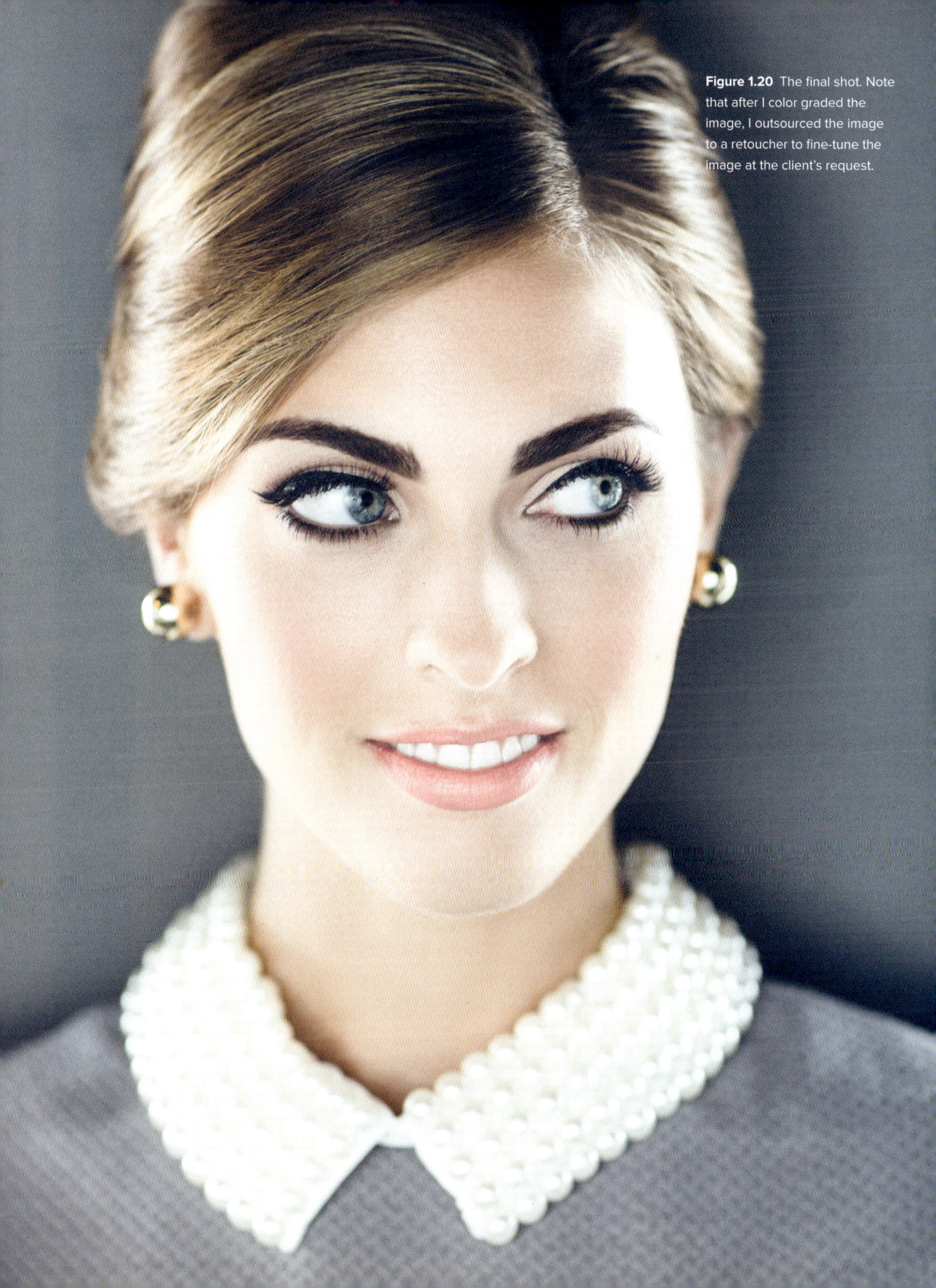

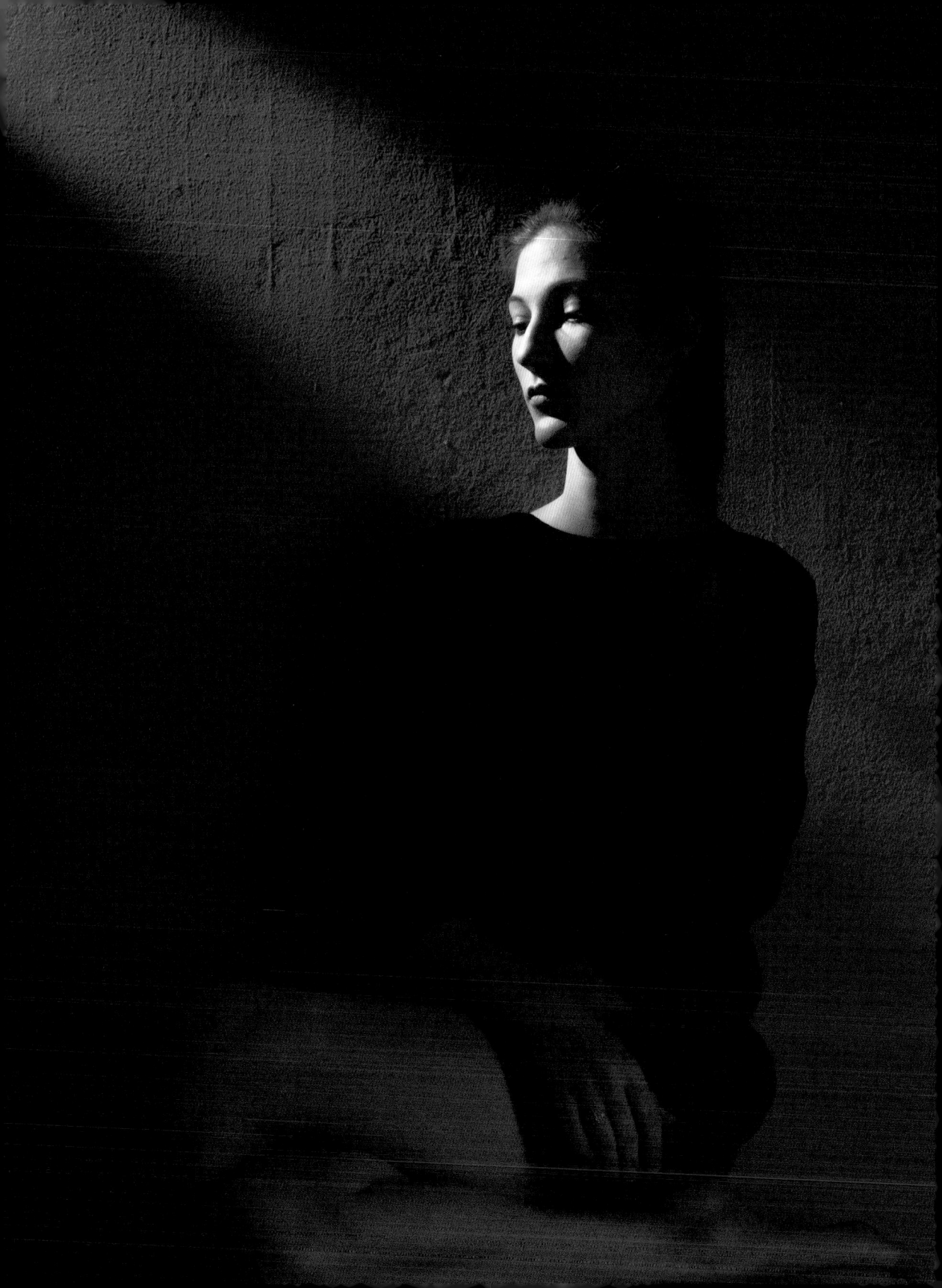

CHAPTER 2

SHAPING FLASH

There are countless ways you can control the spread, quality, color, and shape of a strobe output. This chapter starts out with the basics—firing the flash from the top of your camera—then moves on to a variety of light shapers, such as snoots and barn doors. These modifiers help control and shape the light, rather than soften the quality of the light, enabling you to bend it to your vision for a shot.

FLASH ON A HOT SHOE

In keeping with the plug-and-play mentality, throwing your flash on top of your camera's hot shoe and getting to work is always a viable option. Depending on how close your subject is to a background, how you zoom and position your flash, and how you balance the flash with your ambient light, your results can be quite diverse.

If you are positioning your subject against a wall or backdrop and want a shadowless image, place your flash on your camera's hot shoe and take a horizontal, landscape-formatted exposure (**Figure 2.1**). This camera position will allow your flash to light the left and right side of the subject equally, resulting in little to no shadow. Note that if even if you want a vertically formatted shadowless portrait, you still need to shoot it in a horizontal format and crop it to a vertical in post (**Figure 2.2**).

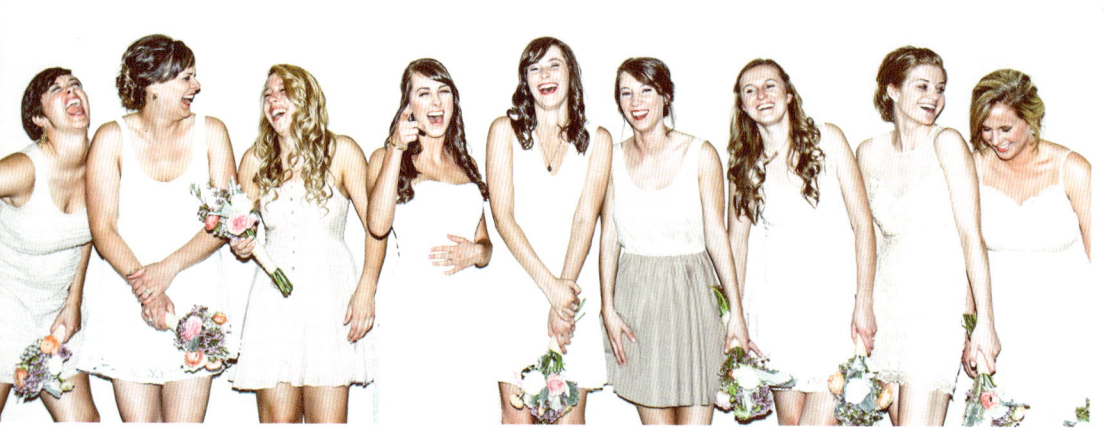

Figure 2.1 By placing a flash on your camera's hot shoe and shooting in a horizontal format, you get shadowless light.

If you were to shoot in a vertical, portrait format, it would result in a hard shadow to the left or right of the subject, depending on the orientation of your camera and flash (**Figure 2.3**). Also, to ensure an even spread of the light across the frame, make sure that your flash is zoomed out to a setting as wide as your lens diameter or wider. For example, if you are shooting with a 35mm lens, your flash should be zoomed out to at least 35mm, or even 28mm or 24mm.

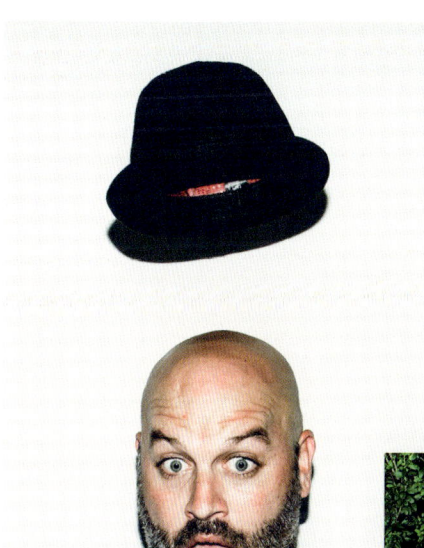

Figure 2.2 If you want a shadowless image with a vertical orientation, shoot it as a horizontal and crop it to a vertical in post. Note that this method will produce a smaller file size.

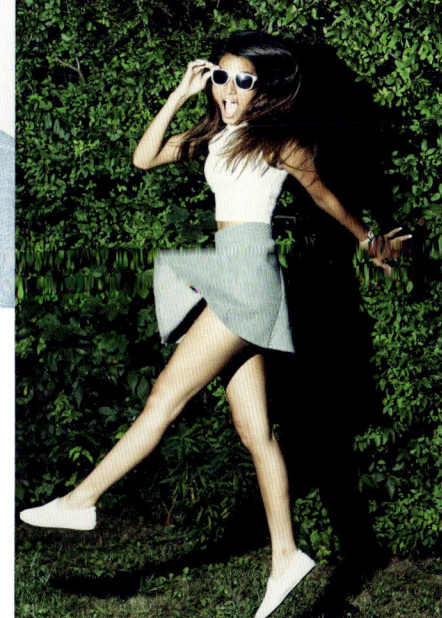

Figure 2.3 In this shot, the camera was oriented in a vertical position with the flash going to the left, which resulted in the subject's shadow going to the right.

THROUGH THE WINDOW GLASS

Once you get your flash off of your hot shoe, you can really start to shape your light—even without adding a modifier to the light. Consider the ordinary front door window in **Figure 2.4**, for example. I placed my flash on a stand outside the door and fired it through the window at the subject. The room was a bit too cramped to back off of the subject enough to fully light him, so I decided to fire through the window to gain some extra space. Doing so also narrowed and dappled the light, giving it a dramatic quality (**Figure 2.5**). Technically, the window glass qualifies as a gobo.

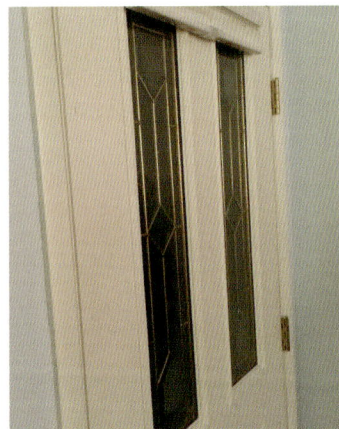

Figure 2.4 By placing my flash outside the front door and firing through these windows, I created a narrow, more dramatic light quality.

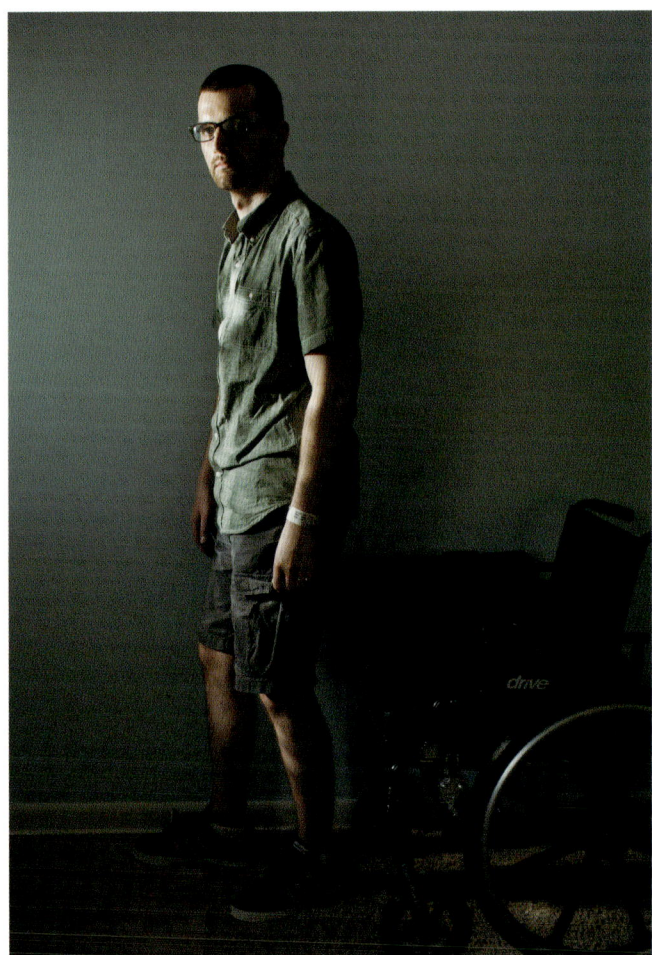

Figure 2.5 The lighting has a much more dramatic quality after it's fired through the narrow window.

RAKED OVER WALLS

One thing I have learned by working in cramped spaces is that placing my subject against the wall or backdrop (as opposed to five feet in front of it) has its advantages. In **Figure 2.6**, you can see the scene. My model is standing in front of a large, blank white wall in a quiet hallway. My light is placed as close to the wall as possible, elevated to about eight feet and fired parallel to the wall. Note that the light is illuminating the narrow side of the subject, leaving the camera side of him in shadow. This helps to preserve the element of drama in the image (**Figure 2.7**). I also zoomed in the flash head to 105mm in order to focus the output into a narrow blast (**Figure 2.8**). The light raking over the wall created a really cool light-ray effect almost like light through a prism. By making a gradient adjustment and increasing the contrast and clarity in Adobe Lightroom, I enhanced the prism effect (**Figure 2.9**).

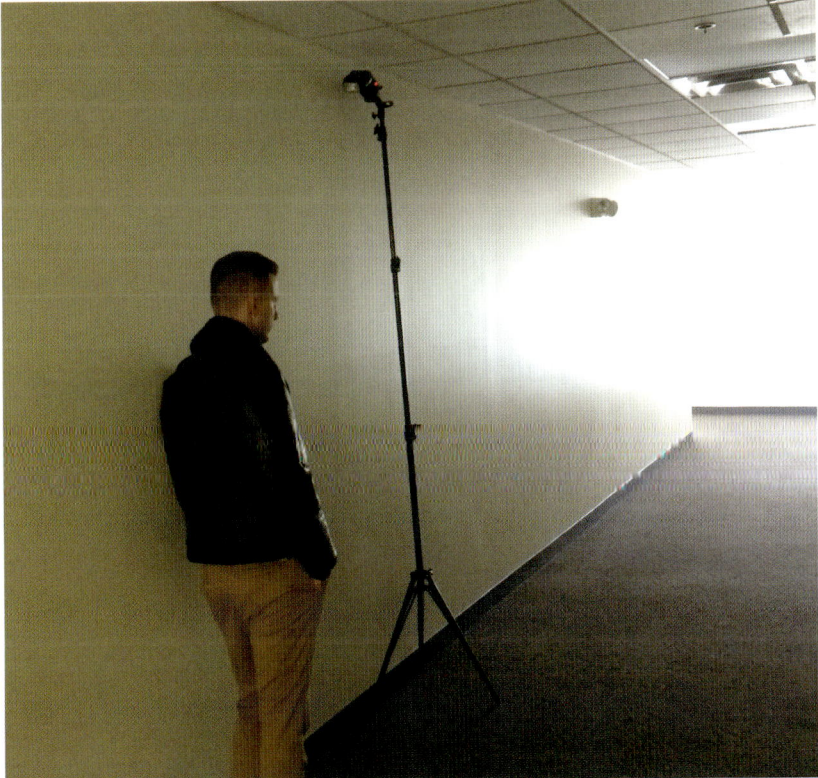

Figure 2.6 When you place a light right against a backdrop or wall and fire it parallel across the surface, you can create a light-ray effect.

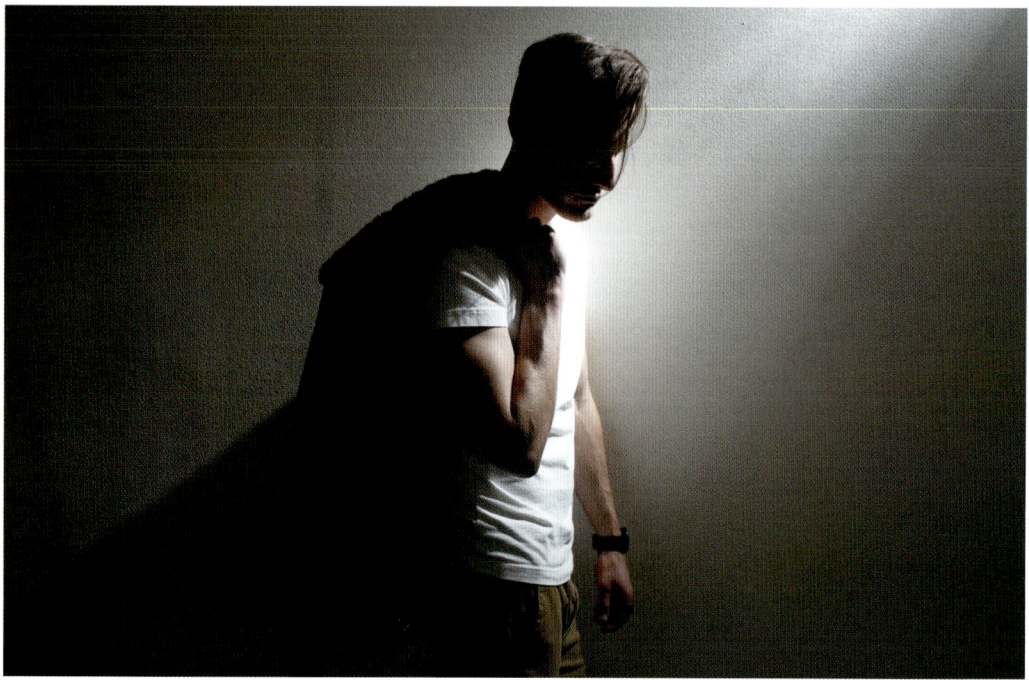

Figure 2.7 The raw file. The light appears as a defined line, creating a nice, dramatic effect.

Figure 2.8 The lighting diagram. The light was elevated to about eight feet and angled down at the subject.

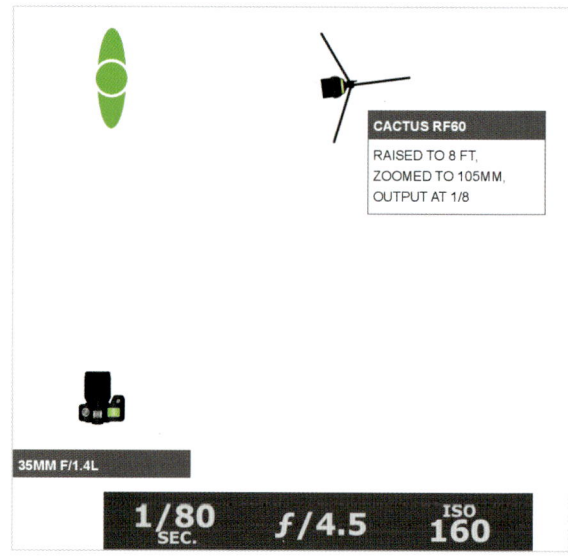

CACTUS RF60

RAISED TO 8 FT,
ZOOMED TO 105MM,
OUTPUT AT 1/8

35MM F/1.4L

1/80 SEC.   ƒ/4.5   ISO 160

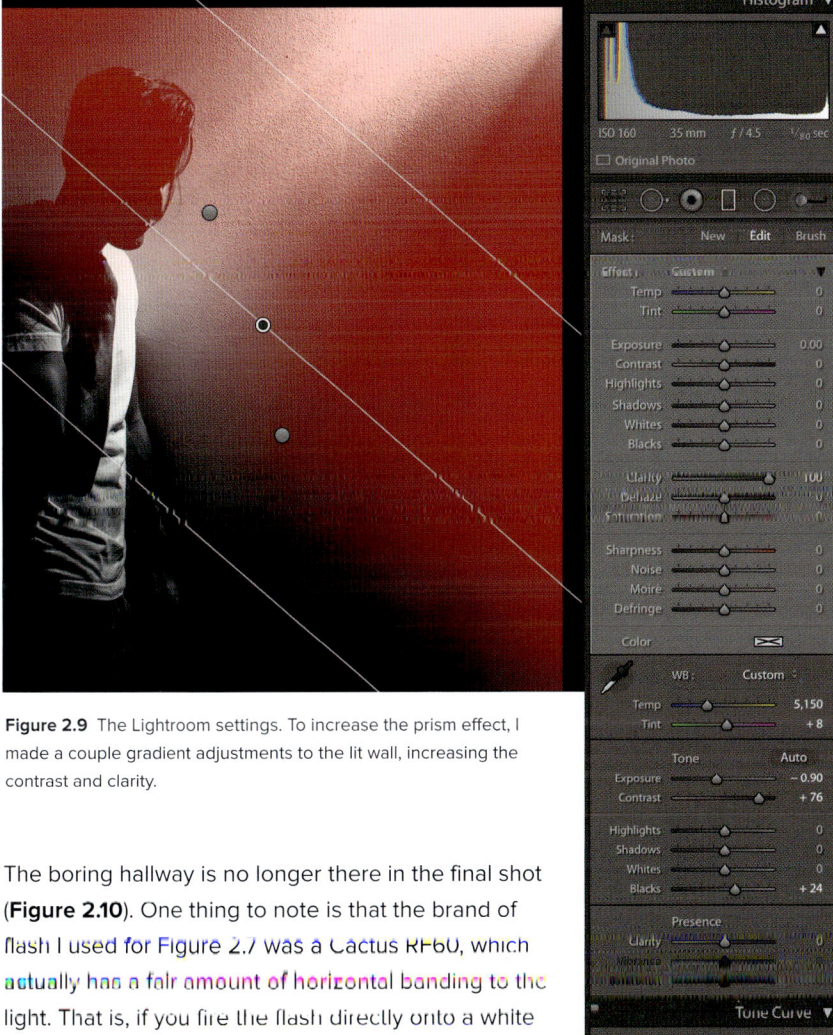

Figure 2.9 The Lightroom settings. To increase the prism effect, I made a couple gradient adjustments to the lit wall, increasing the contrast and clarity.

The boring hallway is no longer there in the final shot (**Figure 2.10**). One thing to note is that the brand of flash I used for Figure 2.7 was a Cactus RF60, which actually has a fair amount of horizontal banding to the light. That is, if you fire the flash directly onto a white background and close down your aperture to under-expose the shot one stop, you will see horizontal lines in the light. I have tested a LumoPro LP180 side by side with the Cactus and know that the LumoPro system does not have the same banding. While the banding is technically a flaw, I actually like using it in my images.

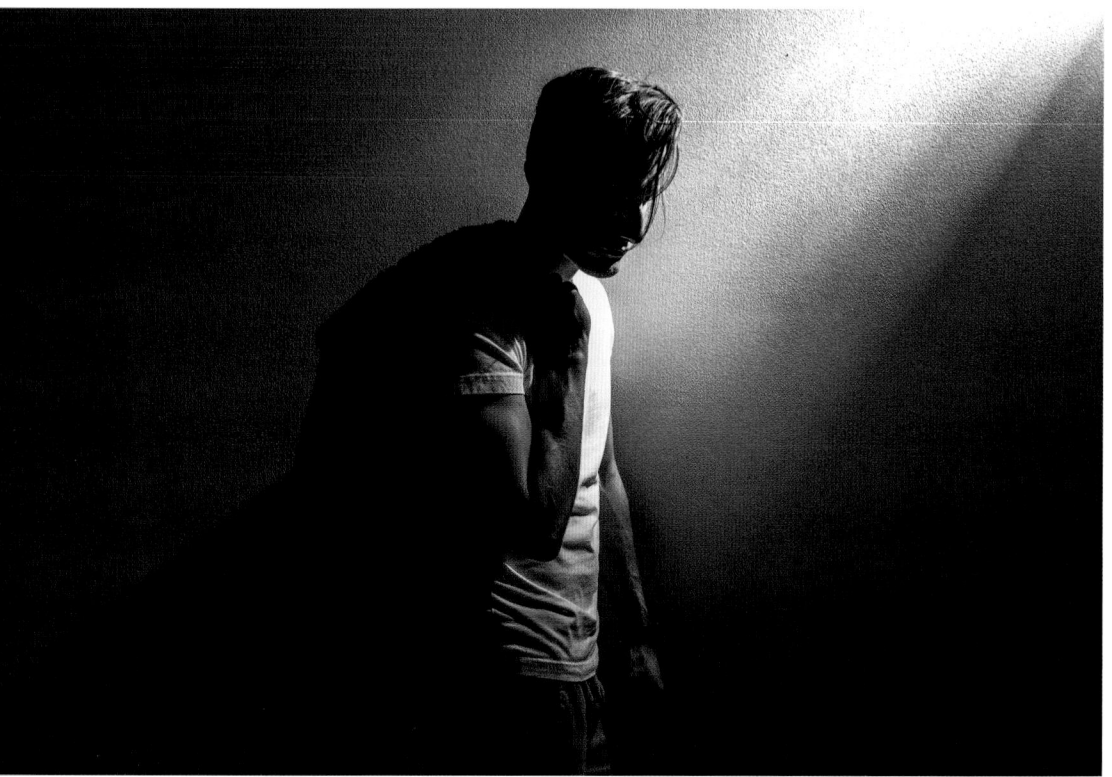

Figure 2.10 The final shot. The boring white wall has been transformed into a dramatic, textured backdrop for my model.

MODIFIER OPTIONS

Most of this book deals with scenarios lit with an unmodified flash. However, I do have a few modifiers that I sometimes use. This section explores those options.

UMBRELLA

I have an umbrella that I take with me if I am shooting more "professional" head-shots on location (**Figure 2.11**). Why put quotes around the word "professional"? Look at the setup in **Figure 2.12**. Although the umbrella provides me with conventional, flattering light, my setups are rarely conventional.

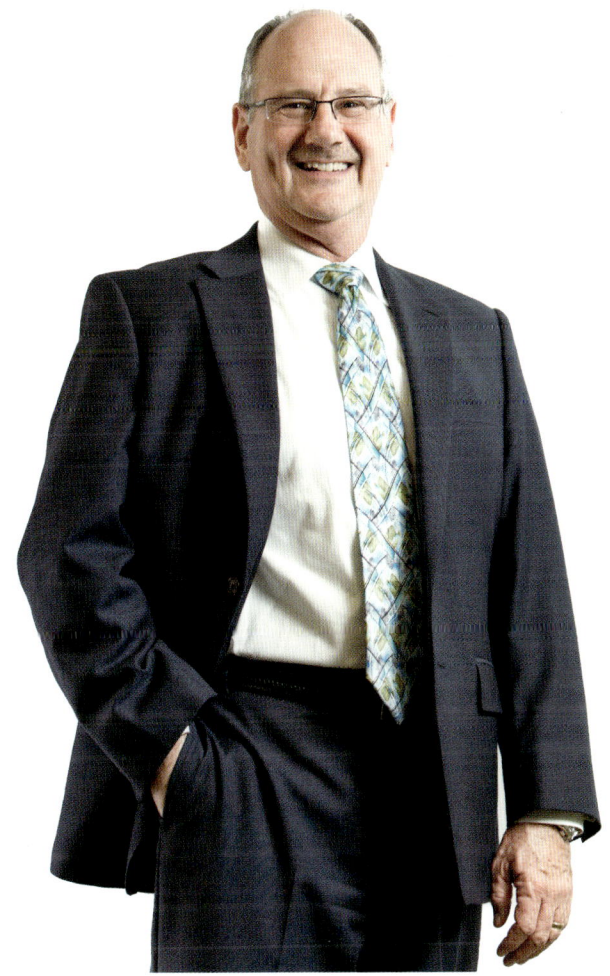

Figure 2.11 When I am shooting more "professional" headshots, I bring my umbrella with me.

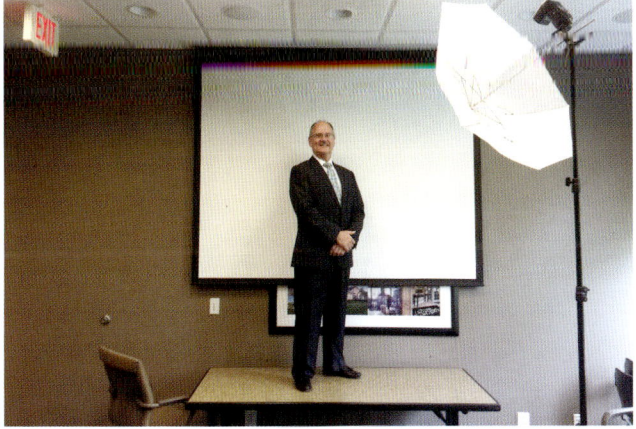

Figure 2.12 Although the umbrella adds a polish to the shot, my setup is often anything but.

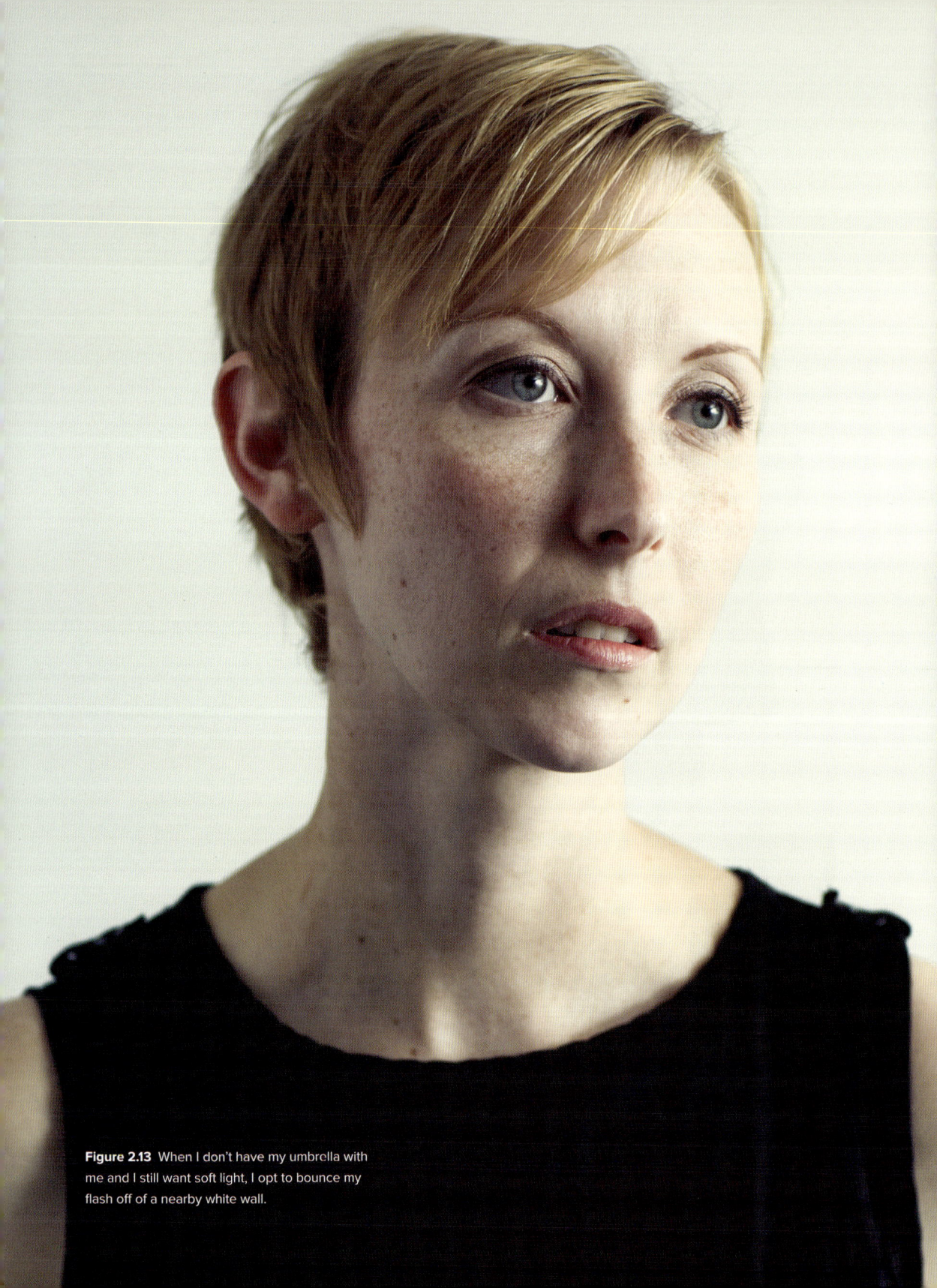

Figure 2.13 When I don't have my umbrella with me and I still want soft light, I opt to bounce my flash off of a nearby white wall.

If I am shooting something less formal, such as an environmental portrait, I usually leave the umbrella at home. If I should decide at the shoot that I want to use soft light after all, I opt to bounce the flash off a nearby wall as I did in **Figure 2.13**. You can find more details on these techniques in my previous book, *Studio Anywhere* (Peachpit Press, 2015).

GRID

I also own a Rogue 3-in-1 Flash Grid, which is a grid and snoot combo, made by ExpoImaging (**Figure 2.14**). I use it when I want to throw a narrow beam of light, as in **Figure 2.15**. This easily removable modifier is small and effective—so effective, in fact, that I can literally place my subject against a white wall (**Figure 2.16**) and have it go to black due to light falloff (**Figure 2.17**). **Figure 2.18** shows the same setup with the grid removed.

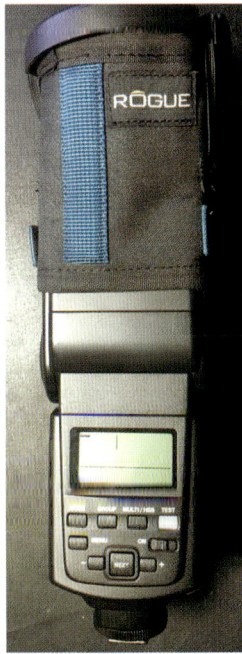

Figure 2.14 This is the Rogue snoot/grid combo that's made by ExpoImaging. It's a small, effective modifier that I use when I want a narrow, focused light output.

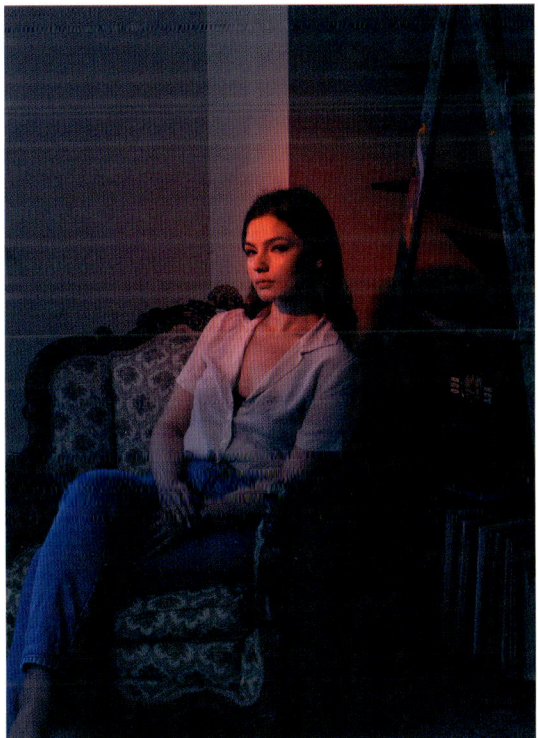

Figure 2.15 This was shot with available light, save for the narrow beam of red light, which came from a red-gelled flash, modified with the Rogue Flash Grid.

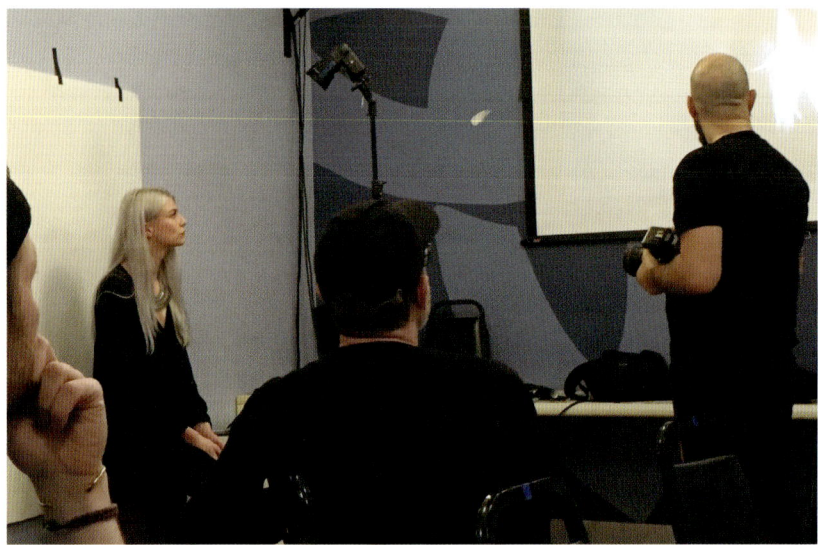

Figure 2.16 The setup. The subject is placed right against the wall backdrop, which, with the help of the grid, goes to black due to light falloff. *Photo by Karen Koenig.*

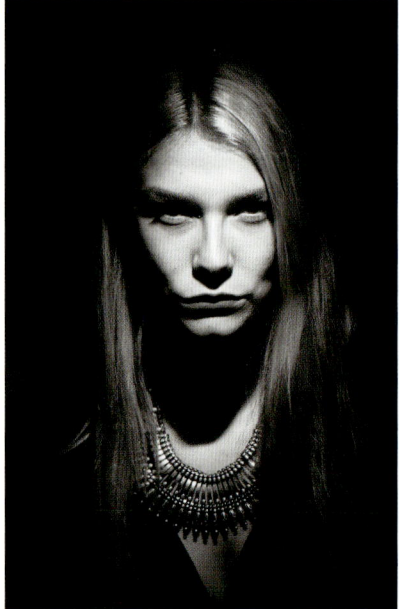

Figure 2.17 The gridded shot. The light falloff when using the grid is so extreme that this white background reads as black in the final shot.

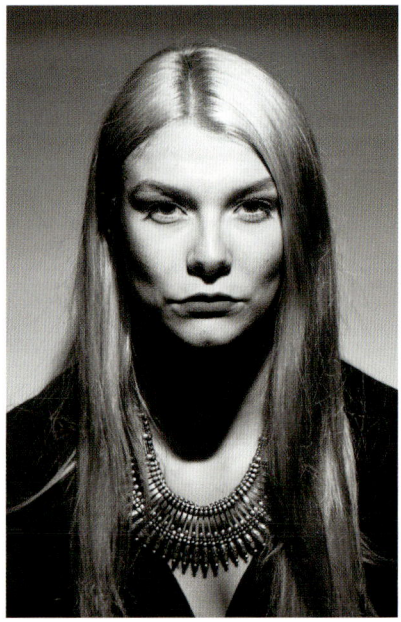

Figure 2.18 The ungridded shot. With the grid removed in this shot, you can see just how much light the grid eliminates.

You may be familiar with the term "invisible black." It's when you are able to create a black background for your subject just by killing the ambient light and illuminating only your subject with your light source, making sure to keep the background unlit. Although I covered the technique in the street section of the first *Studio Anywhere* book (the ballerina scenario), I will improve upon it here.

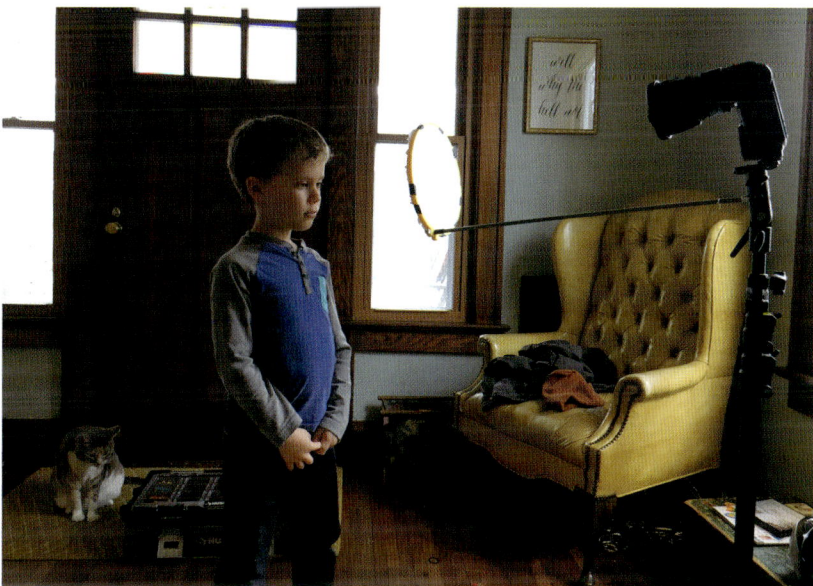

Figure 2.19 The setup. My son Jack is standing four feet in front of a wooden door. My flash, which has a grid/snoot attached, has been rigged to hold a small, shoot-through disc diffuser two feet in front of the flash in order to produce as small, soft light source.

In **Figure 2.19** you can see my setup. My son Jack is standing four feet in front of a wooden door. I have a Rogue 3-in-1 Flash Grid on my flash to produce a small source of light with a fast falloff in order to get an invisible black background. Notice that I also attached a two-foot pole to the light and a small shoot-through disc diffuser to the end of the pole to soften the light. In **Figure 2.20** the image is lit with an umbrella, and you can see that the scene is not pure black due to the light from the umbrella falling on the door behind Jack. In **Figure 2.21** the shot is lit with the Flash Grid only. You can see that, although the grid/snoot provides an invisible black scene, the light is quite harsh. In **Figure 2.22**, which is the result of the setup in Figure 2.19, you can see a softly lit portrait on a black background. Boom.

Figure 2.20 Here, the subject is lit with an umbrella, which results in the background being lit.

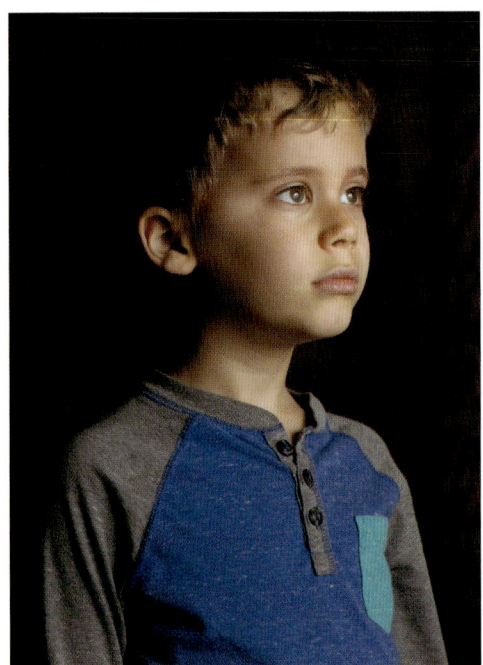

Figure 2.21 This shot is lit with the grid/snoot, and though the background is black, the light on Jack is harsh.

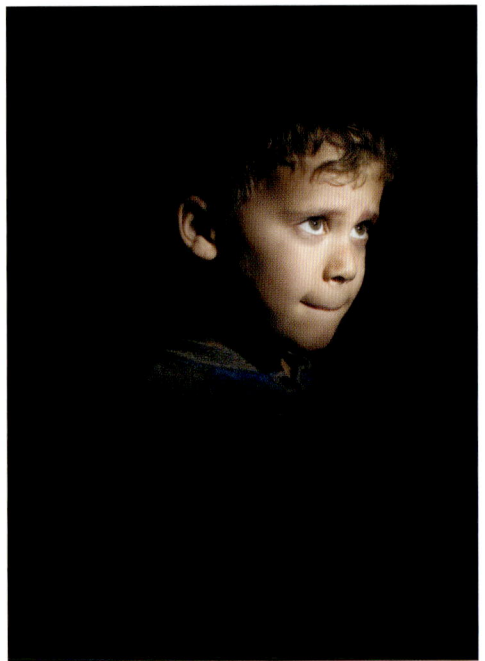

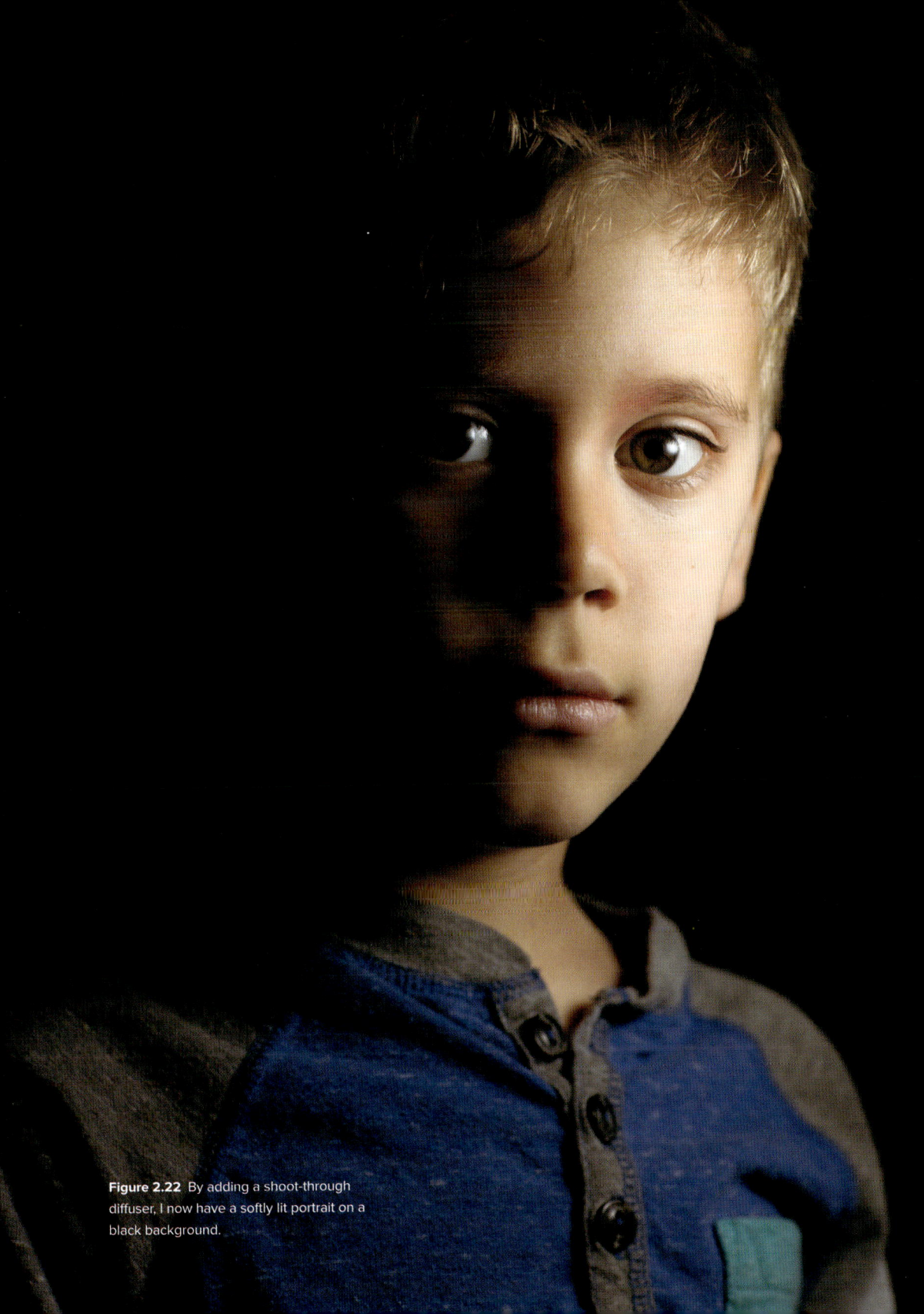

Figure 2.22 By adding a shoot-through diffuser, I now have a softly lit portrait on a black background.

SOFTBOX

When I need soft light with a fast falloff (for flattering, dramatic light), I use a softbox with a grid attachment (**Figure 2.23**). As with the umbrella, however, I typically leave the softbox at home in my basement studio, because I travel with the smallest amount of gear possible. Similar to the scenario in Figure 2.19, I can create an invisible black scene while using the gridded softbox, but because the softbox is larger, I not only have to carry around a bulky modifier and possibly a sandbag if I take it on location, but I will also need more space between my subject and the back wall to avoid lighting the back wall (**Figure 2.24**).

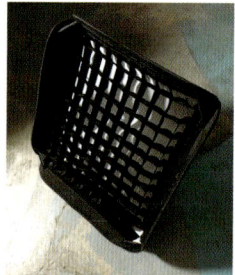

Figure 2.23 This is a collapsible softbox, with attachable grid, made by Cactus. I use it when I want soft light with a quick falloff.

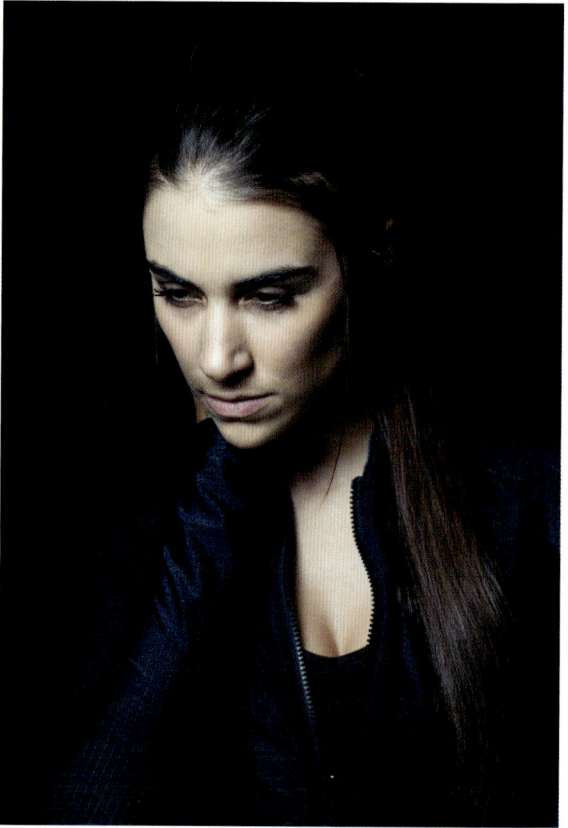

Figure 2.24 This was lit with the Cactus softbox and the grid attached. Although the subject was only a few feet in front of a light-colored wall, the background went to black because of the quick falloff.

BARN DOORS

Recently, I had a portrait shoot with the legendary poet, rapper, and actor Saul Williams. It began with a simple stroke of luck: I saw he was scheduled to perform at a local club near my house, and so I did a quick search for the name of his manager. I easily found it and e-mailed them, introducing myself and explaining that I would like to take his portrait. I said that I could meet him at the venue after the sound check and would need only 15 minutes. To my excitement, they agreed. His art had made quite an impact on my life, so I really wanted to put a lot of thought into a concept for the shoot.

While revisiting his music, I had the thought that his voice, what he has to say, is a light in the darkness. This led me to the concept of putting Saul in a red scene, almost complete shadow, with a thin ray of pure white light illuminating his eyes. I didn't just want a spot of light on him, as the grid provided in Figure 2.15, but instead I wanted a thin line of light that ran across the wall and led through the frame to his face. This would require a light modifier that I didn't own at the time; I would need barn doors for my flash.

Barn doors are metal flaps that can open and close, covering the left, right, top, and bottom of the light. They are typically used on studio strobes or hot lights. It's the tool you need when you want to create a narrow line of light, either vertical or horizontal. The problem is that they aren't available for small flashes. At least, they weren't at the local camera shop I went to hours before my shoot was scheduled to begin (I had finalized the concept for the shoot that morning).

Coming up short at the camera shop, I decided to craft my own barn doors (**Figure 2.25**). I grabbed a sheet of black foam board, some black gaff tape,

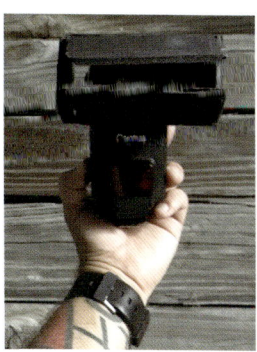 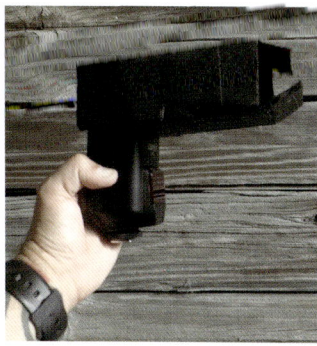

Figure 2.25 I wanted some barn doors for my flash, and when I couldn't find any, I built my own out of black foam board and gaff tape.

and a utility knife. I measured the width and height of the end of my flash and cut pieces of foam board to match it. After taping the four pieces together to make a tight-fitting box for the flash, I cut two additional strips of foam board and taped them over the opening. These flaps were the barn doors. The gaff tape over the seams allowed them to hang open at a rough 45-degree angle. If I wanted an extremely small opening, I could pinch the flaps closed to the desired opening and then hold them in position with a strip of tape. As you can see in **Figure 2.26**, they worked like a charm. The best part about the modifier is that you can smash it flat in your camera bag once it's removed from the flash because there is an opening on the front and back of it. It's the smallest, cheapest, and most effective light modifier that I own.

Figure 2.26
The resulting portrait of Saul Williams, lit exactly how I wanted, with my DIY barn doors.

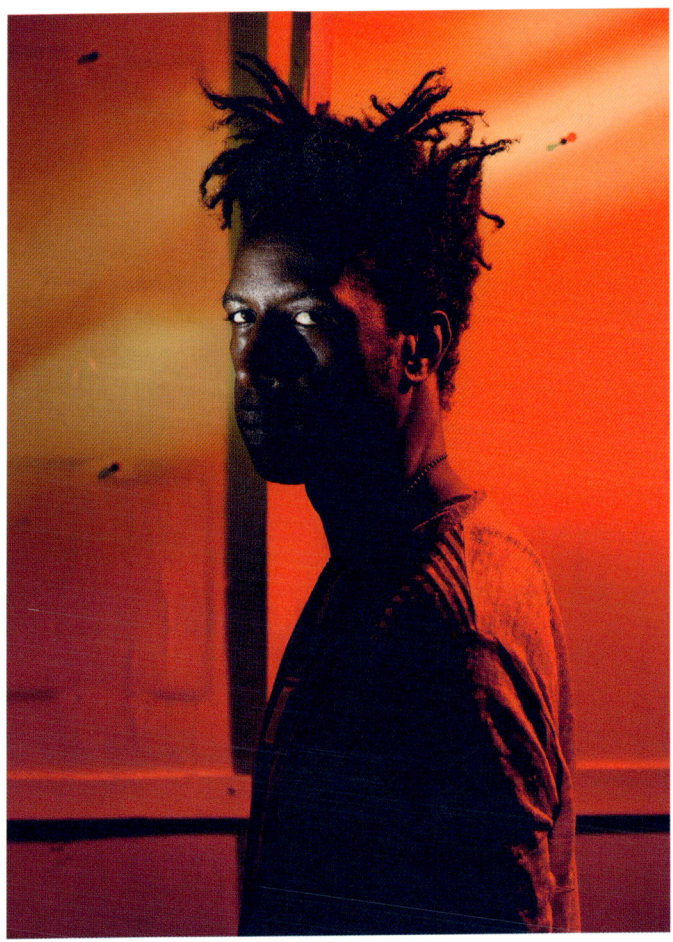

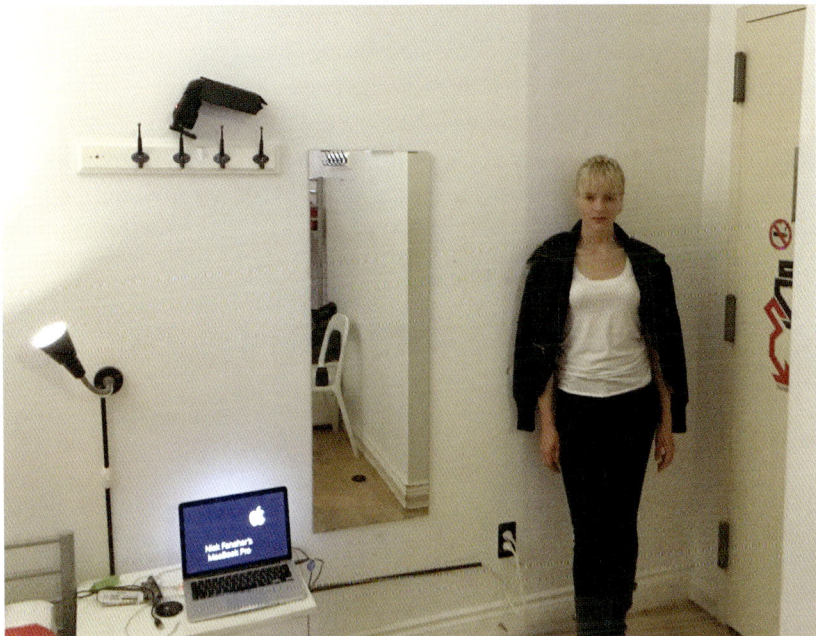

Figure 2.27 The setup. I propped up the flash (with barn doors attached) on a coat hook in my hostel room to create a dark, dramatic scene for a portrait.

A week later I was in New York City on a shoot and was staying in a hostel in Williamsburg. I had an extra day to do some test shooting, so I reached out to a few models. Two of the three models said that it'd be easier for them to come to me. I explained that I was staying in a hostel and sharing a room with two room-mates, so space would be extremely tight. They were fine with that. I knew that with the especially cramped room and limited wall space, I'd really need to get creative with my lighting. Enter my newly crafted barn doors. As you can see, I literally had to prop my light on a coat hook and place my model by the door in order to have a blank wall space behind her (**Figure 2.27**). With the flash's close proximity to the wall and the addition of the barn doors, a cool, unplanned thing happened—lasers (**Figure 2.28**).

As I mentioned earlier, the Cactus flashes make a cool, prism-like effect when fired along a surface. When I place the barn door modifier on the flash and fire it along a surface, the prism effect is even more pronounced, becoming laser-like in appearance. I wanted the wall behind the model to be a little out of focus, allowing some separation from the model, so I shot at a slightly wider aperture of f/2.8 (**Figure 2.29**). In Lightroom, aside from my normal color grading, I also wanted to add a bit of graininess to the image to give it a film noir vibe. This can be done in the Effects panel, as seen in **Figure 2.30**. Experiment with the Amount, Size, and Roughness settings for the grain to find what you prefer. If you plan on doing any retouching to the image, do it before adding grain or the retoucher will hate you. In **Figure 2.31** the tiny hostel room is no more. It's just Larissa, alone in the void.

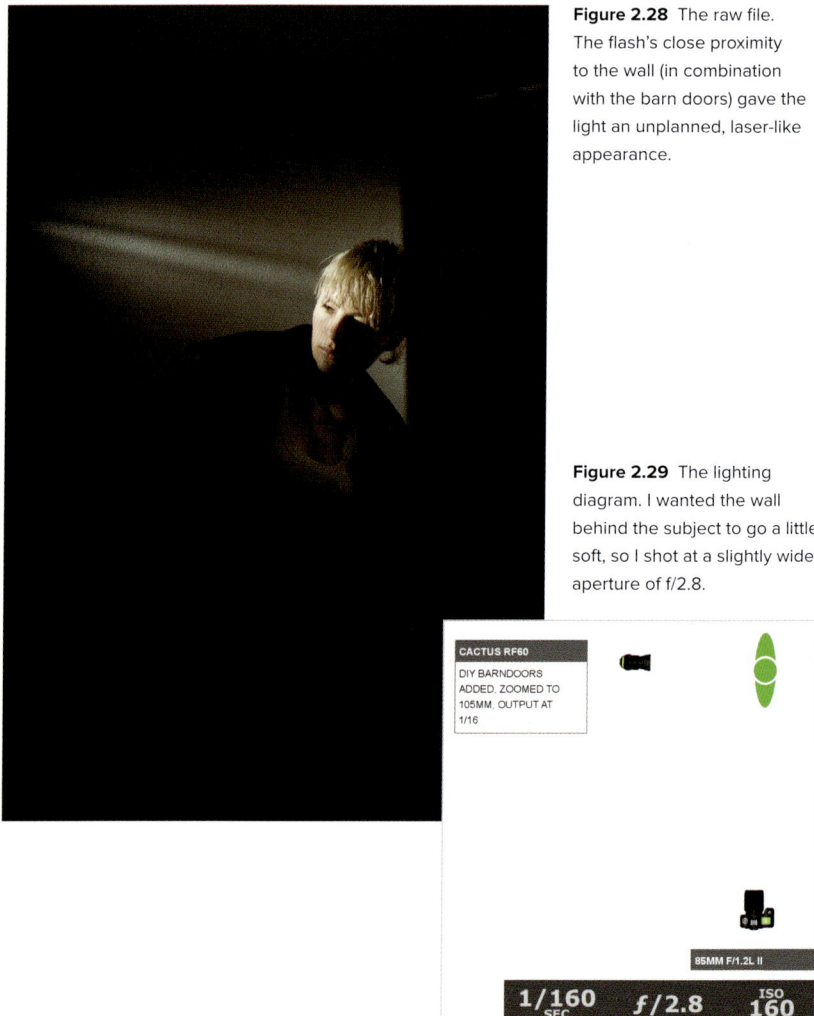

Figure 2.28 The raw file. The flash's close proximity to the wall (in combination with the barn doors) gave the light an unplanned, laser-like appearance.

Figure 2.29 The lighting diagram. I wanted the wall behind the subject to go a little soft, so I shot at a slightly wider aperture of f/2.8.

CACTUS RF60

DIY BARNDOORS ADDED, ZOOMED TO 105MM, OUTPUT AT 1/16

85MM F/1.2L II

1/160 SEC.   f/2.8   ISO 160

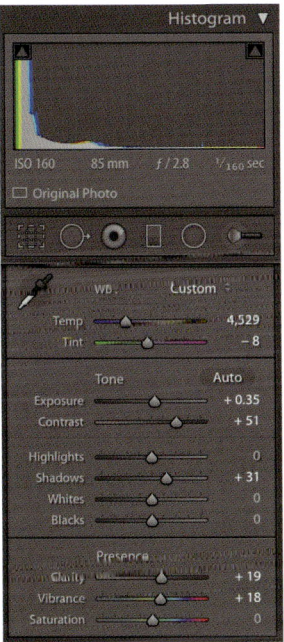

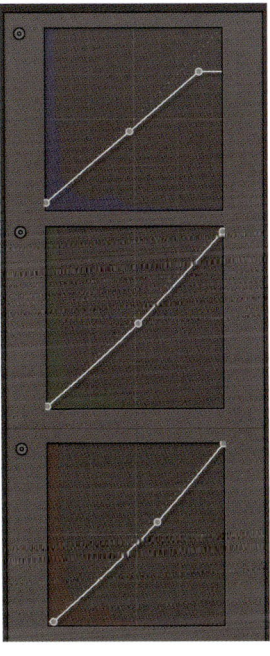

Figure 2.30 The Lightroom settings. I wanted to push a film noir vibe in the image, so I added grain in the Effects panel.

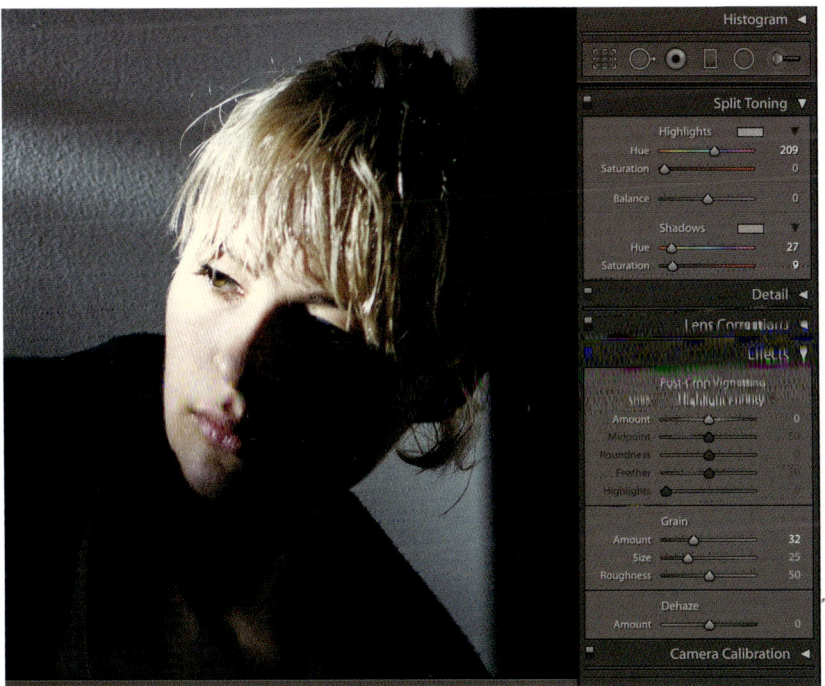

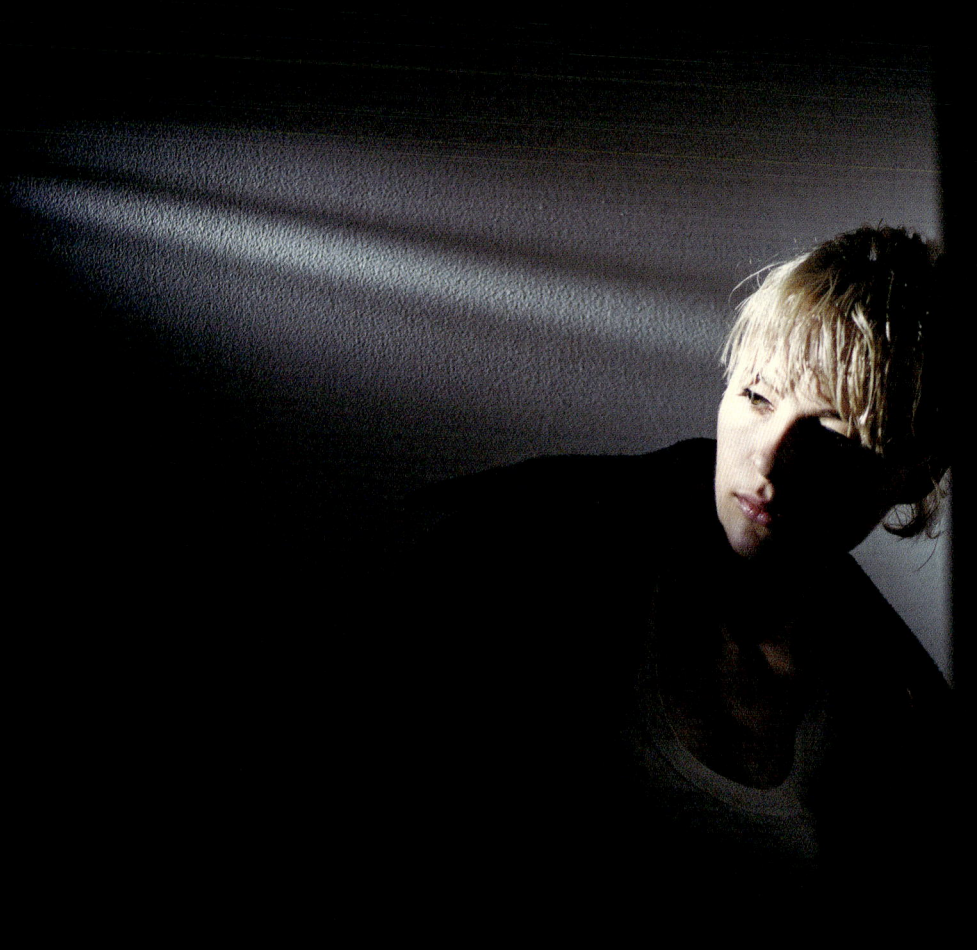

Figure 2.31 The final shot, complete with laser. Dr. Evil would be pleased.

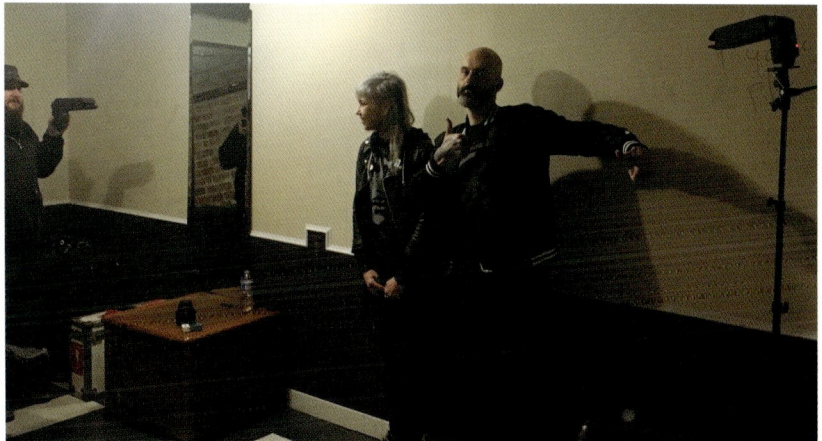

Figure 2.32 I wanted to use this lighting effect on the band Youth Code. Because the light was so narrow, however, I needed to use two lights, one for each subject.

When I was photographing the Los Angeles industrial two-piece Youth Code, I wanted to use this lighting effect. However, because the light is so narrow when lit from the side, it wouldn't work to light both musicians evenly. Instead, I used two strobes, each outfitted with barn doors (**Figure 2.32**). The barn doors were open a bit more this time, allowing the light stream to be a bit wider, as seen in **Figure 2.33**.

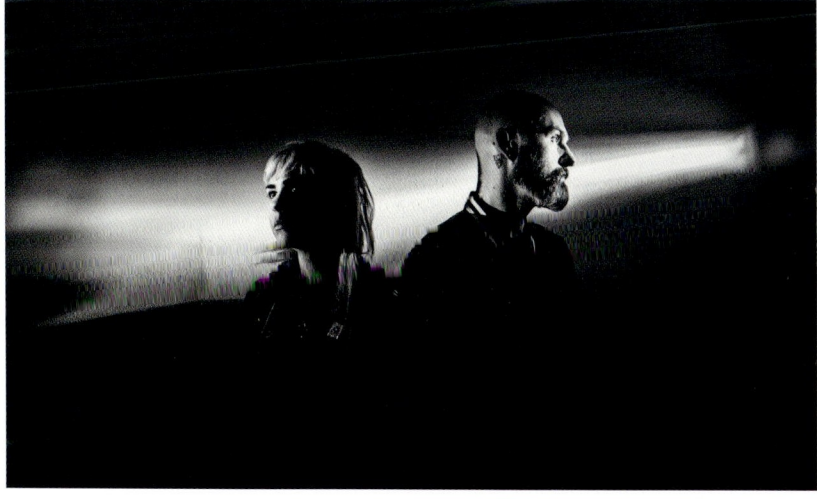

Figure 2.33 The final shot is punchy and epic, just like the band's music.

You can still use the barn doors to create a narrow, linear lighting effect when photographing a group of people. When I photographed the metal band Deafheaven, I wanted to have them isolated against a white seamless background, with their bodies silhouetted and only their faces illuminated. I met them at the venue at the time of their sound check and I set up a white seamless sweep (**Figure 2.34**). I would've preferred to just use a white wall as a backdrop, but this club, like most clubs, didn't have open, white walls. Thankfully, I brought a portable backdrop kit and a roll of white seamless with me just in case.

After setting up the sweep, I placed two flashes on the ground about 5 to 7 feet in front of it, at either end. I aimed them up at a 45-degree angle to get an even spread of light across the white. I laid down a strip of black gaff tape just in front of the background lights, indicating where the band would stand. I placed my main light, with DIY barn doors attached, about 15 feet in front of the tape line and raised it up to 15 feet. I needed the greater distance to allow the strip of light to be wide enough to cover all five band members. Had it been closer, the guys at each end of the group would've been in shadow. By raising the light to a high angle, the light falling on them was making more dramatic light than it would've at a straight-on angle. In the final shot (**Figure 2.35**), you can't even see the background lights because they were behind the legs of the subjects—another bonus of using small flashes. P.S. I had the backdrop extended by a retoucher.

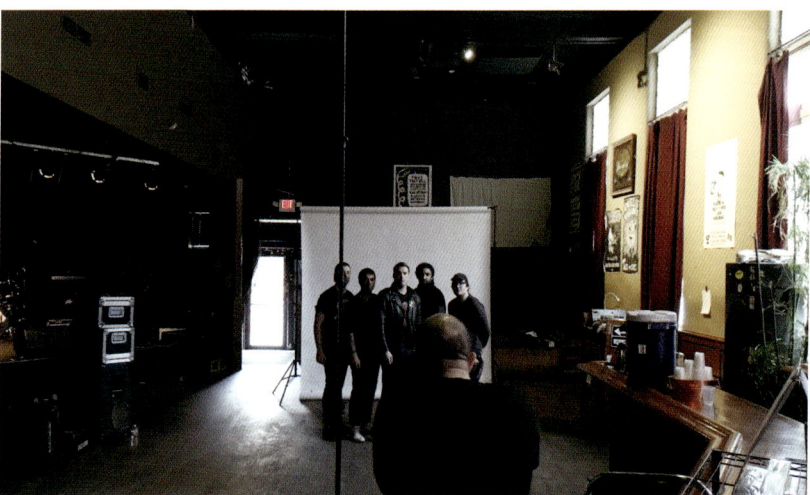

Figure 2.34 The setup. In order to light the whole band, from left to right, my main light needed to be about 15 feet in front of them. *Photo by Adam Lowe.*

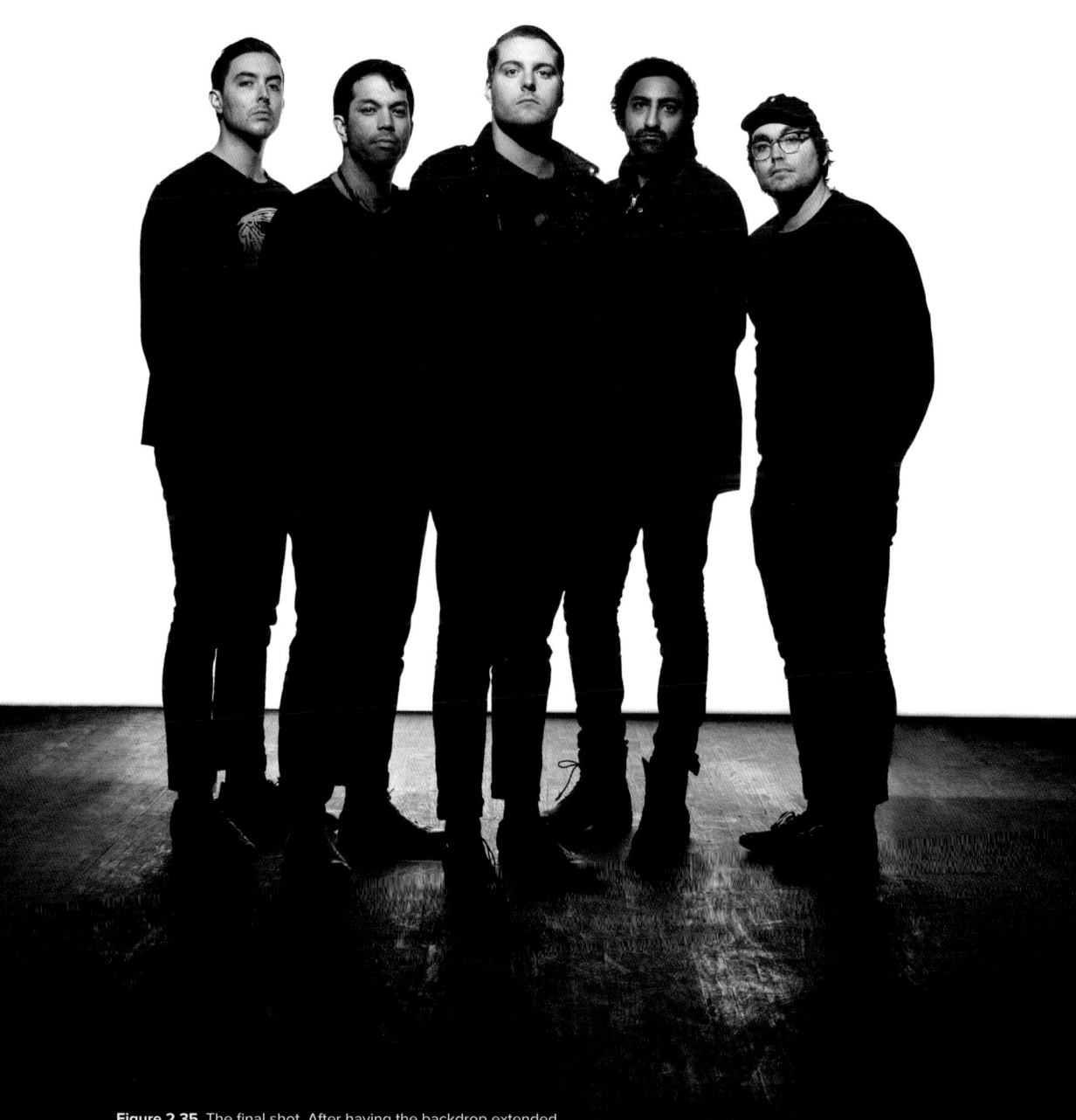

Figure 2.35 The final shot. After having the backdrop extended in post, the band is looking fresh to deaf, heaven.

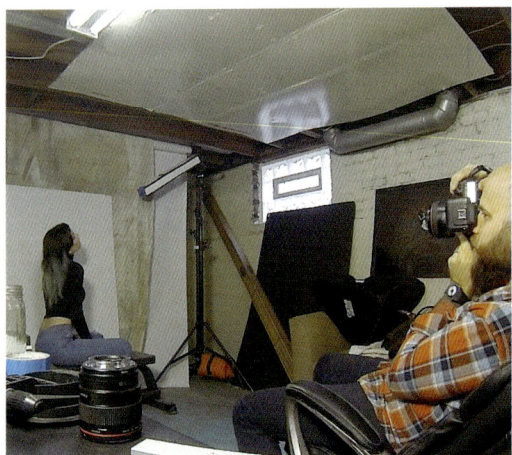

Figure 2.36 This is a DIY, 24-inch snoot, complete with cookie. This extended modifier gives the light a more defined edge than the shorter one I used with the barn doors. This is because the distance from the light source to the cookie is greater.

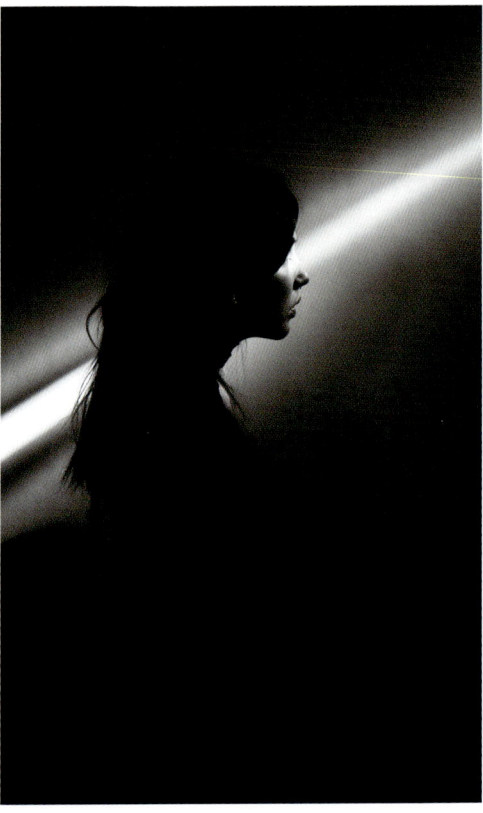

Figure 2.37 The light output from the extended snoot is narrow, defined, and even (right).

In **Figure 2.36** you can see that I am using a homemade snoot that is especially long—two feet long, in fact. I also placed a *cookie* (an object that is placed in front of a light source in order to change its shape or quality) over the opening, leaving only a narrow, horizontal opening for light to escape. The added length of the snoot shapes the light into a narrower, more even and defined line than the shorter barn door snoot, as the cookie is further away from the flash (**Figure 2.37**). The closer the barn doors, cookie, or light modifier is to the flash, the softer the edges of the light output will be.

Finally, you can even get a great effect by placing the barn doors on your flash while it's on your camera's hot shoe. The horizontal banding creates a cool, dramatic effect. Note that, as I mentioned earlier, in order to get a shadowless vertical shot when your flash is on your hot shoe, you need to shoot a horizontal and crop to a vertical, as I did in **Figure 2.38**.

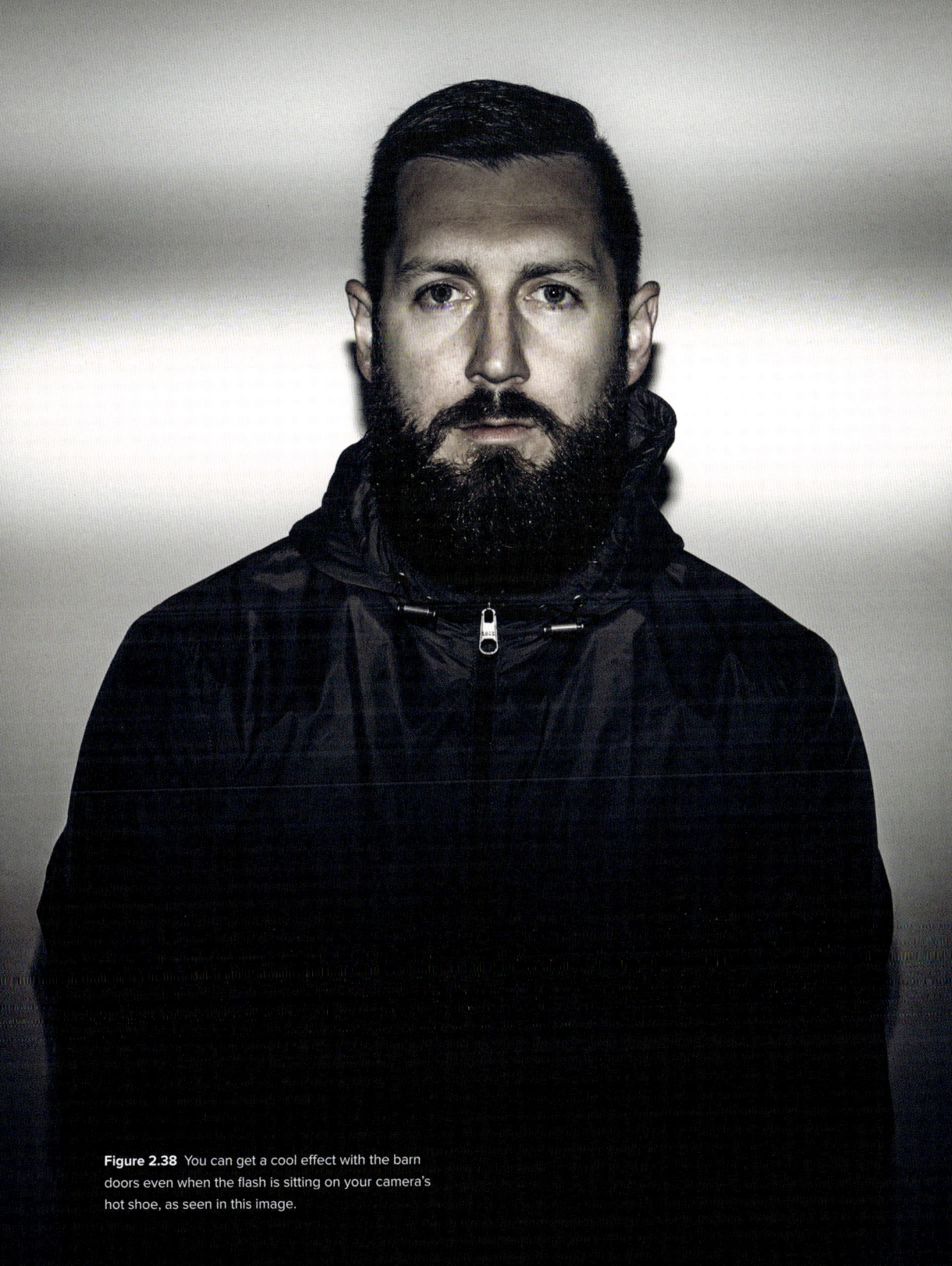

Figure 2.38 You can get a cool effect with the barn doors even when the flash is sitting on your camera's hot shoe, as seen in this image.

LIGHT PLACEMENT

When it comes to shaping light, light placement is just as important as the modifiers you're using—perhaps even more so. Depending on the height or distance of your light in relation to your subject, the light spread and shadows change dramatically. In **Figure 2.39**, you can see an empty glass on a pedestal. I was photographing a new campaign for Jeni's Splendid Ice Creams, and the aesthetic they wanted for it was bright, artsy, and with hard shadows. When I am working with ice cream, my window of time to get the shot is even less than when I'm working with a human subject, because it melts. Thus, I adjust my lighting on empty cups, before adding the ice cream.

Take note that the light is falling off in the top-right part of the frame. If you look at the shadows, you can also deduce that the light is to the left and higher than the glass. For this shot, I wanted even light across the whole frame with a hard shadow.

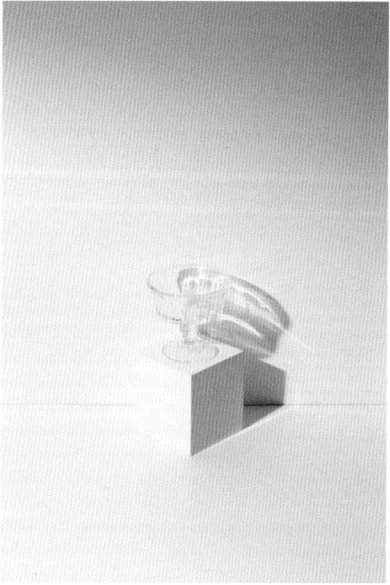

Figure 2.39 If you note the direction of the shadows, you can deduce that the light was to the left and several feet above the product.

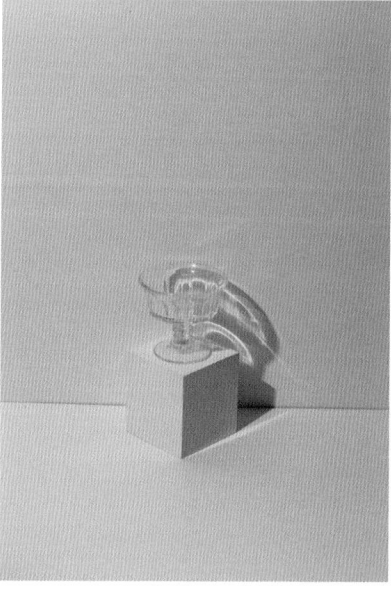

Figure 2.40 Once I adjusted the aim of the flash head and backed the light a couple feet further away from the product, the light spread was even across the frame.

To achieve a broad, even spread of light across the frame, I zoomed the flash out to 24mm and backed the light several feet away from the product. Because I moved the light back, I needed to open up my aperture a stop to compensate and ensure the light was even across the frame (**Figure 2.40**). Note that even though my light output was only set to 1/4 power, I was able to get a small aperture of f/16 due to the close proximity of the light in relation to the small set (**Figure 2.41**). Also, the entire scene being white allowed the light to bounce around, resulting in a brighter scene and thus a smaller aperture. And as you know, small apertures mean sharp images, which is essential in almost all food and product photography.

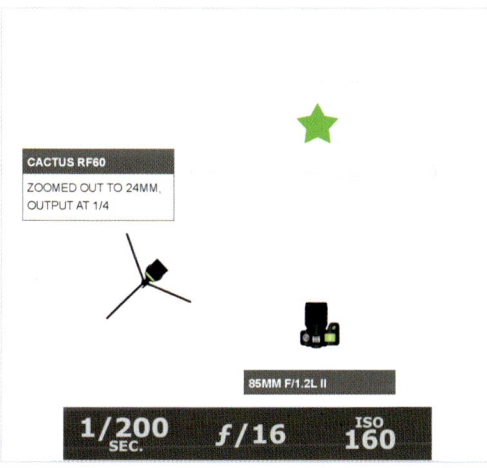

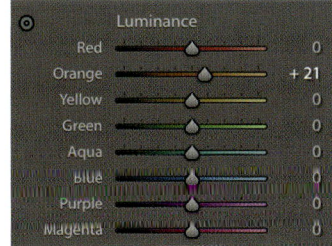

Figure 2.41 The lighting diagram. Even though the light output was only at 1/4 power, my aperture was closed down to f/16 due to the white set and close proximity of the light to the product. The small aperture allowed for a sharp image.

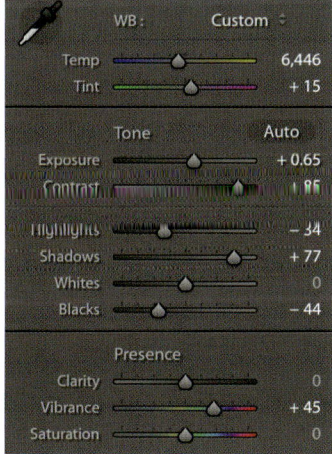

Figure 2.42 The Lightroom settings. The main area I adjusted in the image was the contrast. I cranked it to the right quite a bit, in order to bring out the colors in the image—or should I say, the colors that would be in the image once the ice cream was added to the bowl.

I didn't need to do much in Lightroom to get the image color graded how I liked it. The main thing that I did was crank the contrast, which brings out the color in the image—once the ice cream has been added to the cup, that is. I then lowered the Highlights slider and raised the Shadows slider to retain information in both areas of the image (**Figure 2.42**).

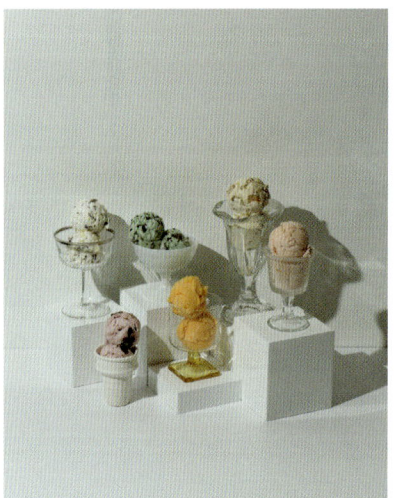 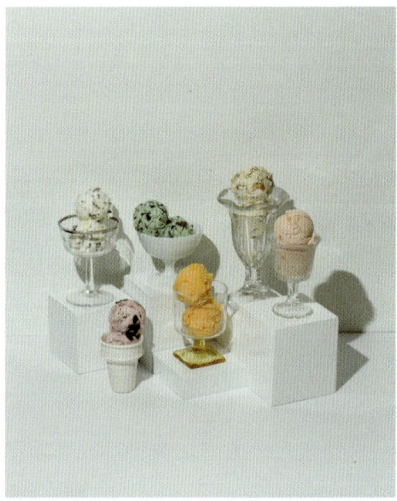

Figure 2.43 The initial shot after the ice cream was added. The shadows were a bit busy.

Figure 2.44 Once I moved the light around to a more frontal angle and elevated it, the shadows decreased in size, allowing for a cleaner image.

Now my light was set and I was ready for the ice cream to be placed in the shot. Although the products closest to the light still looked great (**Figure 2.43**), their shadows were falling on the ice cream to the right of them, resulting in a busy image. To remedy this, I moved the flash stand about a foot to the right, to a more frontal position in relation to the ice cream. I also raised the light about six inches higher. These changes caused the shadows to shorten in length, resulting in a cleaner looking image (**Figure 2.44**). After I applied the Lightroom settings from Figure 2.42, the final image looked good enough to eat (**Figure 2.45**).

When you're lighting with a flashgun as opposed to a studio light that comes equipped with a modeling light, it's a bit harder to figure out what the light is going to do. This will come with practice. In the meantime, one tip is to trigger the flash while looking at the setup, without the camera in hand. See what the shadows are doing before you even put the camera to your eye.

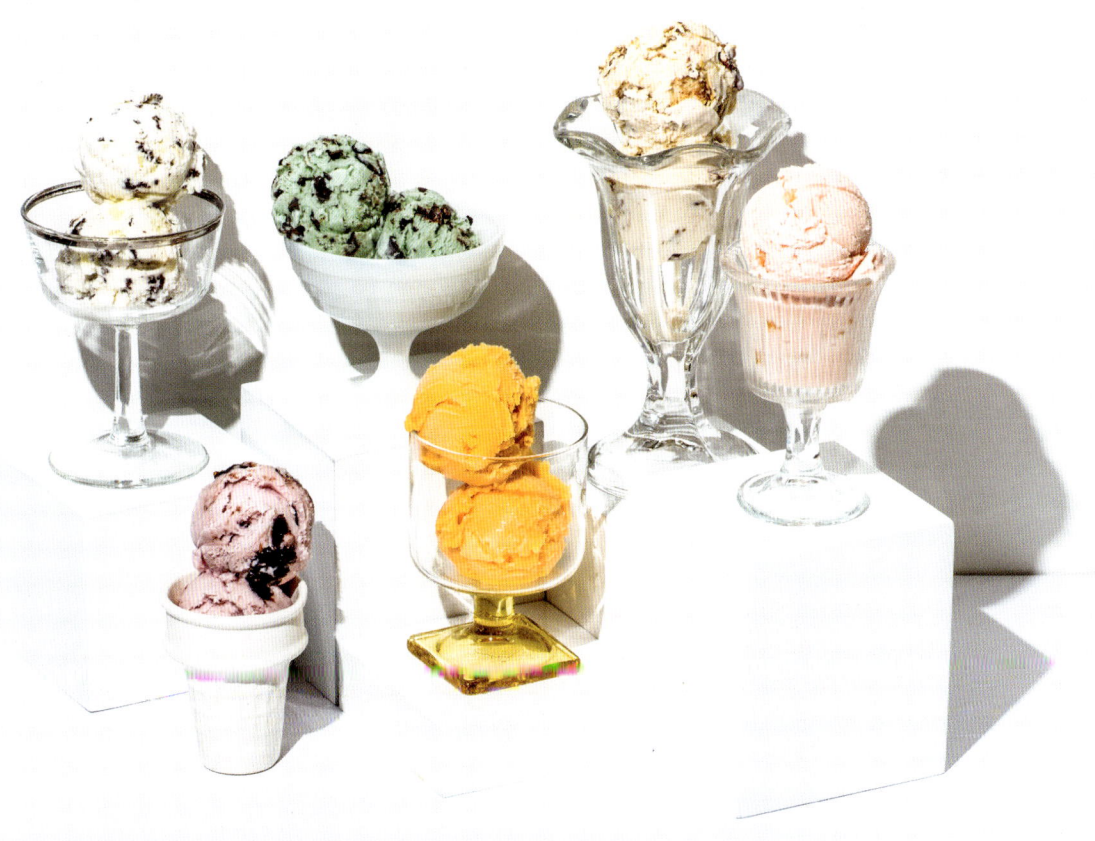

Figure 2.45 The final shot. Creamy.

VARIETY IS THE SPICE OF LIFE

The setup in **Figure 2.46** is the same as the one in Figure 2.45, save for a pink backdrop. My light is unmodified, elevated, and several feet to the left of the product. The result gives the client the desired look for the brand, as seen in **Figure 2.47**. But what do clients love even more than satisfied expectations? Extras. More assets. Options. So after I got the shot that I knew the Jeni's team would like, I took an extra minute to get a second, more dramatic option.

All I did was move my light around to the back of the product and add my barn doors to the light (**Figure 2.48**). The client loved the dramatic image that resulted in **Figure 2.49** so much that Jeni's ended up using it as a teaser for its upcoming season.

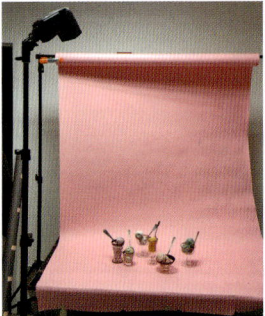

Figure 2.46 The light setup here is the same as for Figure 2.45, but on a pink sweep.

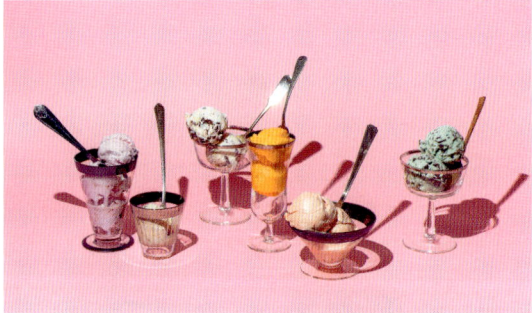

Figure 2.47 This is the look that the brand liked and asked for.

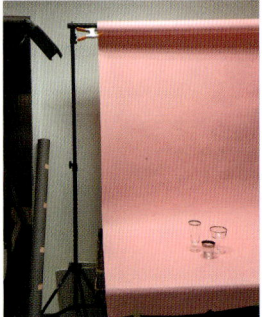

Figure 2.48 I moved the light around to the back of the product and added the barn doors to the flash.

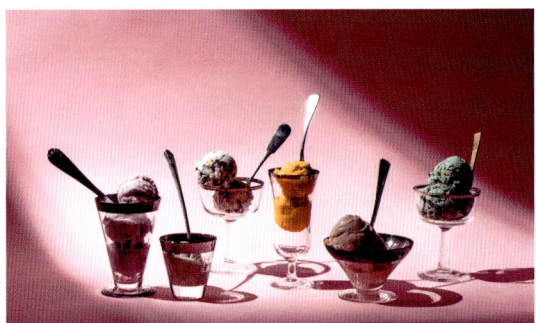

Figure 2.49 This image, which is much moodier and more dramatic, ended up being used by the client as a teaser image for an upcoming campaign.

MAKING A SCENE

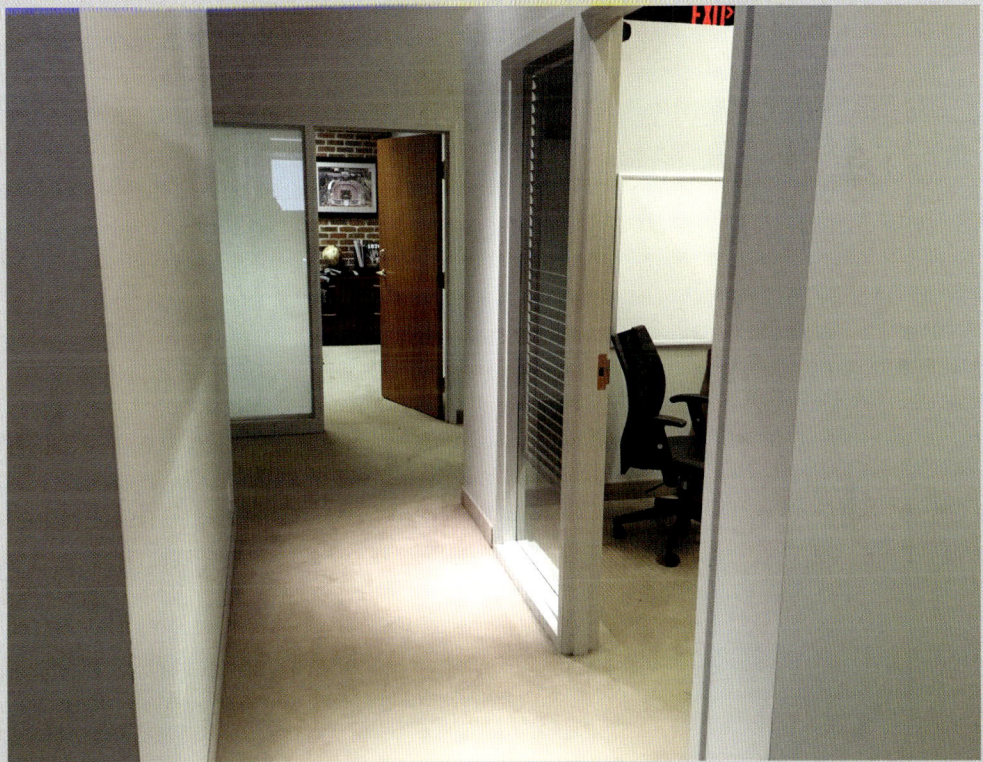

Figure S.1 Where might I place my light(s) and subject if I were creating a moody portrait?

Imagine you are shooting an editorial and the direction you are given by the editor is simple: "Shoot a dramatic portrait of the subject." You are meeting your subject at the magazine and **Figure S.1** is the scenario you walk into. Where might you place the subject and your light (or lights) to get a dramatic portrait? Flip to the back of the book to see where I placed them.

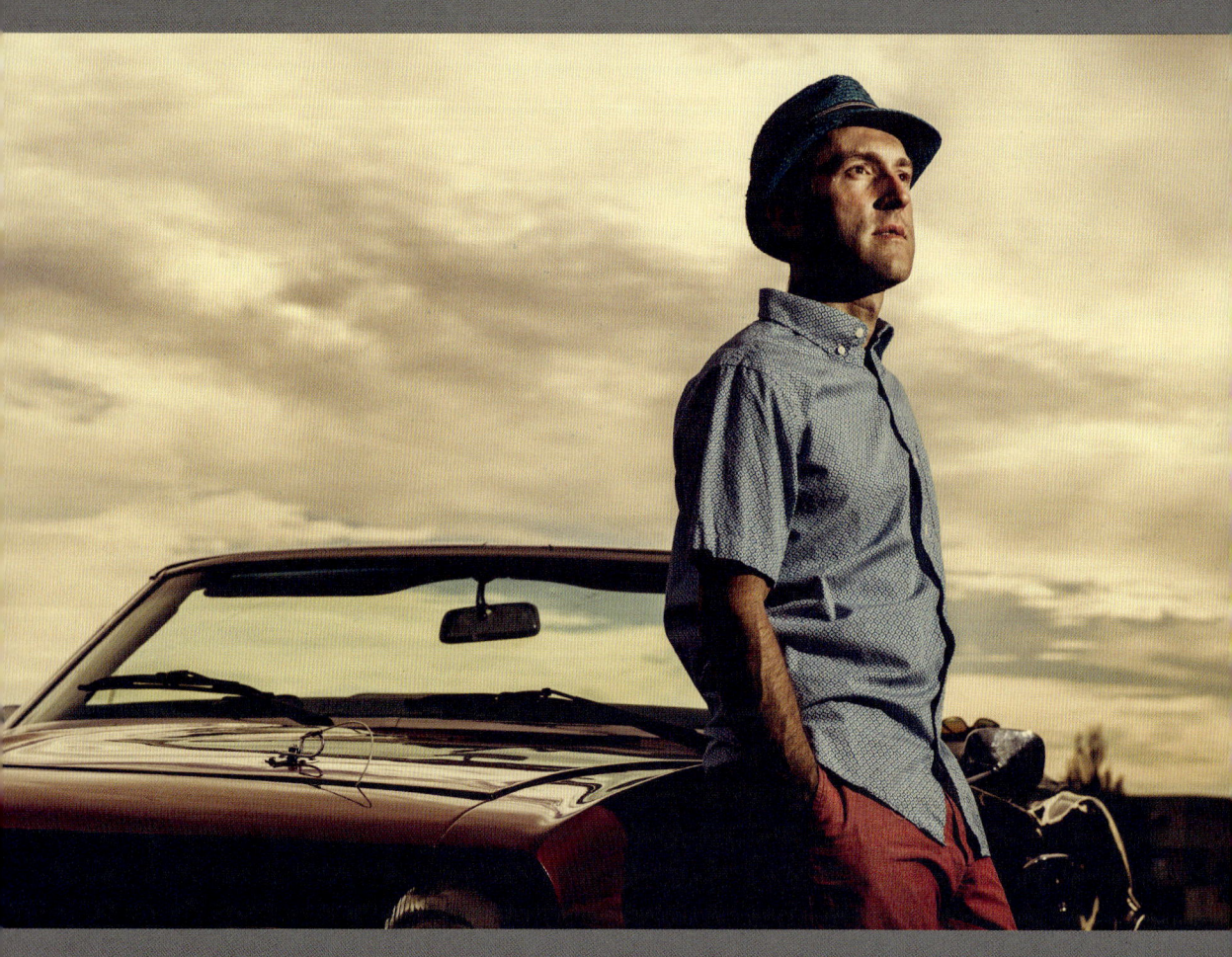

CHAPTER 3

AMBIENT BALANCE

Being able to really see light, let alone control it, is something that comes with much practice and time. Subtly blending ambient light with artificial strobe light is not easy. In fact, it's an art. And it's something you never arrive at, but rather hone. By now you know to keep an eye on what the ambient light is already doing and even how to shape it. You also know your options when it comes to shaping light from a strobe. This chapter delves into how to make these two rogue forces play nicely together (currently imagining a scene from *Tango & Cash*).

DAYTIME: OUTDOORS

Once you know how to shape and control your light, you can start to better understand how to use the light in different situations. Check out the scene in **Figure 3.1**. I was shooting a black-and-white-themed fashion editorial on the street and stumbled upon this cool doorway. Although I loved the spot, I didn't love what the light was doing in it. The sun was in and out of the clouds, which made the exposure unpredictable, and the light that the sun was casting on the model wasn't exactly the dramatic, flattering light I was going for. For **Figure 3.2**, my first attempt, I exposed for the highlights on the model. As you can see, the model's face is well exposed, but the rest of her gets lost in the shadows of the doorway. I tried opening up my exposure, metering for the whole scene. Though it's not as muddy as the previous shot, it's not what I'd call dramatic (**Figure 3.3**). I was going to need to light her in order to dial down the ambient while making sure not to lose her in the shadows.

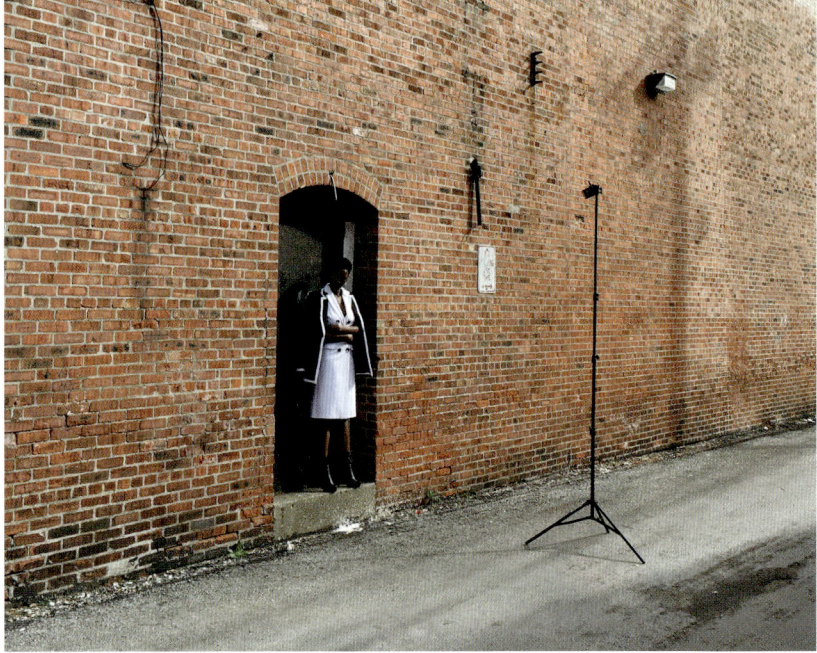

Figure 3.1 The setup. I loved this spot, but not so much what the light was doing. I wanted more drama, so I added a light. Note that I oriented the flash to a vertical position, rather than the normal horizontal one.

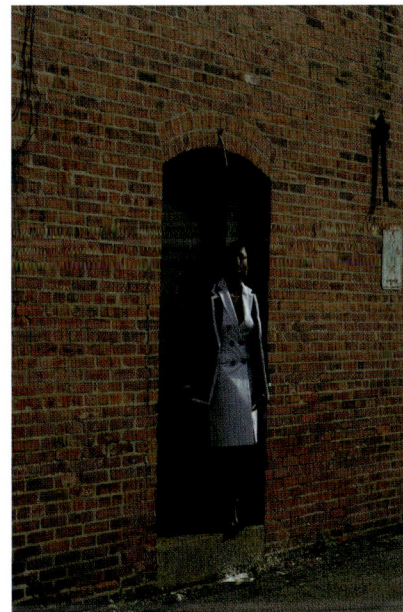
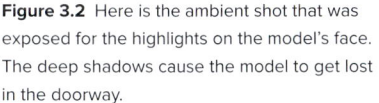

Figure 3.2 Here is the ambient shot that was exposed for the highlights on the model's face. The deep shadows cause the model to get lost in the doorway.

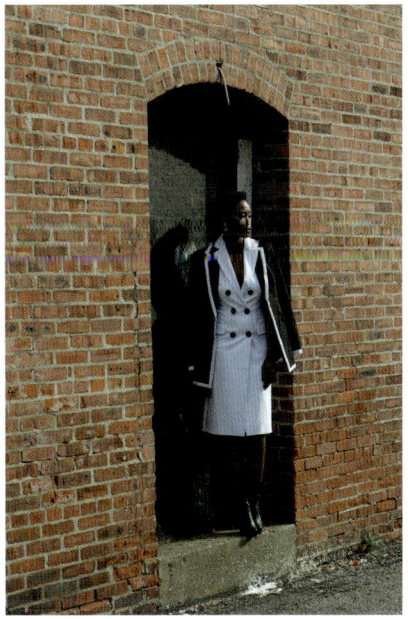

Figure 3.3 In this shot, I exposed for an overall average reading. Although it's brighter, it's not what I'd call dramatic.

My first priority was dialing down the ambient light enough to where the flash would be apparent. Since I was not using High Speed Sync, my maximum shutter speed was 1/200 of a second. After setting that, I lowered my ISO as low as I could, which was 50. The only thing left to do was to start closing down my aperture until the ambient light was a stop underexposed, leaving me at f/8. Now it was time to turn on the flash and turn up the power until the output was bright enough to light my model, which ended up being 1/2 power.

I put an unmodified flash on a stand, raising it up to roughly the same angle as the sun in relation to the model. I set it about 10 feet away from her, allowing for a greater spread of light as well as more defined shadows. My goal was to light the model and not the wall around her. Although a snoot would've worked in minimizing light falloff, I didn't have one on me. Instead, I zoomed the flash in to 105mm, and I positioned the flash to a vertical orientation. This allowed for a narrow, vertical output of light, rather than a broader, horizontal burst (**Figure 3.4**). Now my subject was popping out from the shadows and the brick wall was muted—just how I wanted it (**Figure 3.5**).

Figure 3.4 The lighting diagram. To eliminate as much ambient light as possible, my ISO was at 50 and my shutter speed was maxed out at 1/200. Next, I lowered my aperture until the ambient was one stop underexposed at f/8. Finally, I turned on my flash, increasing the output until the light was bright enough to light the model, which ended up being 1/2 power.

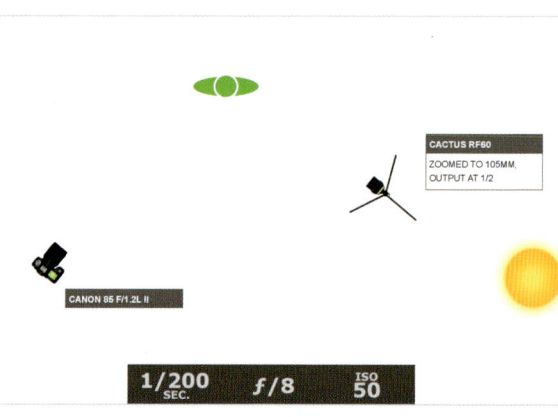

Figure 3.5 The raw file. The model pops out from the shadows, and the brick wall is more muted.

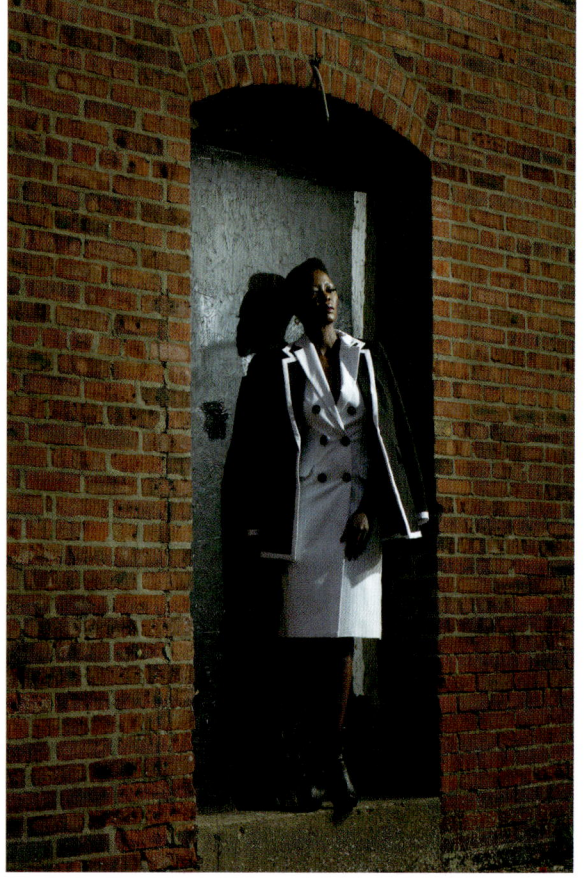

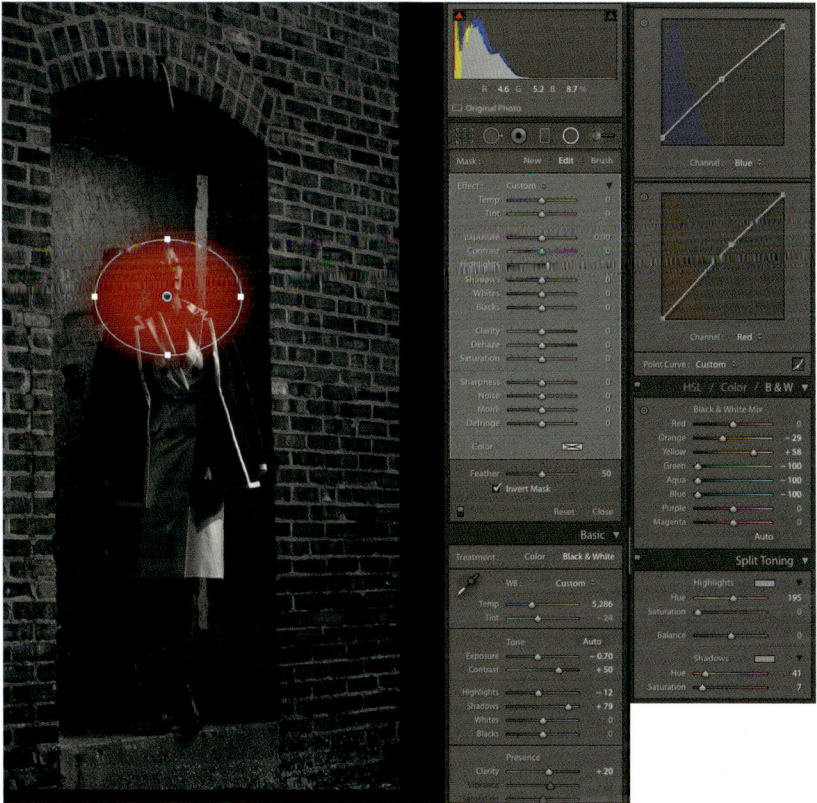

Figure 3.6 The Lightroom adjustments. By making a radial adjustment over the model, bringing up the Highlights slider, as well as tweaking the Orange and Yellow channels in the Black & White Mix, I was able to draw focus to the model's face.

My goal in Lightroom was to push down the presence of the bricks a bit and bring more focus to the model's face. To accomplish this, I made a radial adjustment on her face and increased the Highlights slider. Next, I decreased the Orange slider and increased the Yellow slider in the Black & White Mix panel to further dial back the intensity of the bricks (**Figure 3.6**). To finish the color grading, I increased the contrast, upped the shadows, and added a bit of blue and red in the Tone Curves. Finally, I exported the file to Photoshop to use the more powerful Spot Healing tool to remove any remaining blemishes in the scene. The final shot now looks much more ambiguous, like it could be either moonlight or daylight (**Figure 3.7**). Either way, it's noir as hell, and I'm really happy with it.

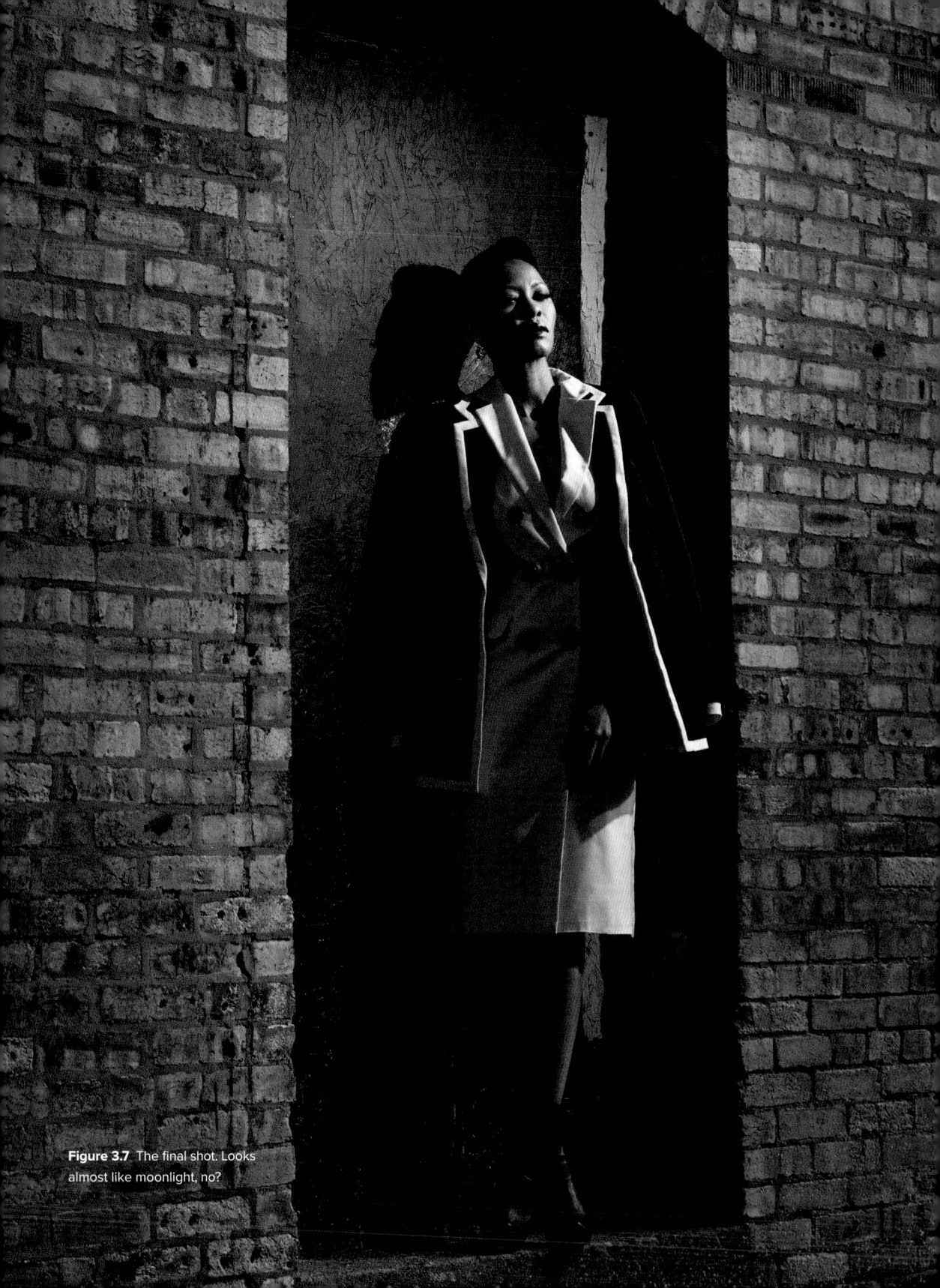

Figure 3.7 The final shot. Looks almost like moonlight, no?

DAYTIME: INDOORS

While doing a two-day shoot for Sears Hardware on location, I needed to capture a variety of scenarios, both indoors and out. In **Figure 3.8** you can see one setup, which was inside a garage, in front of an open door, with the model on a ladder. Although the light from the open door was indirect and thus quite soft, it didn't evenly light the model (**Figure 3.9**) because his head was above the door opening. If the shoot hadn't been for a print ad, I might have just brightened up the top of the image in post. Because the client was so important, however, I wanted to get the shot as close to perfect as I could in camera. That meant adding a flash.

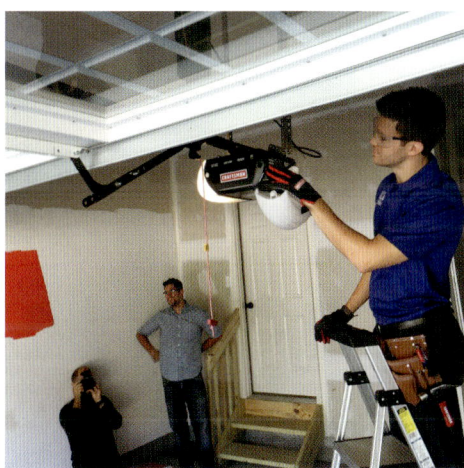

Figure 3.8 The setup. Although the open garage door provided a large, soft light source, it didn't fully light the model on his ladder, so a flash was needed. *Photo by Dylan Stanley.*

Figure 3.9 The available light shot. As you can see, the light falls off at the top of the frame, resulting in uneven lighting.

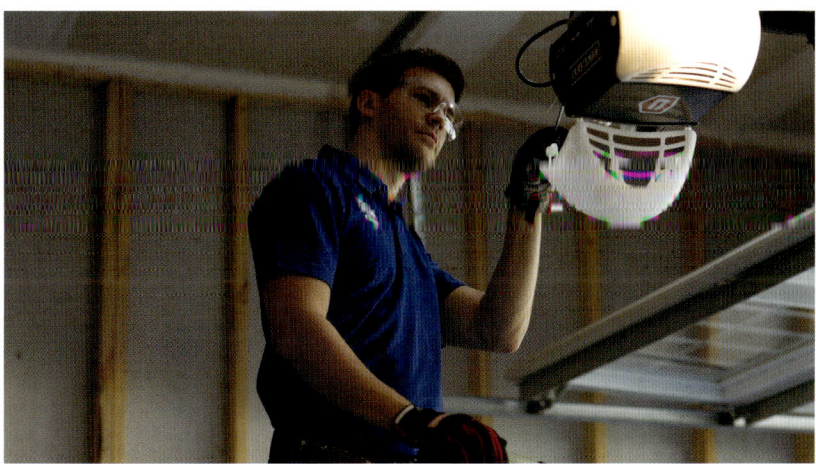

I wanted to fill in the light in the top part of the image, blending it with the light in the bottom, which meant adding soft, cool light. In Figure 3.8 you can see my flash through the window in the garage door. I aimed the light toward the ceiling, pulling the fill card up so that some of the light also kicked toward the subject's face. To get a good ambient exposure in the dark garage, I had two options. The first was to open up my aperture really wide to f/2 or wider, which would lead to a super shallow depth of field. To have a bit of sharpness in my image, I opted instead to keep my aperture at f/3.5, meaning I need to bump up my ISO a bit to 200 to retain a good amount of ambient light (**Figure 3.10**). The added flash filled in the side of the model's face as well as added some separation between him and the ceiling (**Figure 3.11**).

Figure 3.10 The lighting diagram. To have a bit more sharpness in my image, I kept my aperture at f/3.5. So I needed to bump my ISO up to 200 to get a decent ambient exposure. My flash output was moderate at 1/8 power.

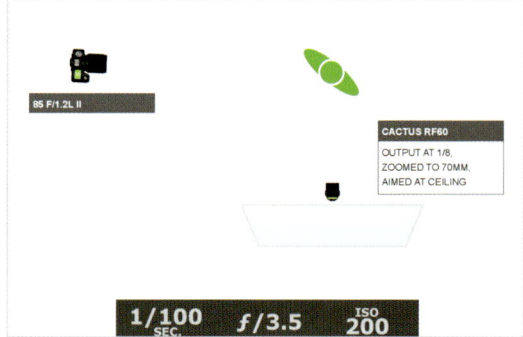

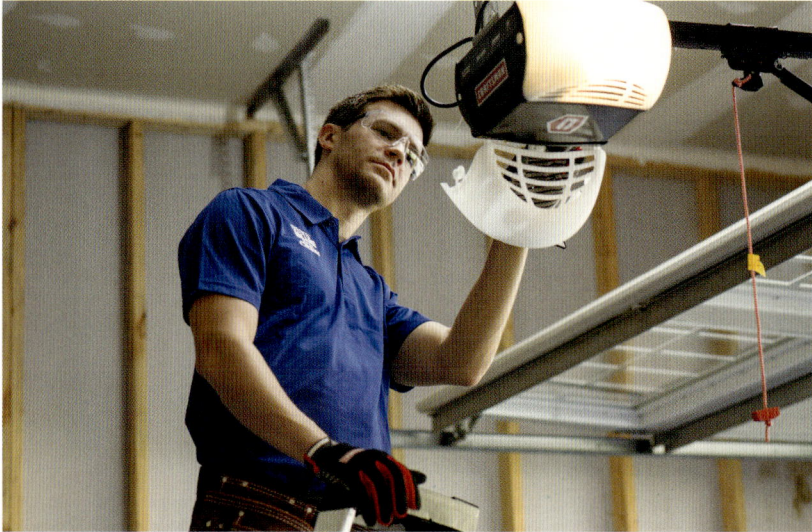

Figure 3.11 The final shot. Now the model is evenly lit and nicely separated from the ceiling.

EVENING: INDOORS

One of the blessings of using small flash is being able to set the output extremely low in order to match dim, indoor ambient light. If you've ever used a monolight, such as Alien Bees, or even more so a power pack like a Profoto system, you know how much more powerful those lights are than the existing ambient light in most indoor scenarios. They are often so strong that photographers sometimes have to "bleed" off extra light in order to get a lower output. This entails attaching an additional, unneeded strobe head to a pack in order to pull power from the main light to lower the output. The technique is helpful when you want to either use a wide aperture to achieve a shallow depth of field or use a higher ISO to bring up the ambient light in a scene. I'm willing to bet that many photographers wouldn't have ever thought that having too much power would be an issue. But it is. In fact, it's an issue whenever you're shooting in a dimly lit room and you want to retain the ambient light, as I was for a recent wedding.

In **Figure 3.12** you can see the stunning interior that was the site of a wedding reception I was shooting. The sun had just gone down, meaning that the light

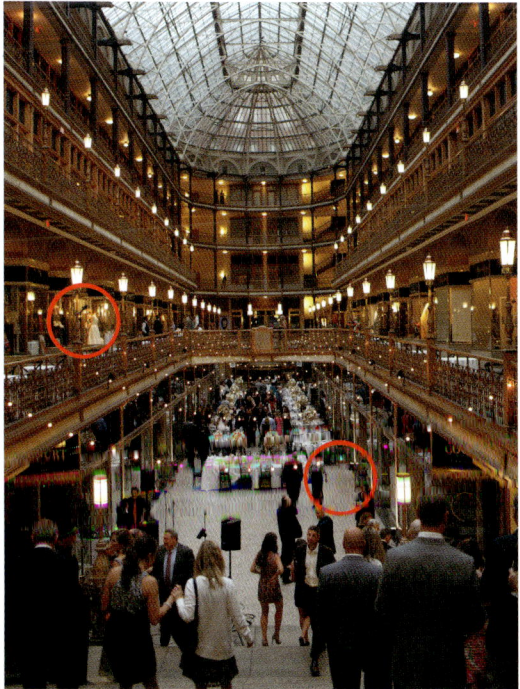

Figure 3.12 This ornate scene was the location of a wedding reception I was shooting. Because it was so dim, I needed to add a light, seen in the left circle, but I couldn't have the output very high because I wanted to retain the ambient light. The circle on the right is where I planned to stand when the bride and groom came down the stairs.

inside was dropping off quickly. The bridal party was just about to do their grand entrance, and I was trying to gauge my exposure and determine whether or not I needed to add a light. I decided that it would be a good idea to have one set up in case it was needed, so I placed one in the upper level, aimed at the middle of the staircase where the wedding party would enter. The left red circle in Figure 3.12 highlights my light placement. Meanwhile, I was posted at the bottom of the steps (Figure 3.12's right circle). My shutter speed was 1/30, which can result in moving objects easily blurring. My goal was to set the light output just high enough to freeze the moving bride and groom, but not so bright that I completely overpowered the dim ambient light, which would have resulted in a black background (**Figure 3.13**). By setting my light 10 to 20 feet away from the middle of the stairs, I was able to get a wide enough light spread with the zoom set to 70mm. And with the output set at 1/8, I could get a fast recycle time on the lights, ensuring I captured the perfect moment (**Figure 3.14**).

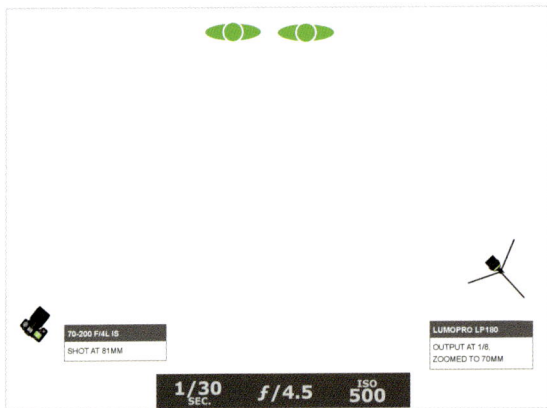

Figure 3.13 The lighting diagram. I zoomed the flash in to 70mm because the light was far enough away from where the action was happening that a wide spread would result in not much light reaching the subject. My ISO was raised to 500 and shutter lowered to 1/30 in order to get a decent ambient exposure.

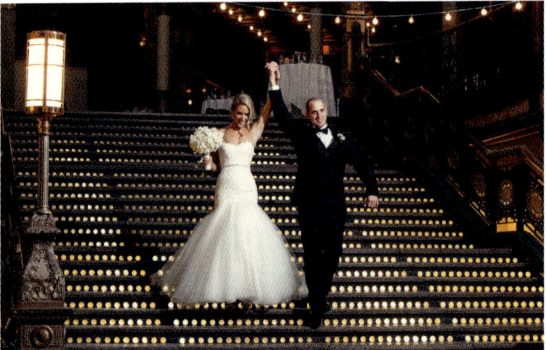

Figure 3.14 The final shot. The bride and groom are crisply captured, and there is still information in the background.

EVENING: OUTDOORS

You've heard the expression "the best of both worlds"? That's exactly what I needed to capture on a recent shoot for The Crest restaurant. It was kind of a unique scenario in that it was both an indoor and an outdoor shoot at the same time. I needed to photograph the details of the new restaurant's space as well as how customers were interacting with it. The only way to do it was to shoot when it was open for business, during the dinner rush. This meant that space was especially limited, and wherever I stood, I was in someone's way. I also needed to go up to every table that was in my shot and get the diners' permission to photograph them. For a natural introvert, this was way outside my comfort zone, so I made my assistant do it for me. (Yes, I sometimes bring assistants on bigger shoots.) That said, I was looking for any excuse I could find to shoot from the recesses of the restaurant, keeping the customers far away and even out of focus, if possible.

We had actually just wrapped up shooting and were about to head inside, when I noticed the restaurant name on the front window and thought it'd make for a rad shot to have the name highlighted with a full restaurant out of focus in the background. I knew that I was going to need to a strobe to pop out the letters and that I would need to have a thin line of light coming from the side in order to illuminate only the letters, so I added the Rogue Flash Grid to my flash and placed the light parallel to the glass (**Figure 3.15**). I set the white balance to Flash to cause the tungsten-lit dining room to go more orange than it naturally appeared to the eye. Now, there was a separation between the words on the glass and the background created not only by differing brightness and depth of field but also by the differing color temperatures (**Figure 3.16**).

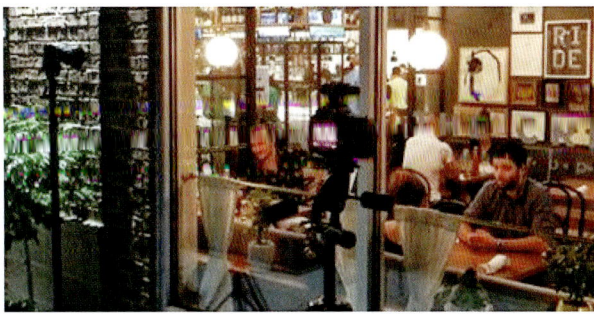

Figure 3.15 The setup. I was shooting the lifestyle images for The Crest, a new restaurant in town, and wanted to get the logo on the window with a full dining room out of focus in the background.

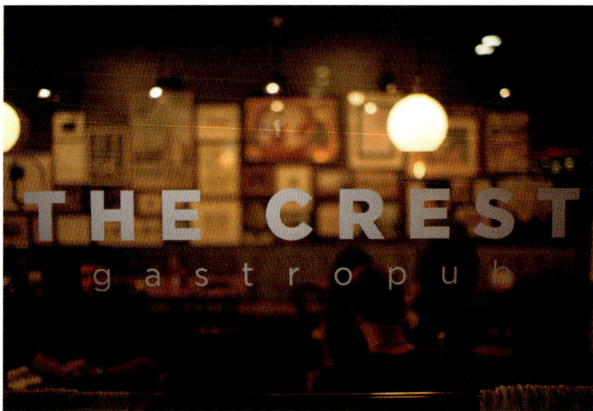

Figure 3.16 The raw file. The words are now separated from the background by the contrasting color temperatures, depth of field, and strobe light versus ambient light.

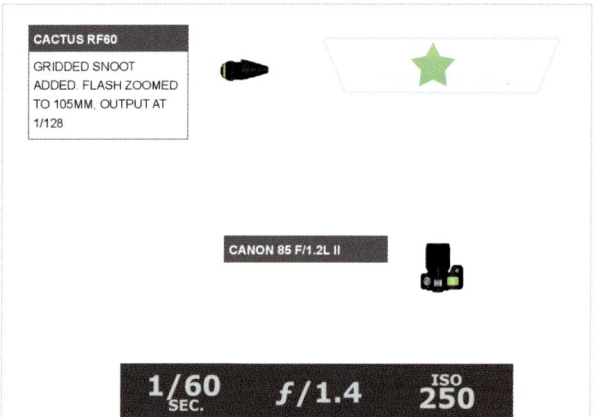

Figure 3.17 The lighting diagram. The dim dining room light and the matching low strobe output results in a really wide aperture.

Because of how dim the indoor lights were, my output was all the way down at 1/128, even though I was shooting at f/1.4 (**Figure 3.17**). In Lightroom, I really pushed the orange of the dining room to communicate a cozy feeling (**Figure 3.18**). To further flush out this warm feeling, I added a warm tone to the highlights in the Split Toning panel. Finally, to round out the color grading and bring a bit of balance in the overall colors, I added a cool tone to the Shadows slider. The final shot (**Figure 3.19**) ended up being used by the client as a header image on a design contest submission, which went on to win Best of Category. I'd like to think that my images helped give the restaurant a one-up over its competition, although The Crest didn't need much help.

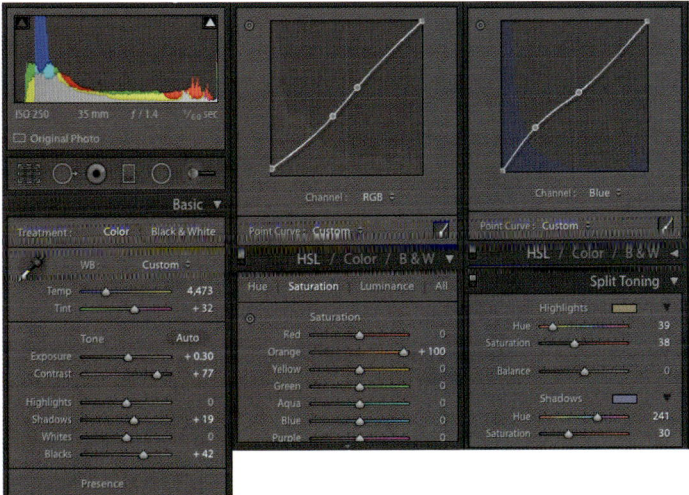

Figure 3.18 The Lightroom settings. I wanted to push the warmth of the background, so I increased the saturation in the Orange channel. I also added warm highlights and cool shadows in the Split Toning panel.

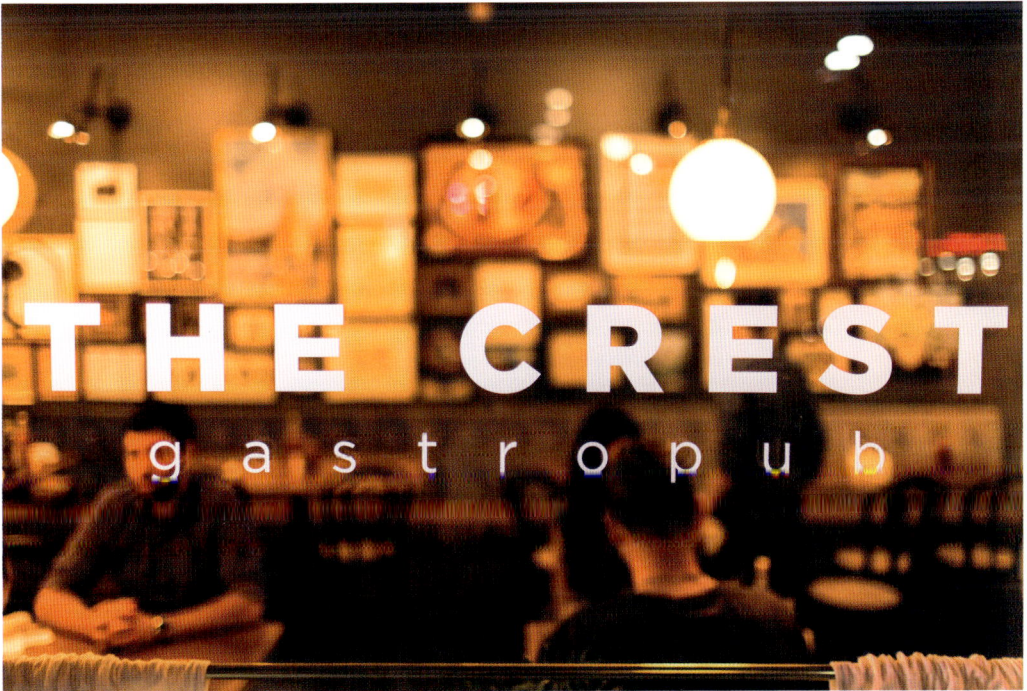

Figure 3.19 The final shot. The client ended up loving this image so much that the restaurant used it as a cover for its design contest submission.

PRO TIP:
SMARTPHONE PHOTOGRAPHY

You may have heard Chase Jarvis's expression "The best camera is the one you have with you." I 100% believe that this is true. When said camera happens to be a smartphone, however, you should know how to make the best of it, because it's a fairly rudimentary piece of gear.

I have an iPhone 6S. When I am using my smartphone's camera in optimal conditions—in a well-lit scenario where a wide focal length is needed—and in combination with the app Snapseed, I can get some pretty fantastic images. The only things my iPhone camera can't do well are low-light scenarios, situations where I want a longer focal length, or when I want a shallow depth of field.

One fantastic feature that my phone's camera does have (which I only recently discovered) is the ability to do an exposure lock and adjustment. This is essential if you are taking a photo of a shadowy scene, for example, and want to retain the overall mood, rather than getting an average exposure of the mid-tones, which often results in blown highlights or overexposed shadows.

Imagine, for a moment, you are leaving your friend's house late one evening to find that the moon is especially bright and casting a beautiful glow over the cars on the dark street. You quickly pull your phone out of your pocket to get a shot of the scene. When you take a photo, the image is all blown out and grainy because the camera was metering for the midtones of the dark houses and cars. Not only that, the moon and the rest of the sky is blown out white with no detail. Before you post this fantastically shitty photo to your Instagram with the hash tag #epicmoonrise, try taking another shot using the following directions.

Pick up your phone and open your camera. Pick a highlight or shadow that you want to make the focus of your photo, such as the sky area in **Figure 3.20**. Touch that area on your phone's screen and hold it there for three seconds. You will see an exposure lock indicator as well as a sun icon next to a slider (**Figure 3.21**). By dragging the slider up or down, you can raise or lower the exposure.

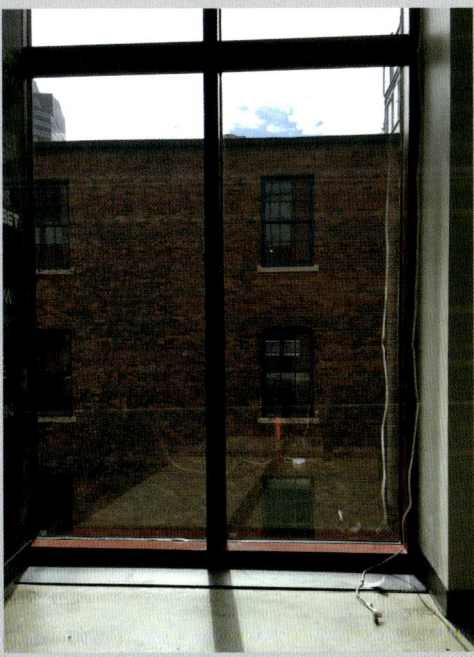

Figure 3.20 The "auto" exposure. Note that when the phone does the metering for you, it often results in blown highlights, as seen in this shot.

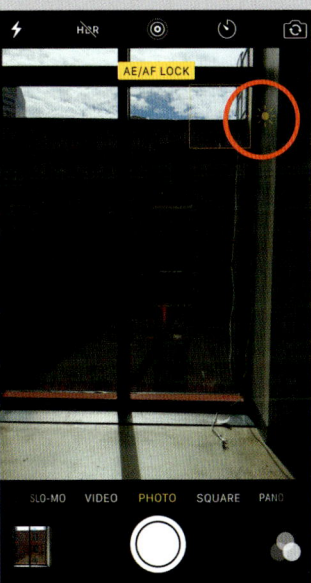

Figure 3.21 The metered exposure. By touching for three seconds the part of your screen that contains the detail you want to preserve, you can make an exposure lock. By dragging the slider next to the sun icon up or down, you can further adjust the exposure.

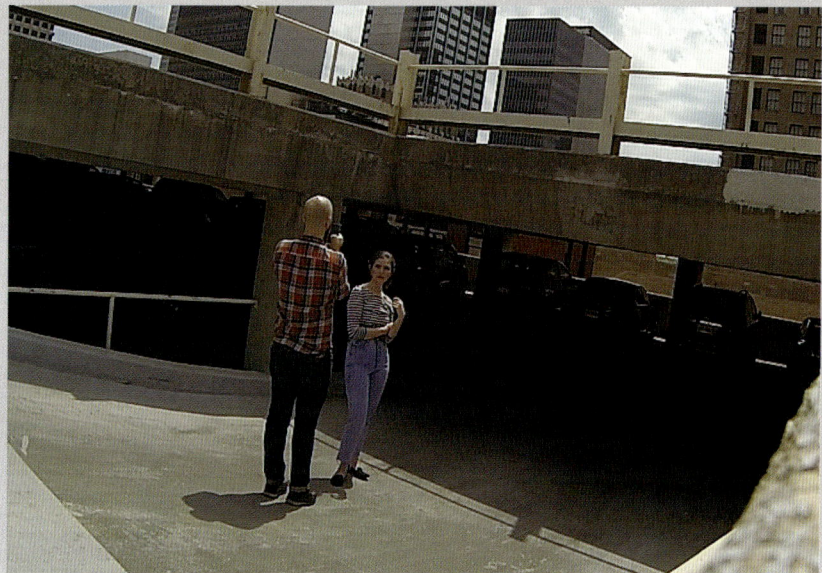

Figure 3.22 The setup. If you want to isolate your subject in a black scene, look for a spot that offers both bright light and dark shadows.

Using the exposure lock technique, you can also make studio-like portraits with an "invisible black" background, using nothing more than an iPhone, as long as you have an existing hard light source. As long the scenario has a spot of bright (typically hard) light and shaded area, you can pull off this technique (**Figure 3.22**). I found a spot on top of a parking garage, where I could place my subject at the edge of the shade so the sun outlined her hair.

My goal is to get as close as I can to the subject without getting too much lens distortion, due to the wide angle. I also try not to use the phone's zoom ability, because it is a digital zoom and results in a pixelated final image. Rather, I save much of the composing for post, when I crop any unwanted portions of the resulting photo (**Figure 3.23**) after the fact.

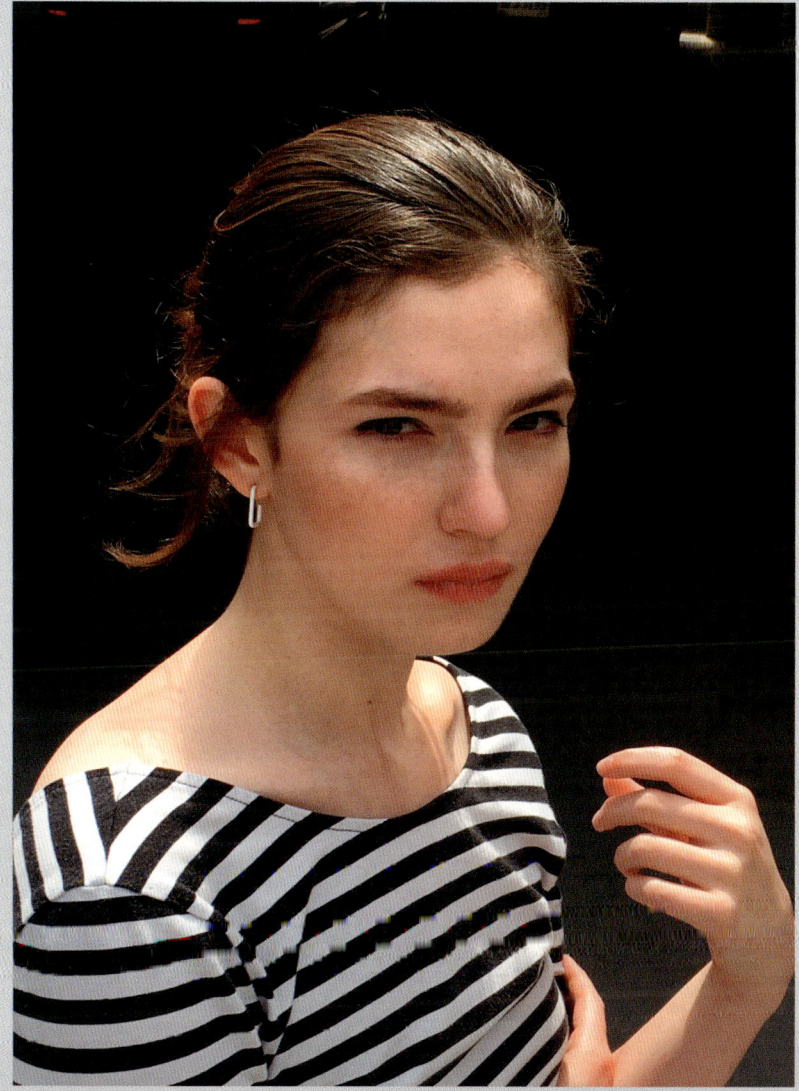

Figure 3.23 The "raw" file. I moved in as close as I could to the model without getting wide-angle lens distortion. Rather than using the phone's digital zoom, I will crop the unwanted portion out of the photo after the fact.

Using the app Snapseed, I am able to quickly crop and edit the image. The features I most often use in the software are found in the Tune Image section (**Figure 3.24**). In this photo, I reduced Ambiance, Contrast, Saturation, and Shadows, and raised Highlights to give me a polished, studio-like portrait, as you can see in **Figure 3.25**.

Now back to our hypothetical moonscape. Recompose your moonlit master-piece, touching the moon on your phone's screen and holding it there until the exposure locks. Now you can pull down the exposure until there is adequate detail in the moon and the shadows are black, as they should be. Now you have an image deserving of an epic hash tag.

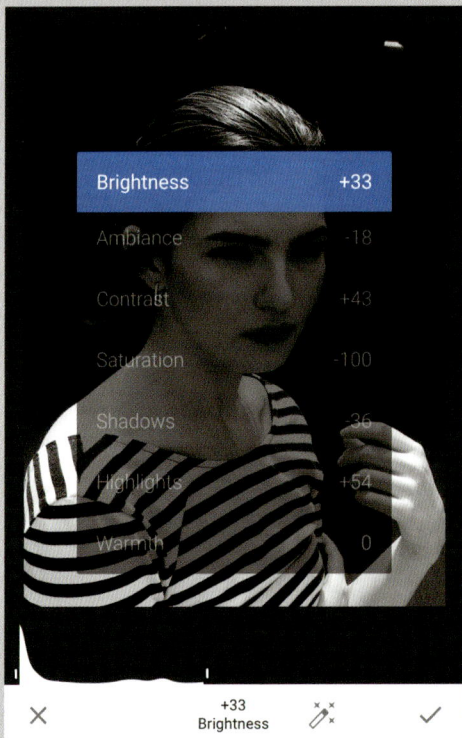

Figure 3.24 The adjustments. I use Snapseed, adjusting the ambiance, contrast, shadows, and highlights to get a polished result.

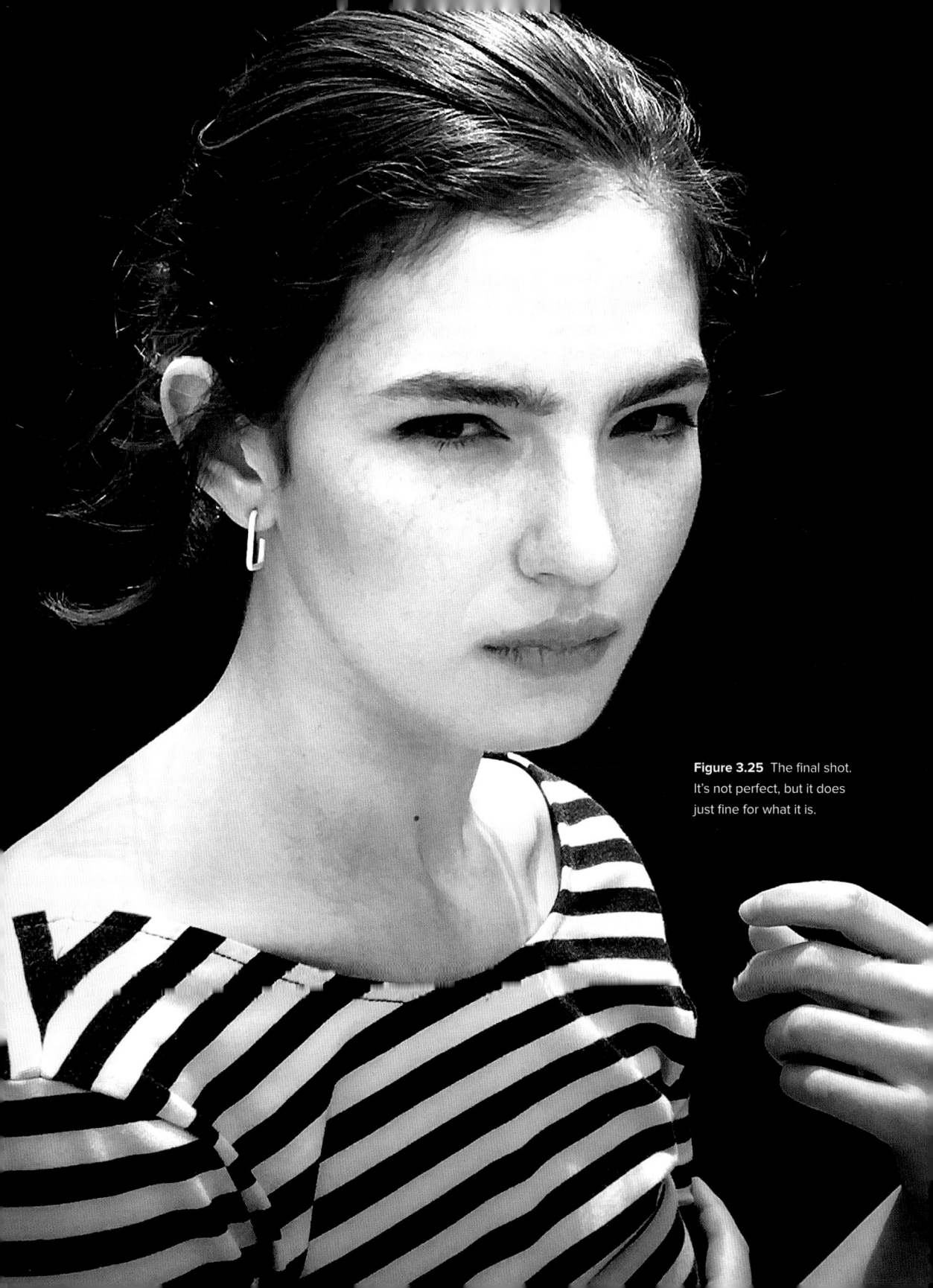

Figure 3.25 The final shot. It's not perfect, but it does just fine for what it is.

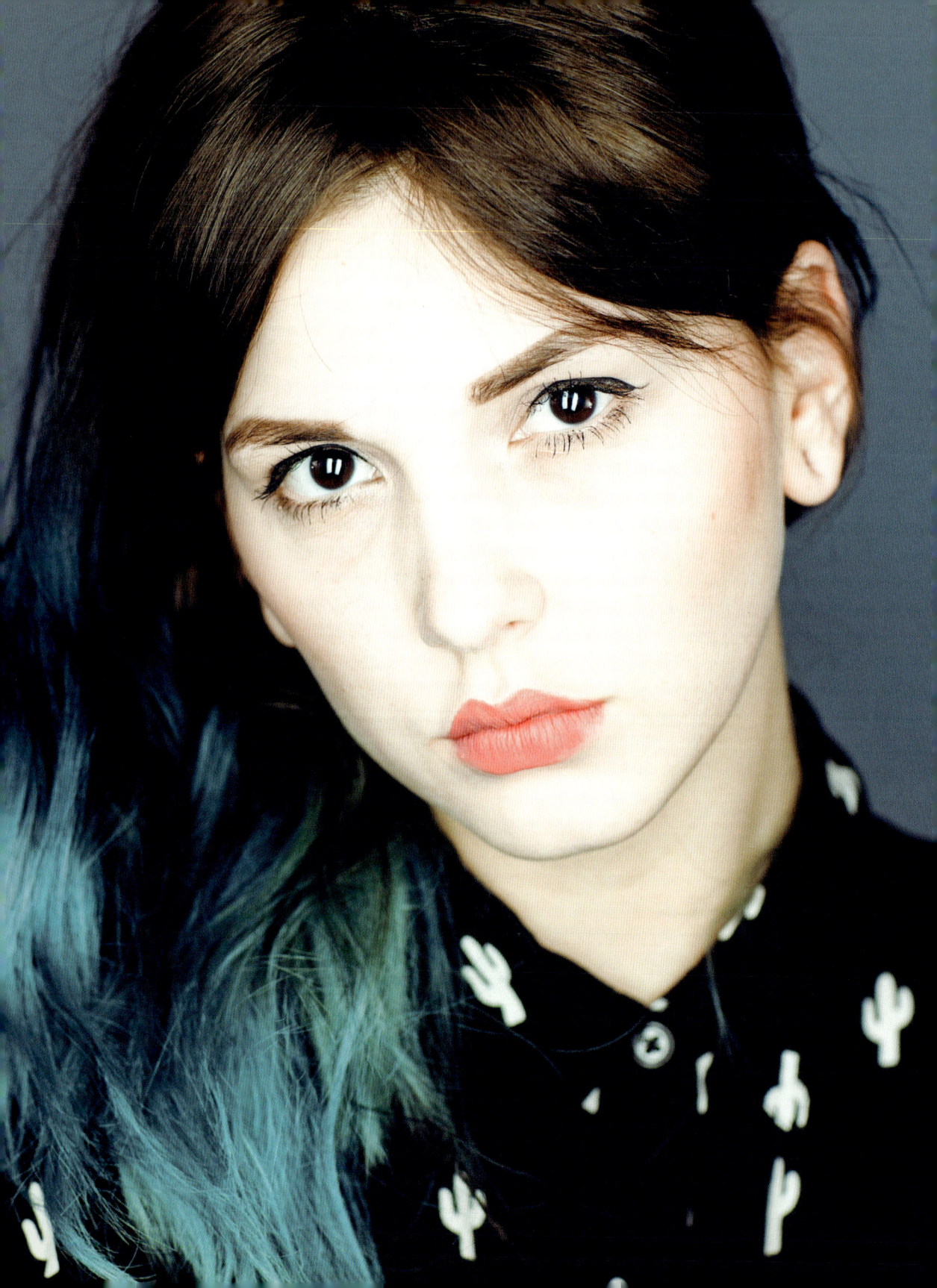

CHAPTER 4

LIGHT BILLIARDS

If you've ever played a game of billiards, you've certainly used this next technique: the bank shot. You know that if you aren't in an ideal place to make a clean shot, you have to get creative. It comes down to simple angles and a bit of (dare I say it) math. If you shoot the cue ball at an angle into the side rail, you know that it will bounce off the rail at the same angle. The same principle applies to lighting. If the space you're shooting in is too small, by getting creative with the placement of your light you can manipulate the size and quality of your small, hard light source.

Although the techniques in this chapter have to do with softening the light, they still rely on the existence of a narrow stream from a hard light source to work. Yes, they are essentially nothing more than bounce-light techniques, but these light bounces are a bit trickier than just pointing your flash at a ceiling during a wedding reception. This chapter moves from light shaping to light manipulation, transforming your flashgun into a flash laser.

MONEY IN THE BANK

When I am focusing in my flash to 105mm, it becomes a laser of sorts—a bright, narrow beam of light. In **Figure 4.1** you can see that I was shooting in a normal hallway with white walls. The nice feature to this spot was the small outcrop of wall, behind the model, which was the perfect spot for me to tuck a flash on a stand. You may be asking yourself, "Why the hell didn't he just use an umbrella and light the model from the front, like a normal person?" Well, since you asked, the hallway I was shooting in was a bit too narrow to put a light with an umbrella in front of the subject without having it creep into my camera frame. Yes, if I had moved the subject to the left and placed him against the wall, there would've been the space, but then the wall behind him would have been lit, resulting in a brighter, less moody scene.

Placing the light behind Alex meant that the bounced light lit the narrow side of him, leaving the side closest to the camera in shadow (**Figure 4.2**). This gave the portrait a moodiness and mystery that I really enjoy.

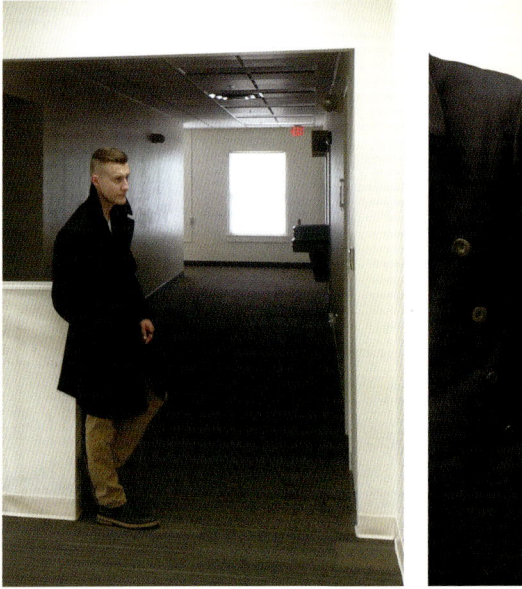
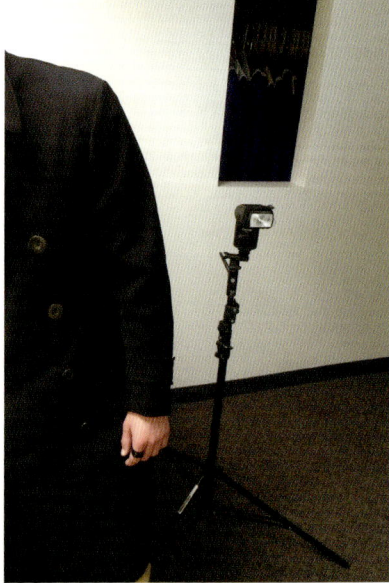

Figure 4.1 The setup. The small wall outcrop served as a perfect spot for me to hide my light, which was aimed at the wall in front of the model.

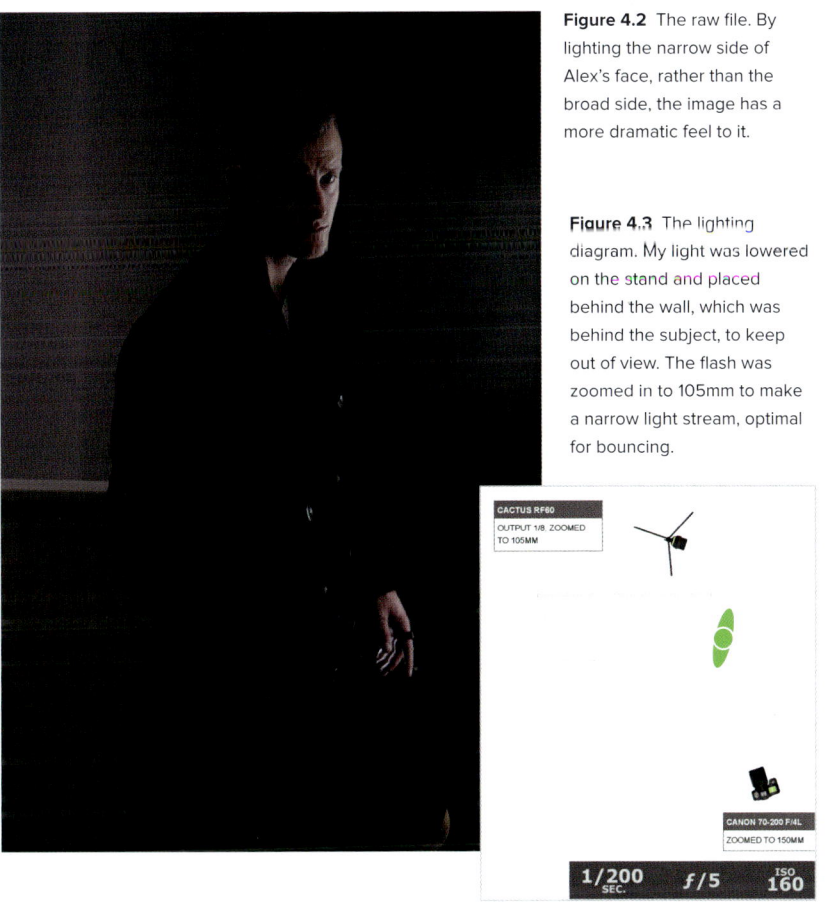

Figure 4.2 The raw file. By lighting the narrow side of Alex's face, rather than the broad side, the image has a more dramatic feel to it.

Figure 4.3 The lighting diagram. My light was lowered on the stand and placed behind the wall, which was behind the subject, to keep out of view. The flash was zoomed in to 105mm to make a narrow light stream, optimal for bouncing.

CACTUS RF60
OUTPUT 1/8 ZOOMED TO 105MM

CANON 70-200 F/4L
ZOOMED TO 150MM

1/200 SEC.   f /5   ISO 160

Note the lighting diagram in **Figure 4.3**. Imagine if I had set up my flash in the same position behind Alex, but forgot to zoom the flash to 105mm, leaving it at 24mm. Can you guess what the image would look like? Because the light spread would've been much more broad (think shotgun versus rifle), the light would have been much more even and spread out by the time it hit the wall in front of him, meaning less light would return from the bounce, leaving him several stops underexposed.

When it came time to color grade my image, I knew that I wanted to convert it to black and white, with a blue colorcast to it. I started by adding a gradient adjustment to the left half of the image, lowering the exposure (**Figure 4.4**).

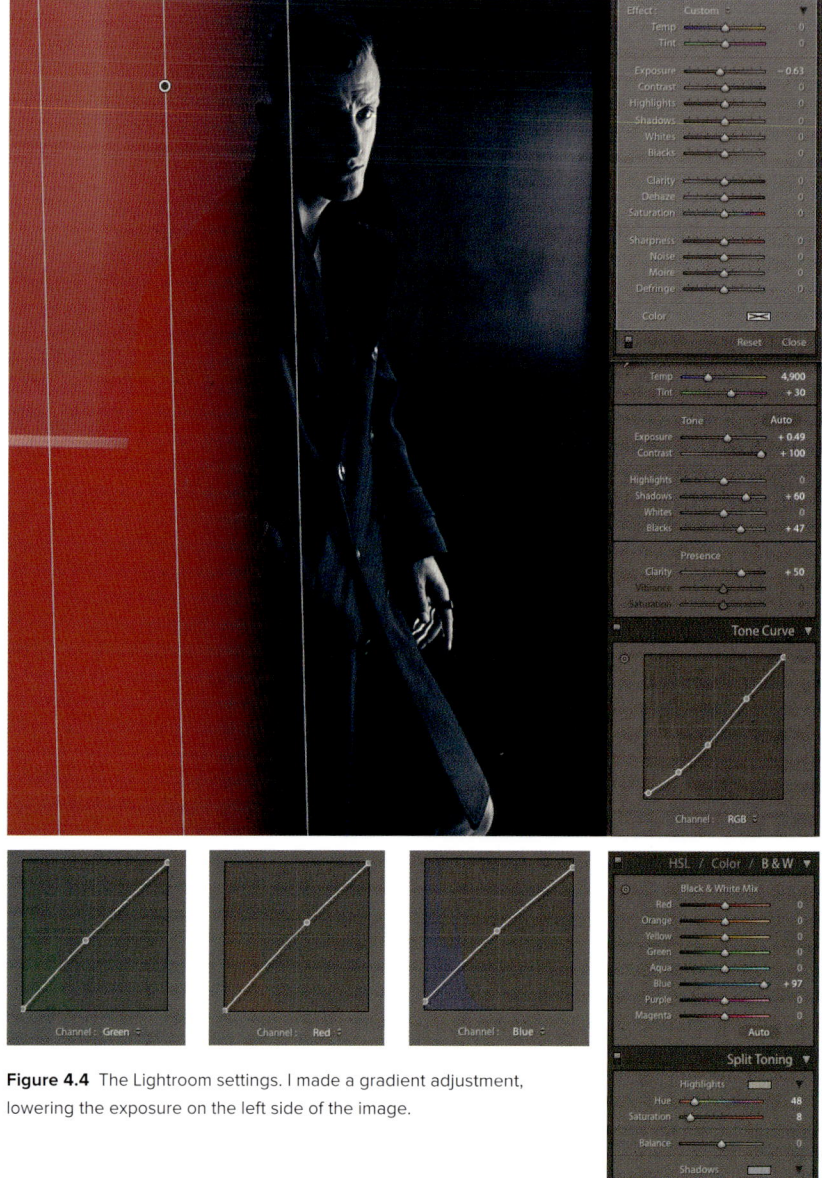

Figure 4.4 The Lightroom settings. I made a gradient adjustment, lowering the exposure on the left side of the image.

After selecting Black & White mode, I increased the slider in the Blue channel, which raised the ambient light (because it was cool-colored daylight) in the background of the photo. I added a gentle curve to the Red, Green, and Blue channels in the Tone Curve panel. Finally, I added a colored overlay in the Split Toning panel, adding a warm tone to the highlights and a cool tone to the shadows. You can see the final image in **Figure 4.5**.

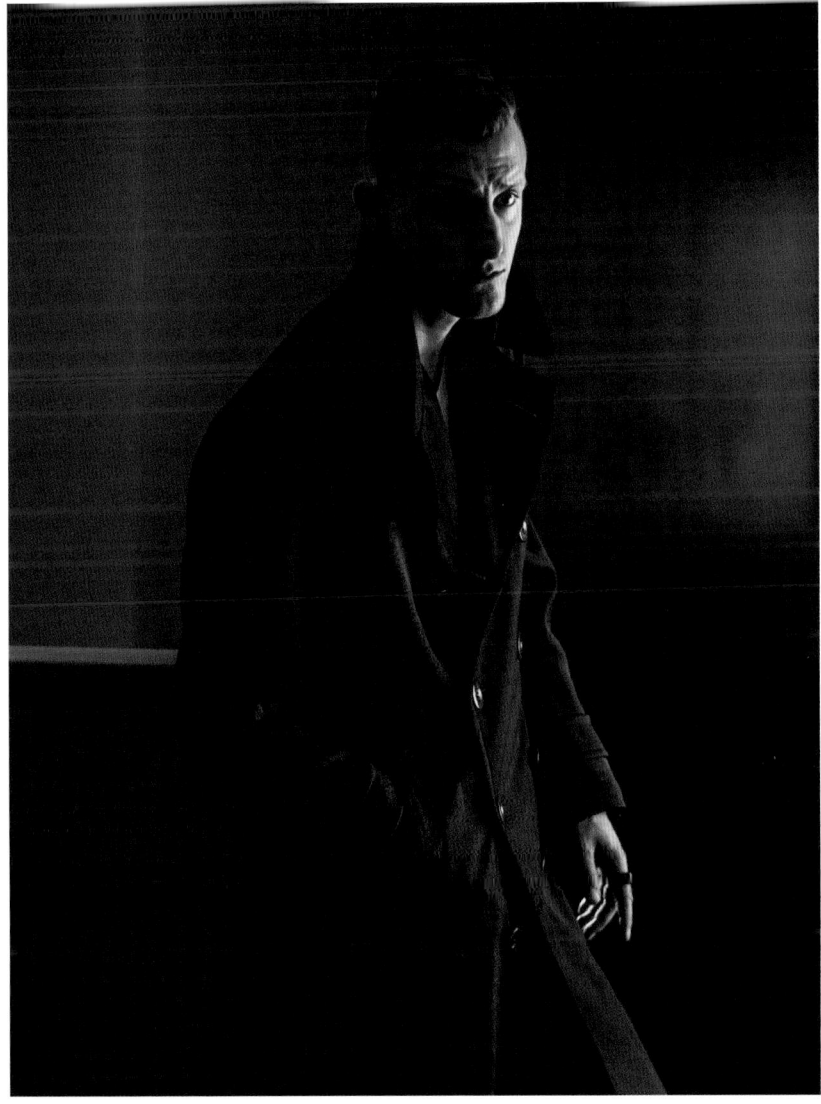

Figure 4.5 The final shot. Alex is looking too cool for school.

Part of what makes the portrait of Alex so powerful is the drama, which was created by placing the light on the narrow side of the subject (the side furthest from the camera). What would happen if the light was bounced into a wall on the broad side of a subject (or product), as illustrated in **Figure 4.6**? You'd get an almost shadowless image like **Figure 4.7**.

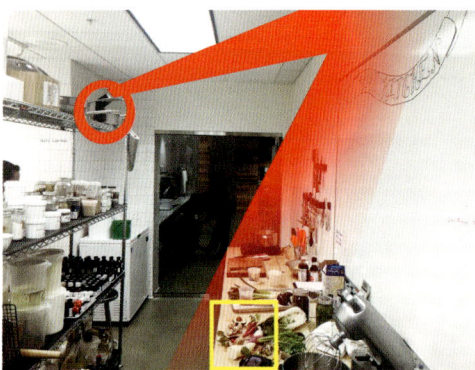

Figure 4.6 The setup. In this scenario, my light was placed on the broad side of the product. (To be fair, there is no narrow side in an overhead product shot.)

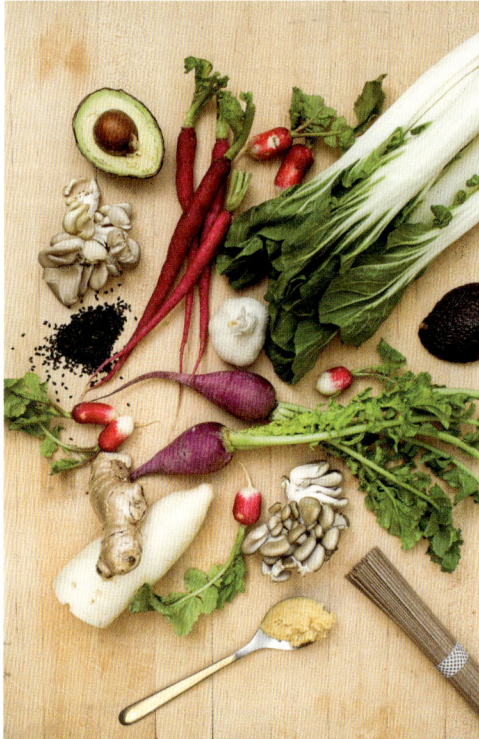

Figure 4.7 The final shot. Almost shadowless, soft light, as if shot under a skylight.

IN A TIGHT SPOT

Not long ago I was doing a commercial shoot in a home, which was both a blessing and a curse. The blessing was that the home was beautiful, so no additional props or styling were needed. The curse was that I was stuck with what the space provided, which meant tight quarters in the kitchen, where the shoot was taking place.

I was photographing a line of home water coolers, and the client wanted the kitchen as a backdrop. This meant that the model needed to be slightly in front of the kitchen, with the visually recognizable kitchen items, such as a sink, cabinets, and the like, in the background. The problem was that there was a wall just to the right of where she needed to stand, which made it impossible to put a soft light source there. Even if I could rig up a flash to the wall so that it was out of sight, no light-softening modifier could be used without interfering with the shot. So I once again needed to bounce some light.

The lighting setup ended up being quite similar to the previous setup, except that in this one, the room for error was much smaller. The final image needed to be a well-lit lifestyle image to be used commercially by the client. This meant that I couldn't just skate by on moody lighting and a ton of stylized color grading in post. To boot, I had an extremely picky client looking over my shoulder at every shot. Because we weren't on a set, where walls could be easily moved around, I needed to go full MacGyver on this one.

Just as for the shot of Alex, I placed my flash on a stand behind the model (**Figure 4.8**). Because the model needed to be facing toward the camera in this shot, rather than in a profile like the previous scenario, I needed to position the light to bounce in a more wrapping manner. I placed it on the side of the model closest to me and put a grid on my flash to cut down on light spill. The light needed to pass right in front of the model without lighting her directly, which would result in harsh lighting, as seen in **Figure 4.9**. Once I moved the light a bit more toward me and away from the model, the light was able to cleanly pass her and bounce off the wall to the right, resulting in only soft light falling on her (**Figure 4.10**).

Figure 4.8 The setup. The technique is the same as the previous shot, only the room for error is much smaller.

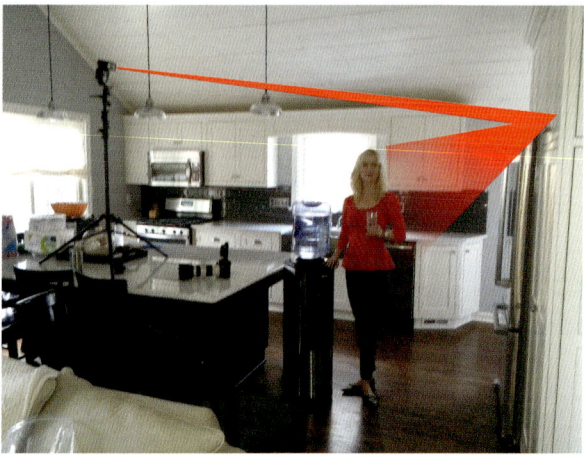

Figure 4.9 This is what it looked like when a bit of the hard, direct light fell on the model. Note the shadows especially on her left hand.

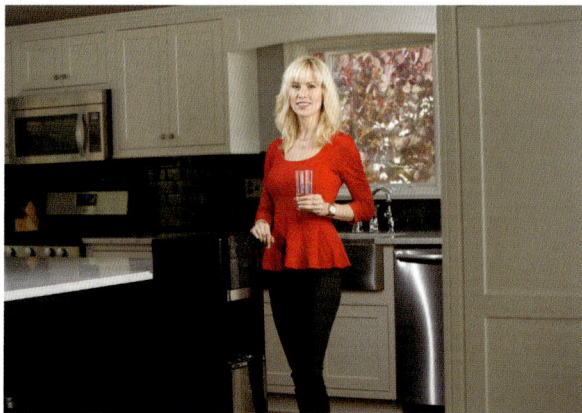

Figure 4.10 The raw file. This what it looks like when the model was lit with only bounced light.

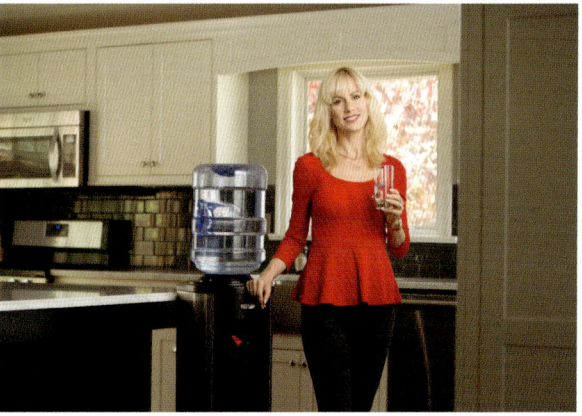

Because the grid absorbed a great deal of the flash output and because the light first had to bounce off a wall before returning to the model, my output needed to be very high. I had the flash set to full power and still needed an ISO of 500 to get an aperture of f/4 (**Figure 4.11**). The result: My model was lit with soft, wrapping light and looked as clean as the filtered water in her hand (**Figure 4.12**).

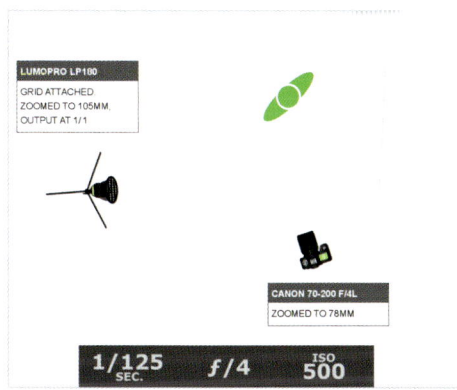

Figure 4.11 The lighting diagram. Because the grid absorbed much of the light output and because much of the output was lost by bouncing into the wall and spreading before returning to the model, the flash output was at full power.

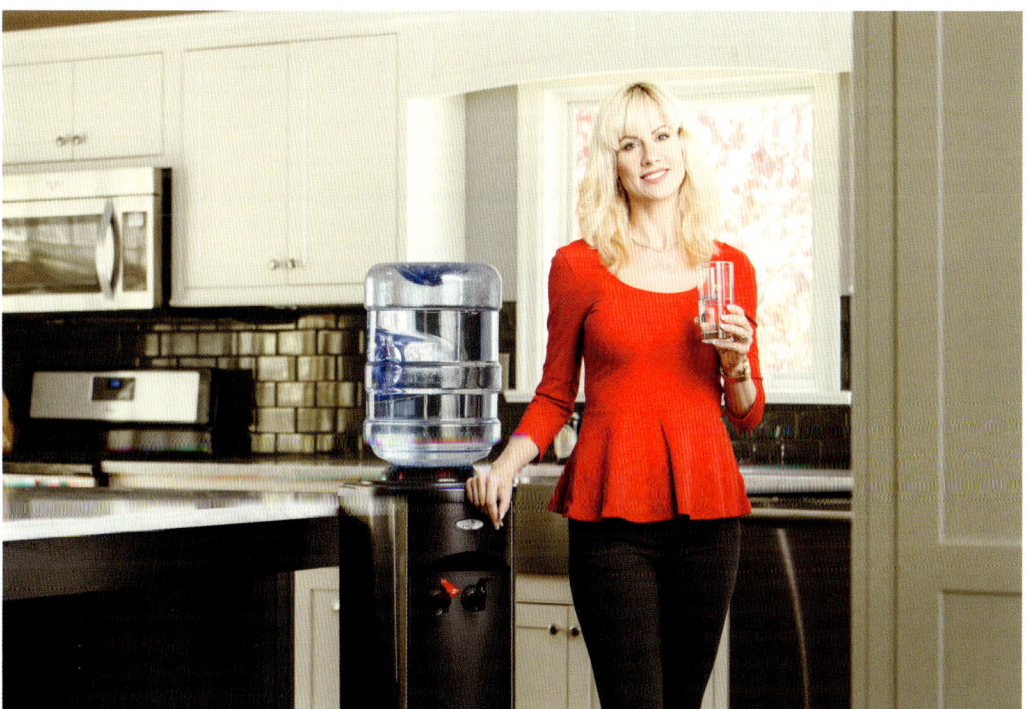

Figure 4.12 The final shot. The light looks as clean as the filtered water.

GETTING INTO SHAPE

By now, I think you can agree that we are thinking about light in different ways. It can be narrowed and directed and used in unconventional ways. This leads us to this next technique, which I refer to as "custom catch light." In **Figure 4.13** you can see an odd-looking scene where the model (my patient, lovely wife) is surrounded by a bunch of foam board. This setup is my original beta test wherein I was attempting to recreate Martin Schoeller's iconic portrait lighting by using nothing more than flashes and foam board.

I have long admired Schoeller's work, and the catch light in his portraits is instantly recognizable. I had seen several photographers attempt to recreate it, and they had all come up short. To boot, they were using expensive strobes with expensive modifiers. I was determined to not only come closer to Schoeller's lighting than they had, but also to do so by using minimal gear (yeah, this is the kind of stuff I do in my free time).

I started by trying to use just one flash, but realized that this was an impossible undertaking. I just couldn't light my subject's face evenly with one light. I eventually figured out that by placing one light behind each side of the subject and aiming them into a reflective surface in front of her face, I could get the result I was looking for. The only thing was that I needed to flag the lights from spilling hard light onto the subject (hence the side v-flats), and I needed the subject to sit really, really close to the front foam board (which meant that I needed to use a wide-angle lens). Also, because the board in front of the model was large and white, the light was overall kind of flat. I then used black gaff tape to narrow down the white bounce area to shape the light (and thus the catch light) into two vertical strips, like Schoeller's. It was kind of a hot mess (**Figure 4.14**), and though the wide-angle lens distortion wasn't ideal for portraiture, I was satisfied with my lighting (**Figure 4.15**).

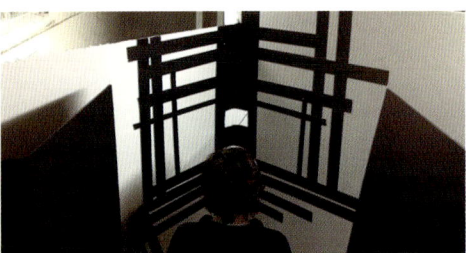

Figure 4.13 The first setup. This rig was from my original beta test of using bounced light to mimic Martin Schoeller's iconic portraits.

At the time that I was doing these experiments, I was a staff writer for Fstoppers. I posted the results of my experiments on the site, which garnered a range of responses from "Wow" to "Who cares?" One comment stood out to me, however. A reader wrote something along the lines of "What's the point of giving the subject snake eyes?" This triggered a line of thinking in me. Why did the shapes need to be two vertical strips? I was essentially creating the shapes by using gaff tape, so why not make a range of reflective shapes? Wouldn't this result in cool shapes appearing in my subject's eyes? I needed to find out.

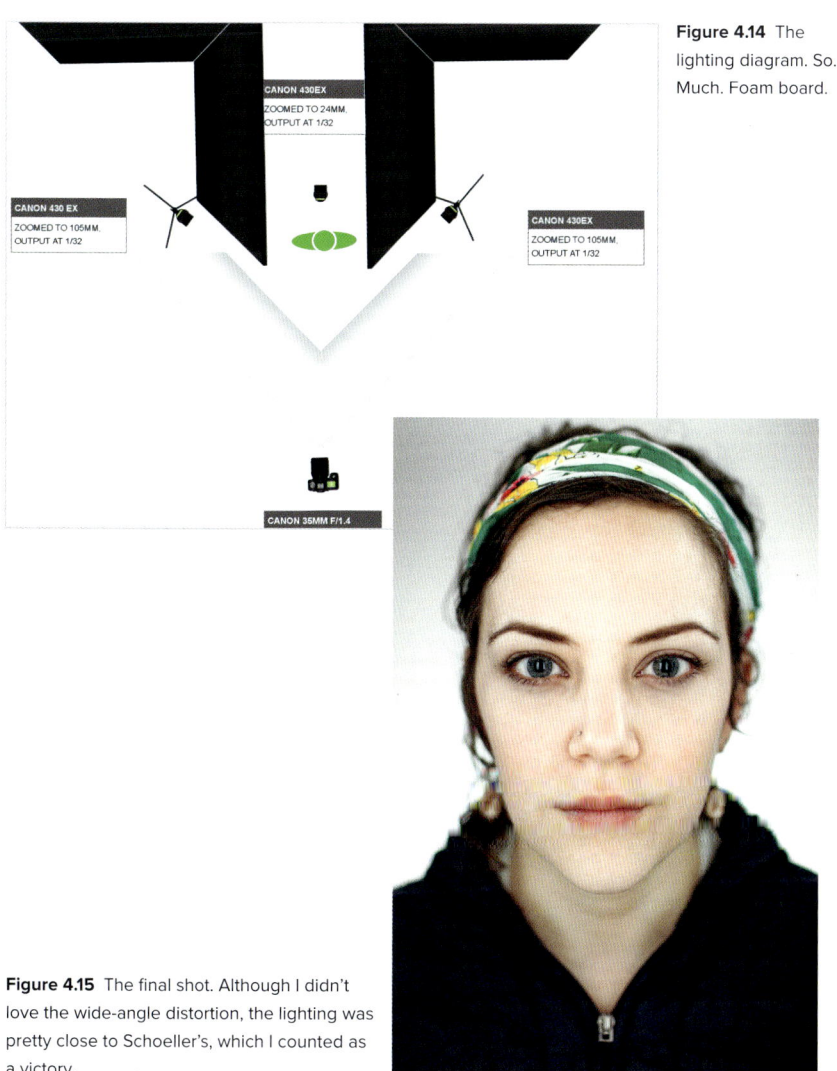

Figure 4.14 The lighting diagram. So. Much. Foam board.

Figure 4.15 The final shot. Although I didn't love the wide-angle distortion, the lighting was pretty close to Schoeller's, which I counted as a victory.

For my second setup (**Figure 4.16**), I switched to using a black board in front of the subject and using white gaff tape to shape the reflective surface area. It worked like a charm (**Figure 4.17**). The only issue was that I was still getting quite a bit of lens distortion, which I wanted to reduce.

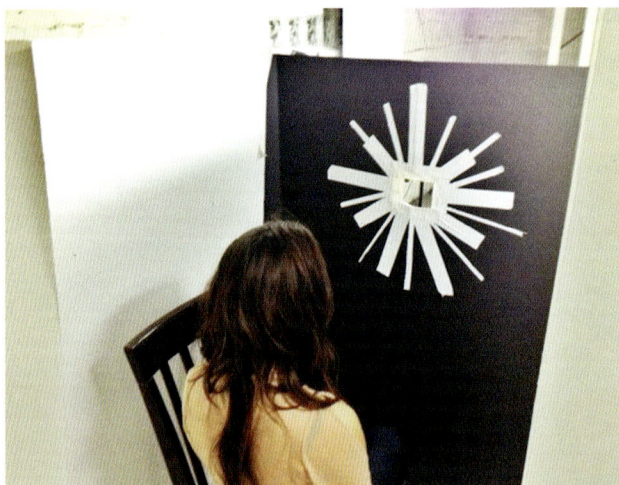

Figure 4.16
The second setup. I switched to using a black board in front, with white gaff tape to shape the reflective surface area.

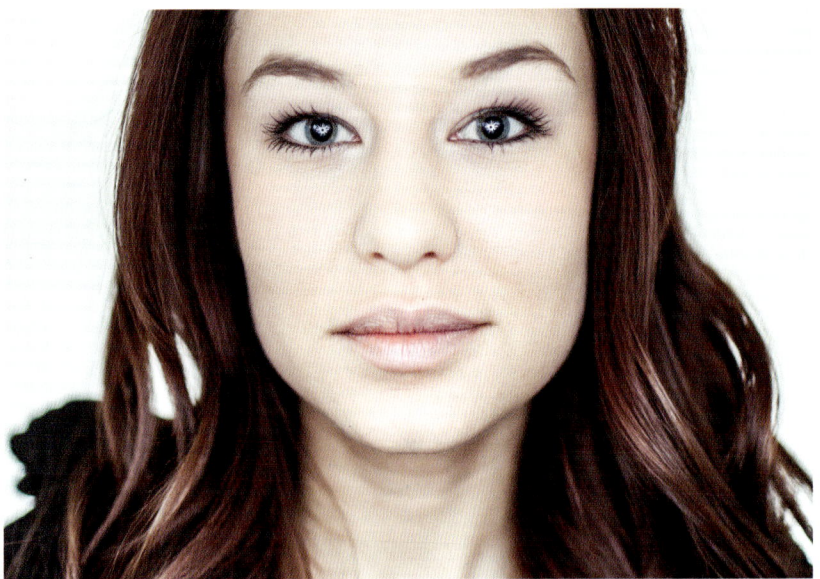

Figure 4.17 The final shot. The custom starburst shape is in full effect.

After my successes, I tried a few other shapes before losing interest in the technique. I shelved it for a couple years until a client asked me to use the technique during a session. Because this was a spur-of-the-moment request and I no longer had my old v-flat rig, I had to quickly improvise the setup you see in **Figure 4.18**. I used a white v-flat covered in grey paper; I didn't have a black v-flat at the time, but I did have a roll of "Thunder Grey" paper, which I used to minimize and shape the white reflective area. This time I decided to enlarge the shoot-through hole, which allowed me to back up from the bounce board a bit, using an 85mm lens to remove the distortion. I also experimented with using small flags on the sides of the flashes rather than entire v-flats. They did the job just fine (**Figure 4.19**).

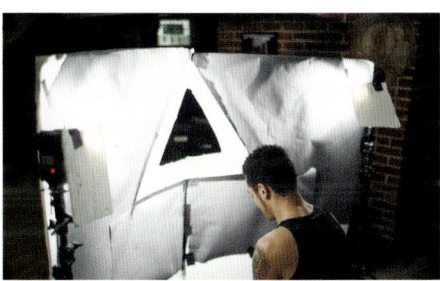

Figure 4.18 The third setup. I enlarged the shoot-through hole in the bounce board, which allowed me to back up and use a longer lens to remove lens distortion. I also tried using small flags on the lights rather than full-sized v-flats.

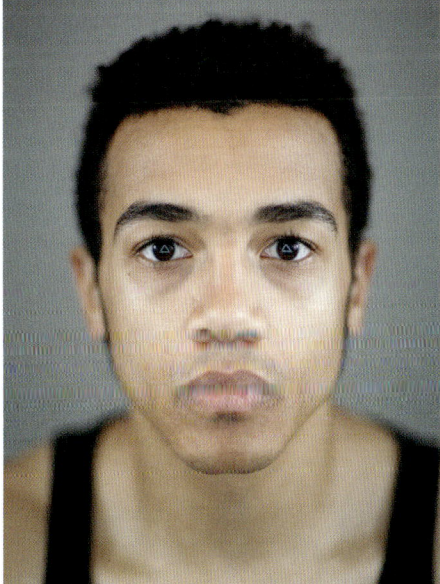

Figure 4.19 The raw file. Now the distortion is gone, and I have a nice, shallow depth of field, which brings focus to the subject's eyes. I just need to pop out the catch light a bit in post.

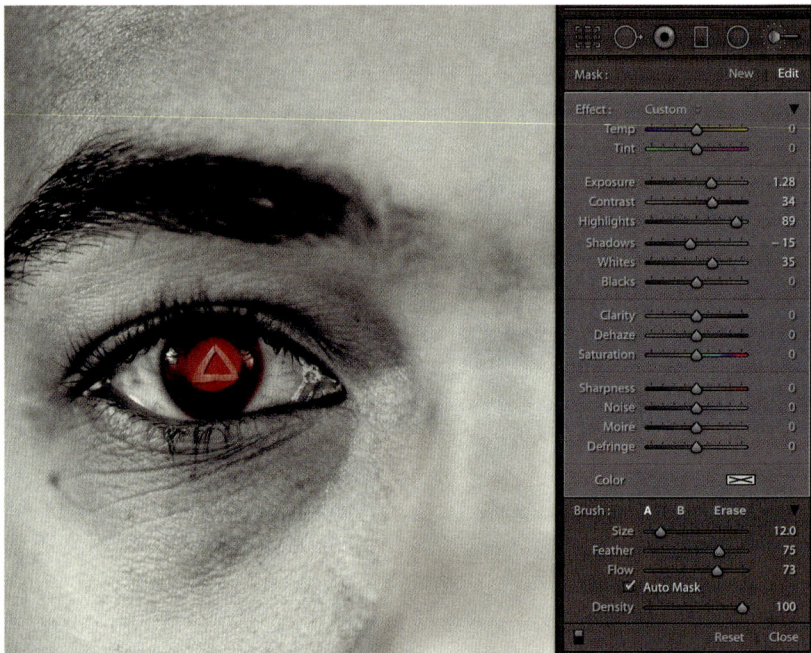

Figure 4.20 The Lightroom settings. To brighten the triangle catch light, I made a Brush Adjustment to the area, increasing the Exposure, Brightness, Whites, and Contrast sliders while reducing the Shadows slider.

I wanted the catch lights to pop out more than they did in the raw file, so I tweaked them in Lightroom (**Figure 4.20**). I made a quick Brush Adjustment to the area, increasing the Exposure, Brightness, Whites, and Contrast sliders, and reducing the Shadows in order to get the final shot (**Figure 4.21**).

Two years after I first began experimenting with this catch light rig, I ended up with the setup seen in **Figure 4.22**. I created a single black v-flat and attached collapsible light flags on each side, where the flashes would be placed. I also cut out a larger-than-necessary shoot-through hole. My idea was to make removable panels that had different white shapes on them, which could be easily swapped out and taped over the opening. This would save not only time but also quite a bit of gaff tape—which ain't cheap.

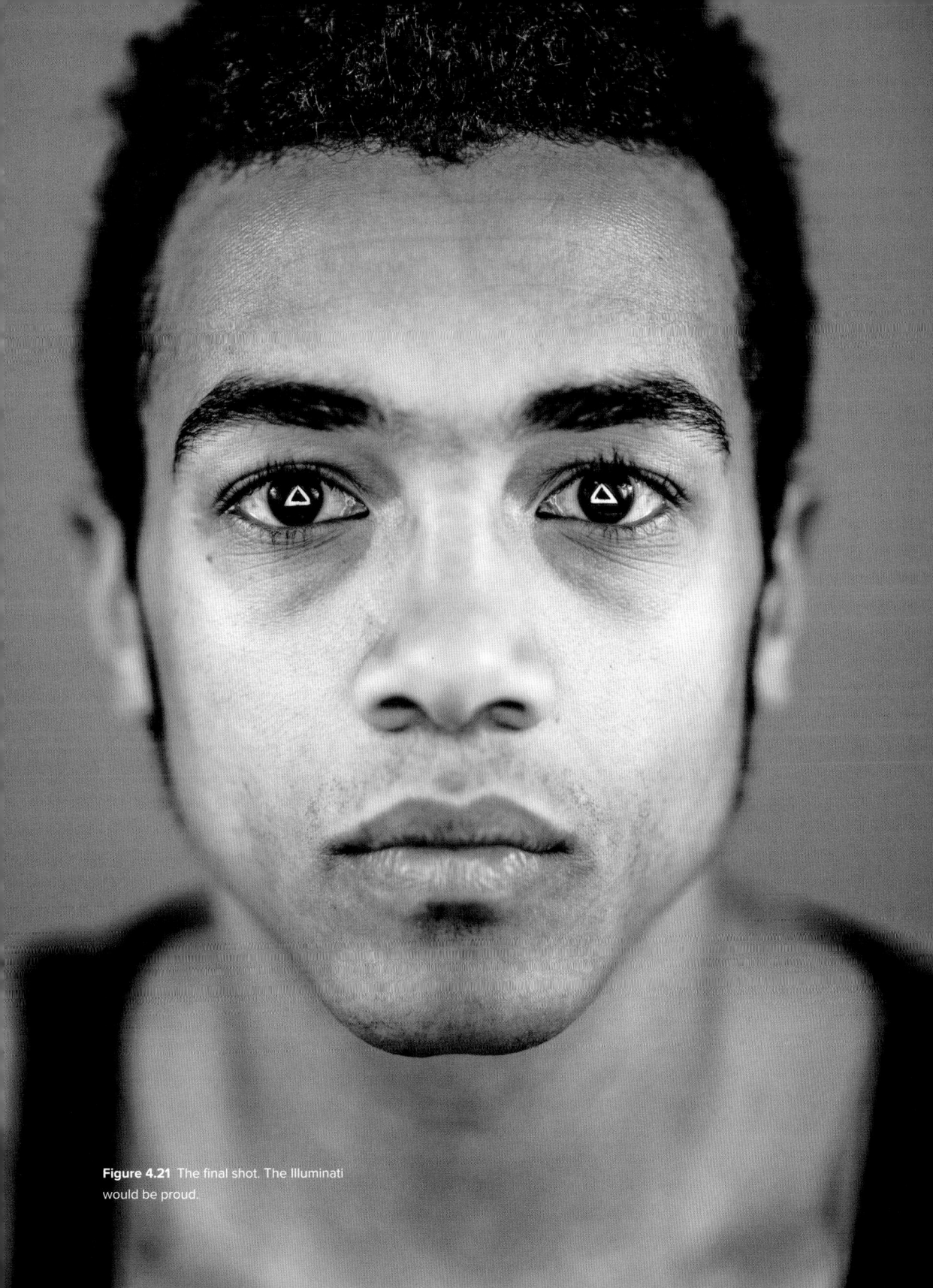

Figure 4.21 The final shot. The Illuminati would be proud.

Note my flash and camera settings in **Figure 4.23**. Because I wanted to have an extremely shallow depth of field in my portrait, I shot at f/1.2. This meant that my ISO needed to be low (set to 50) and my flashes turned down (both at 1/128). Note that this won't work if you are shooting in a bright space, because the ambient light will overpower the strobes at that low of an output. If you want to use this technique but your room is either too bright or your lens doesn't open up to f/1.2, just increase your flash output to make up for the smaller aperture. The only difference is that your portrait won't have as quick of a focus falloff, but the technique will still work fine.

Figure 4.22 The final setup. What you are looking at is a black v-flat with a hole cut out to shoot through. Note that the white shape affixed around the shoot opening is interchangeable.

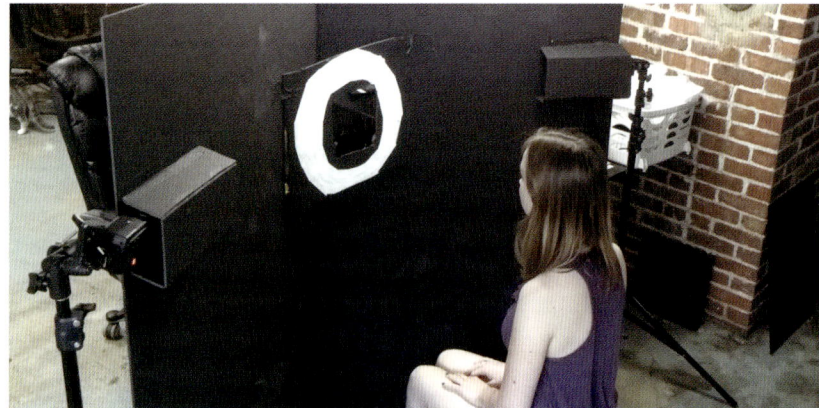

Figure 4.23
The lighting diagram. Note that the flashes were powered all the way down to 1/128 because I wanted to shoot at an extremely shallow depth of field of f/1.2. My ISO was also all the way down at 50.

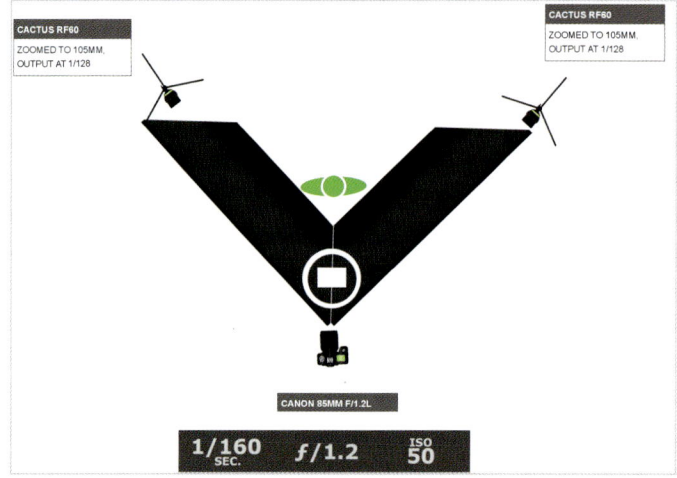

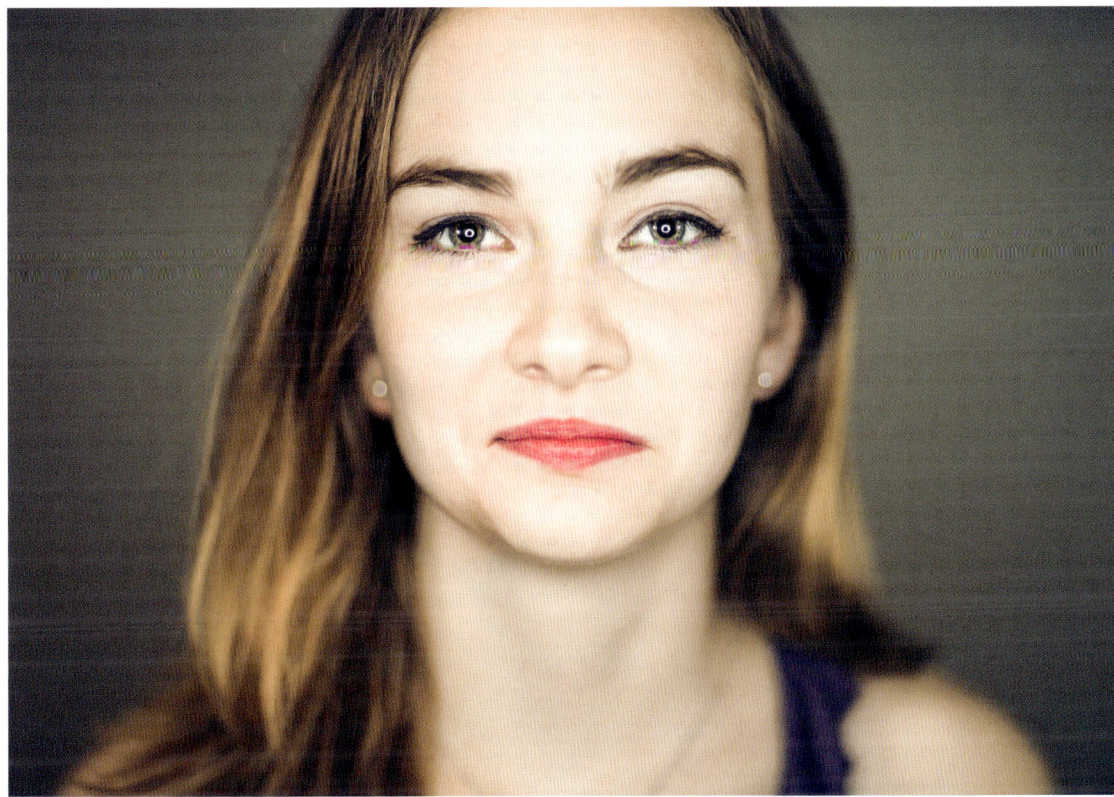

Figure 4.24 The final shot. Looks kind of like a ring flash, right?

In the final shot (**Figure 4.24**), you can see that the white, circular shape that I placed in the v-flat makes a fantastic ring-light effect, but ring lights can't transform into triangles, sun bursts, or other rad shapes. With my latest v-flat, the rig is as portable as it could ever get. I've even taken it on location for staff headshots (**Figure 4.25**). The main thing to keep in mind when using a rig like this is that the smaller the white shapes are, the less recognizable they will be in the subject's eyes. Make sure that the reflective area is a couple of feet across. Finally, and most importantly, you need to make sure that your lights are positioned in a way that the light spread covers the entire surface area of the reflective shapes. Otherwise, only part of the shapes will reflect light, marring the shape of the catch light and producing an under-lit portrait.

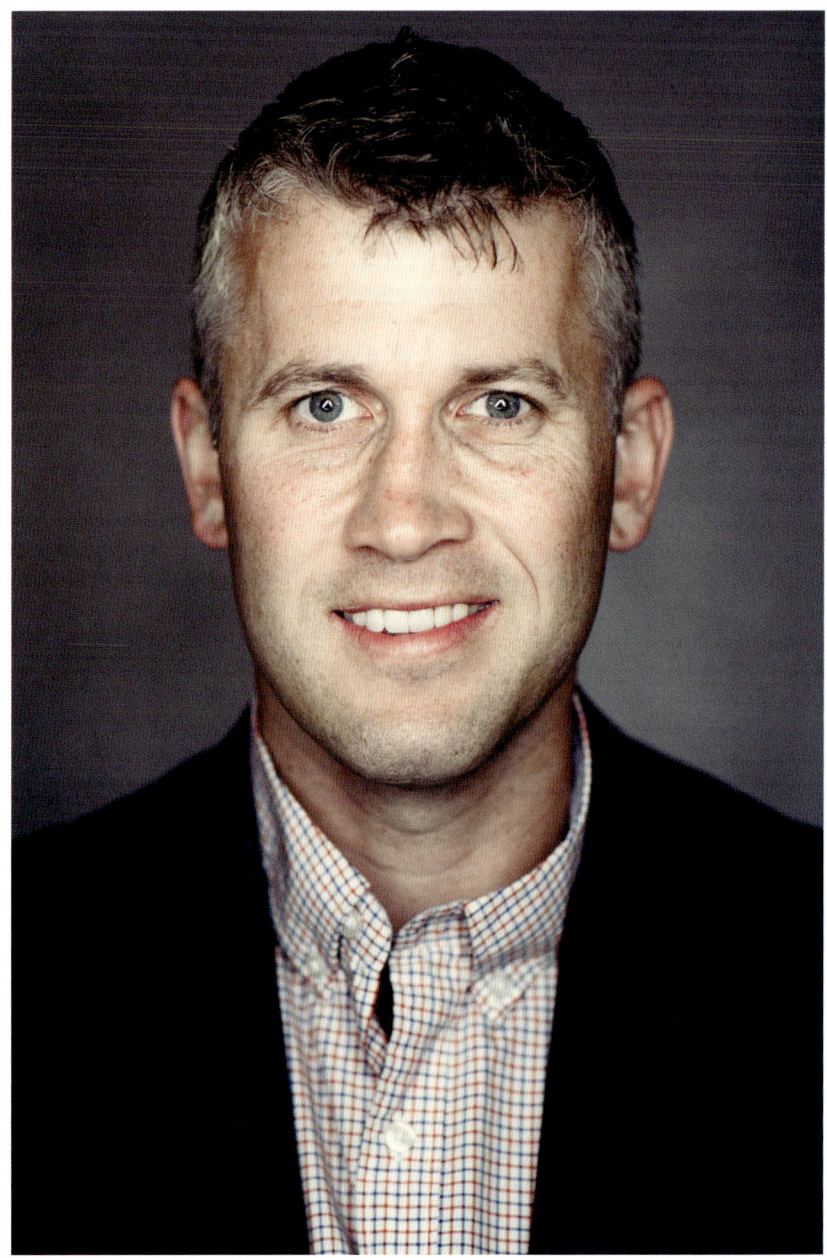

Figure 4.25 The staff headshot. Now that my rig is fairly mobile—it being a single, collapsible piece—I've been able to take it with me on shoots. This is a portrait of a dentist who requested an edgier-than-normal staff headshot.

MAKING A SCENE

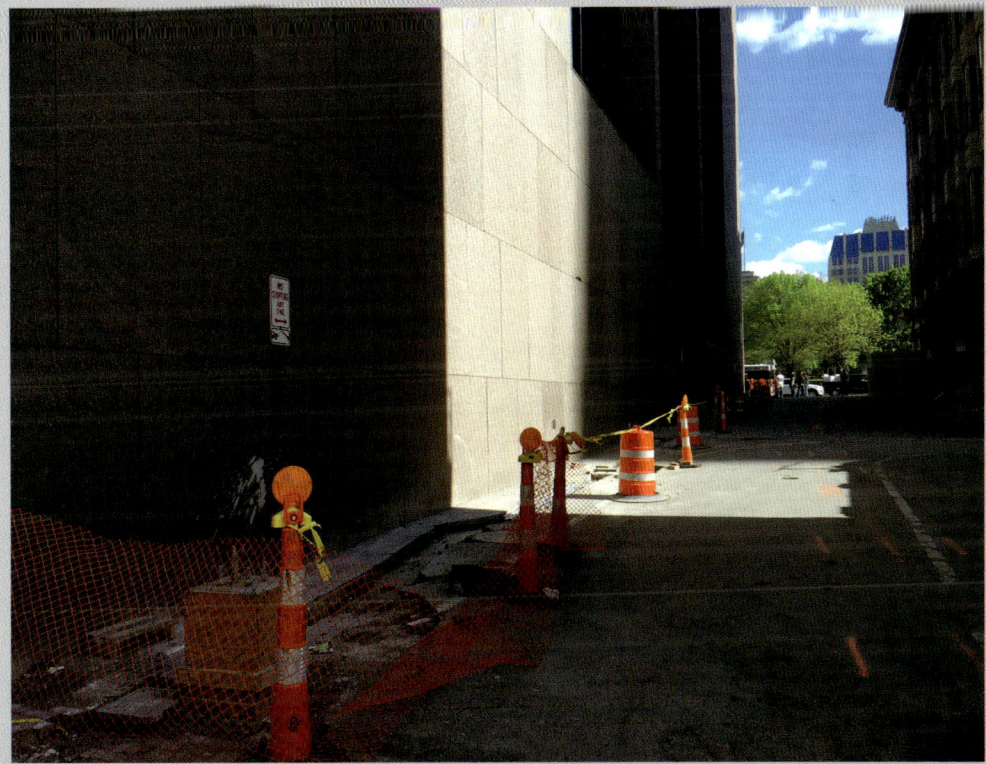

Figure S.2 Where should I place my subject if I were creating an available light portrait on a pure white background?

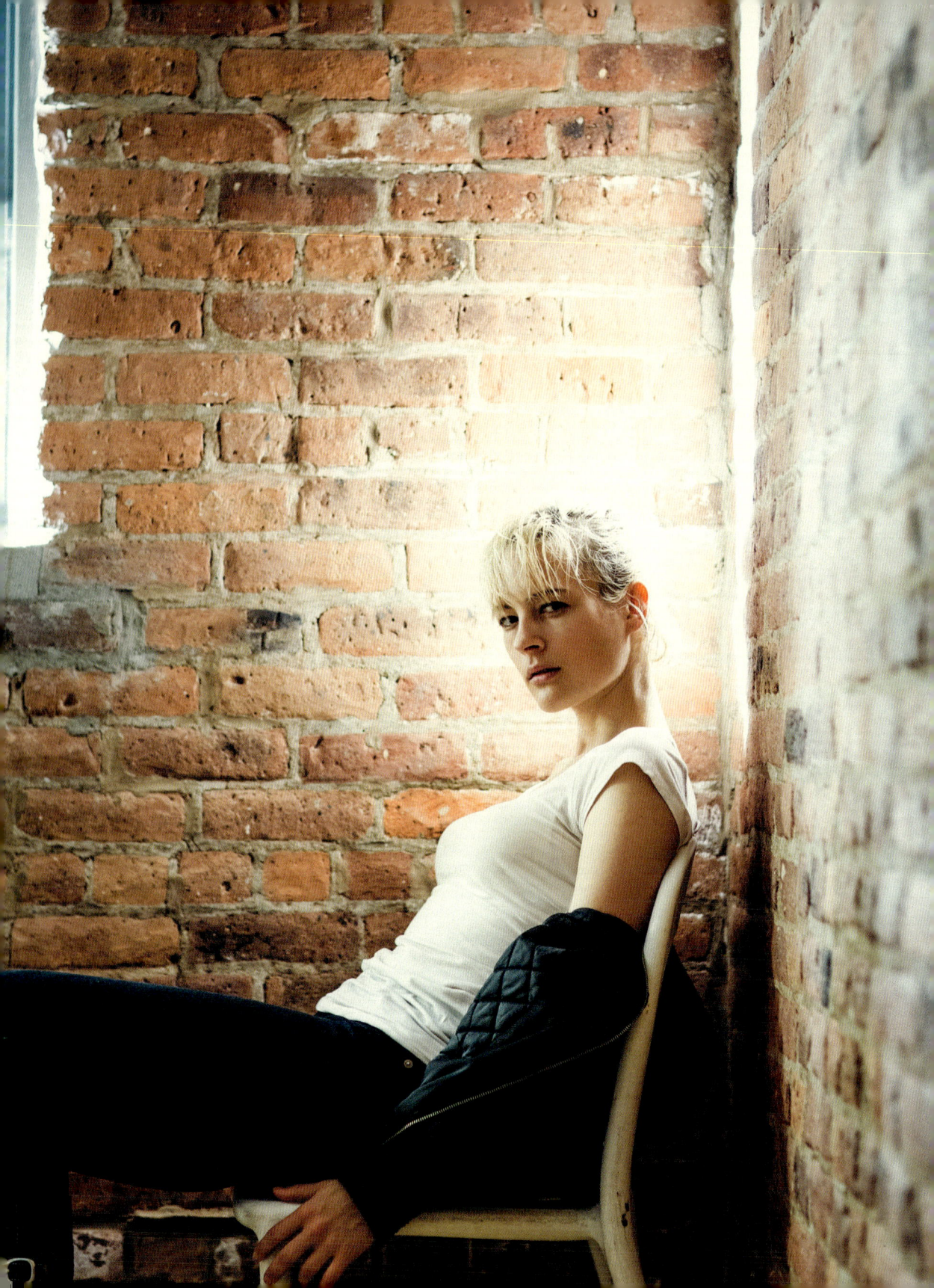

CHAPTER 5

FAKING THE SUN

Sometimes the best natural light is not natural at all. Let's face it, being an "available light shooter" is great...until the only available light is shitty light. As much as I can appreciate natural light and the airy aesthetic that comes with it, good natural light is not always available. So what are your options when it's cloudy, raining, or dark outside? This chapter will cover both indoor and outdoor scenarios wherein you can recreate sunlight in a space that it didn't otherwise occupy.

When you look at the image on the previous page, what does your eye see? Mine sees a warm patch of sun peeking through the window, falling on a pretty girl. But that light didn't actually exist (**Figure 5.1**). Because I placed a flash in the window, behind the curtain, my light mimicked what the sun might have done, had it actually been out that day (**Figure 5.2**). Our eyes are used to seeing sunlight in certain contexts, such as on the brick façade of a building or inside, beside a window. By placing a flash in scenarios such as these and matching it to the relational height of the sun to the model, you can fairly easily create a scenario that your eye will read as a sunny day.

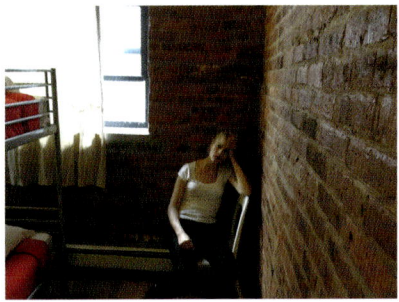 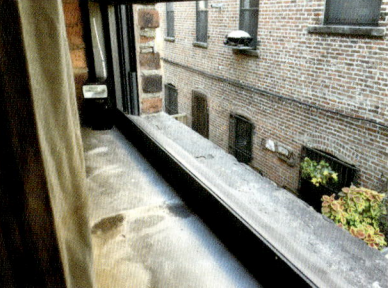

Figure 5.1 The setup. The image on the previous page wasn't lit with natural light, but rather with a flash placed in the window, behind the curtain.

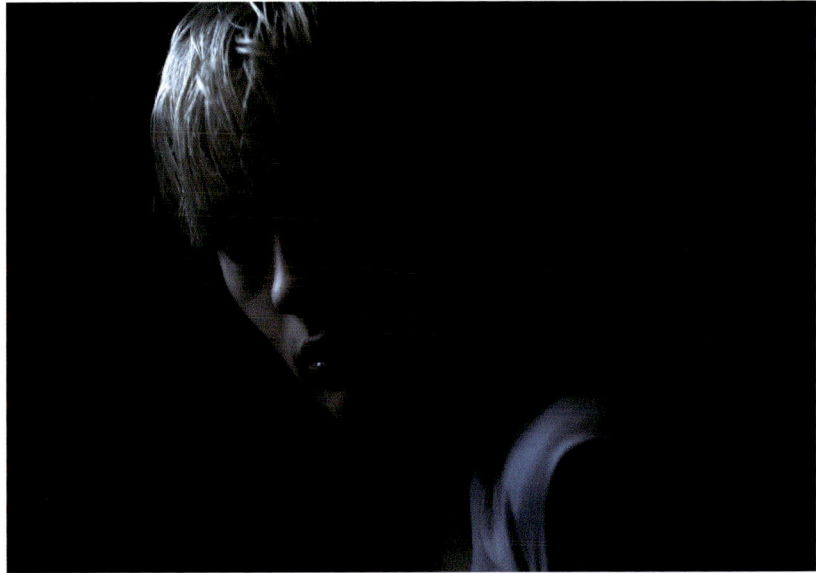

Figure 5.2 The unlit shot. This is how much ambient light was in my exposure. Makes for a nice alternate shot to the unlit one.

ETHEREAL LIGHT

Remember in Chapter 1 when you learned about hacking your reflector? That modifier comes in handy again here. For this scenario, the light was placed behind the subject, aiming away from the camera, in order to create soft, wrapping light. In **Figure 5.3** you can see my subject, Hana, standing three to four feet in front of a white door. If you look closely, you can see my flash on the ground behind her foot, aiming at the door behind her. Because I was shooting in a windowless area, the dim room lights were easy to overpower. Note my settings in **Figure 5.4**. By bumping up my ISO to 320, I was able to use a slightly lower flash output of 1/4 power, which allowed for a faster refresh time and conserved my batteries. Because my only light was behind my subject, I needed to open up my aperture enough such that the light would flood around her and also bounce off the reflector, lighting her face. The closer I stood to Hana with the reflector, the more light was bounced back onto her, increasing the fill light on her face and catch light in her eyes. Conversely, the further away I moved, the less light was bouncing back on to her, resulting in more facial shadows and zero catch light.

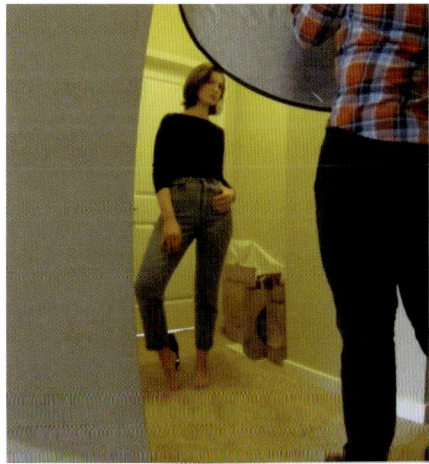

Figure 5.3 The setup. In this scenario, the light is behind the model and aimed into the wall behind her, creating a soft, wrapping light.

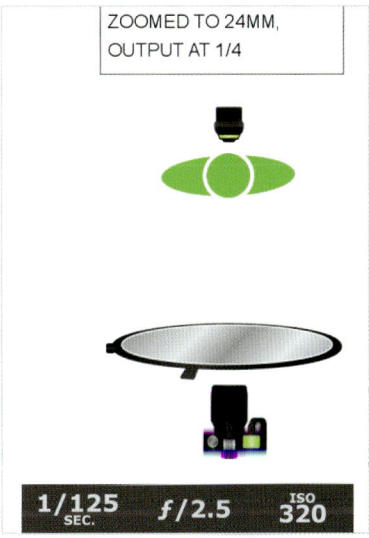

Figure 5.4 The lighting diagram. I bumped up my ISO to 320 to enable me to use a smaller flash output of 1/4, which allowed for a quicker refresh and conserved my batteries.

There are a couple of things to note when using this technique. The first is that you need to make sure that you allow several feet of space between the model and the wall/door/whatever behind the person so that the light from the flash has enough space to spread out, covering the whole background. For example, if the subject is too close to the wall, the light spread will be small, causing light to fall off at the edges of the frame. The second thing to keep in mind is that this technique will not produce crisp, clean light, as you may want when shooting a corporate headshot. This technique produces glowing, ethereal light, perfect for beauty shots.

In **Figure 5.5** you can see the raw file. My white balance was set to Sun/Daylight, which gave the image the blue colorcast. Aside from the blue tone, it appears as though Hana may be standing in front of an open door or large window with the sun streaming in behind her, rather than the dark, windowless hallway where she was actually standing. And although I personally like the blue colorcast, I will show you how to correct it in post.

After I corrected my white balance, using the Eyedropper tool, I noticed that the top third of the frame was shifting really orange in color. The ambient tungsten light creeping by under my strobe light may have caused this. For whatever reason, it wasn't visible in the raw file. It wasn't until I started warming up the color temperature that I noticed the top part of the frame shifting warm a lot quicker

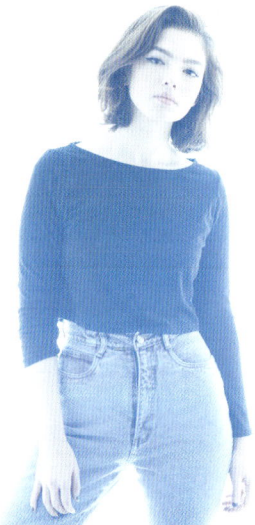

Figure 5.5 The raw file. Besides the blue colorcast (which I will show you how to correct), it looks like Hana is standing in front of an open door or giant window.

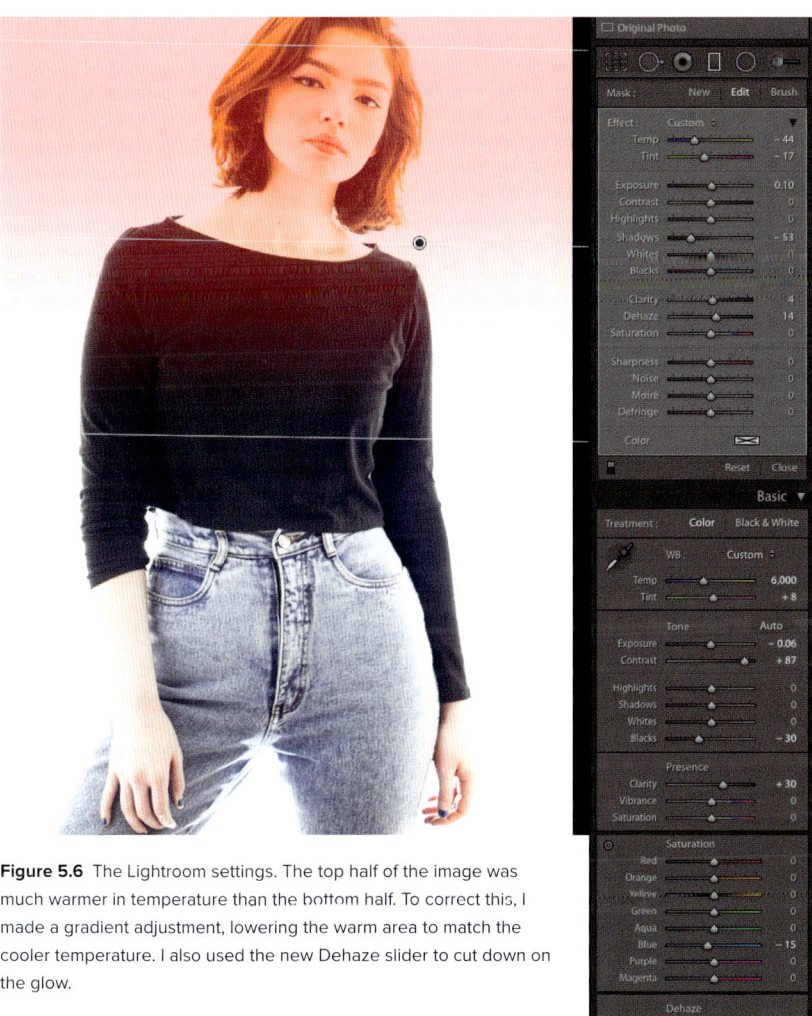

Figure 5.6 The Lightroom settings. The top half of the image was much warmer in temperature than the bottom half. To correct this, I made a gradient adjustment, lowering the warm area to match the cooler temperature. I also used the new Dehaze slider to cut down on the glow.

than the bottom part. I easily corrected this by making a gradient adjustment to the top half of the image, cooling down the temperature until it matched the rest of the image (**Figure 5.6**). Note that I also desaturated the Blue slider in the HSL panel and took advantage of the powerful new Dehaze slider. This effect is like Clarity on steroids. It defines edges and reduces glow like a mother. Just a dab will do ya. Now Hana isn't looking so blue (**Figure 5.7**).

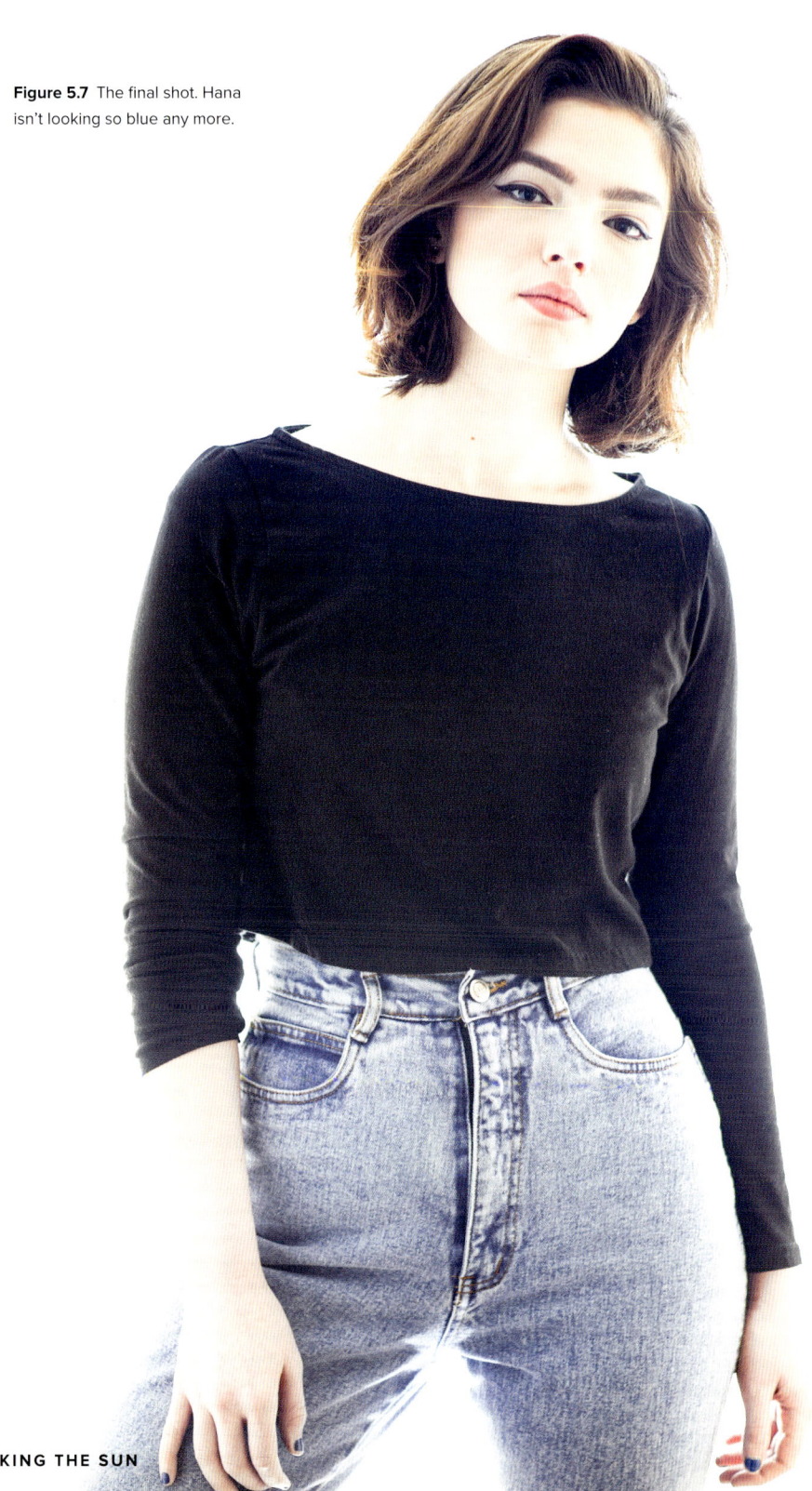

Figure 5.7 The final shot. Hana isn't looking so blue any more.

LENS FLARE

Don't you hate it when you're shooting at a client's apartment and you're asked to transform the room into a sunny day at the beach? Oh, that's never happened to you? Well, me neither actually, but it's still a fun thing to do, so let me teach you how to do it. The white wall seen in **Figure 5.8** could be in any room. No ambient light is necessary. All you really need is one unmodified flash. Adding a star-filter to your lens is a bonus (**Figure 5.9**). I use a Hoya star filter when I want to add an extra twinkle to my light.

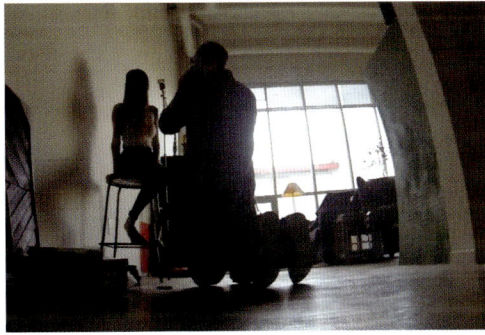

Figure 5.8 The setup. In this scenario the light is behind the model, aimed toward the camera to create a lens flare.

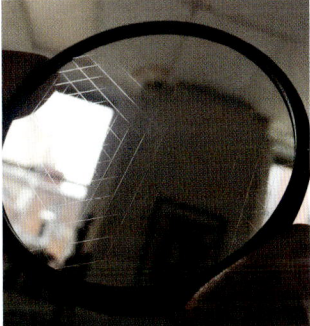

Figure 5.9 Although this Hoya star filter is not required to pull off this technique, it did increase the lens flare effect in my shot.

In this scenario, the light is once again behind Sam, my model, but this time it's aimed back toward the camera, which will provide the lens flare that I'm going for. When you're faking sunlight, raise your flash to a height that is higher than your subject and aim it back down at the person. Because the flash was above Sam, I needed to get lower than her, making sure that the light was in my line of site, behind her. I also had her wet down her hair and whip it back and forth a bit, to drive the beach vibe home. The combination of lens flare and wet hair helps to sell the idea that this was shot outside on a sunny day (**Figure 5.10**).

As you may know, when shooting something like motion and movement, it's best to shoot in bursts to make sure that you get a great frame. That means using a smaller flash output to avoid misfires (**Figure 5.11**). To make up for the lower output, I raised my ISO to 400. I also wanted to make sure to keep an f-stop of f/4 because I didn't want the depth of field to be too shallow; there was already a lot of movement in the shot.

Figure 5.10 The raw file. The combination of the lens flare and wet hair helps to sell the image as having been shot outside on a sunny day.

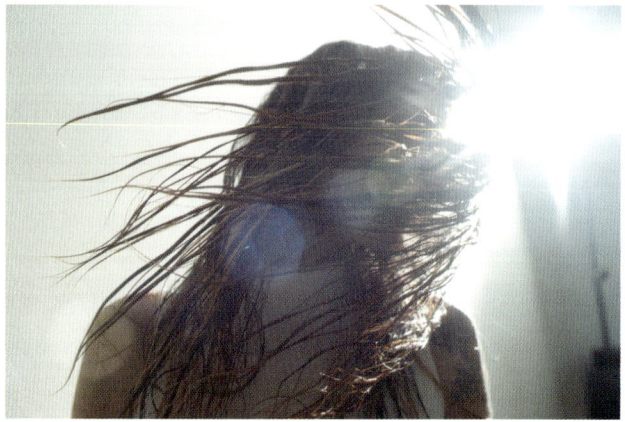

Figure 5.11
The lighting diagram. The smaller flash output allowed for a faster recycle, which was good because I was shooting in bursts.

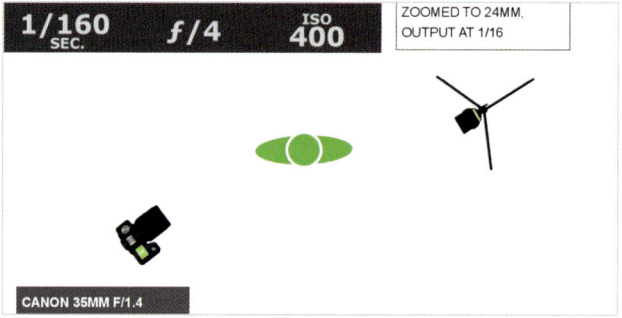

Figure 5.12 The Lightroom settings. To bring home the beach vibes, I added a warm wash to the highlights by lowering the highlight point in the Blue Tone Curve.

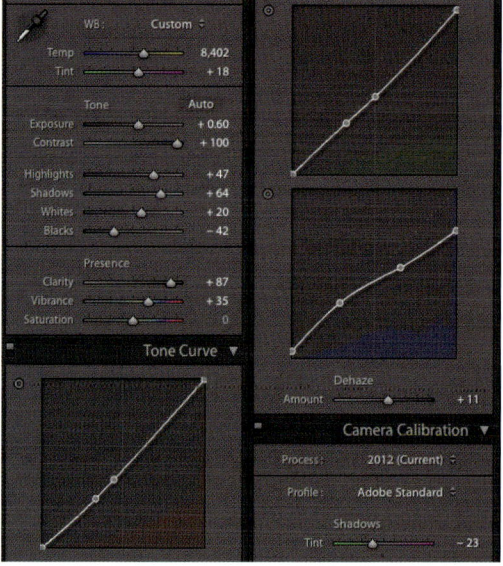

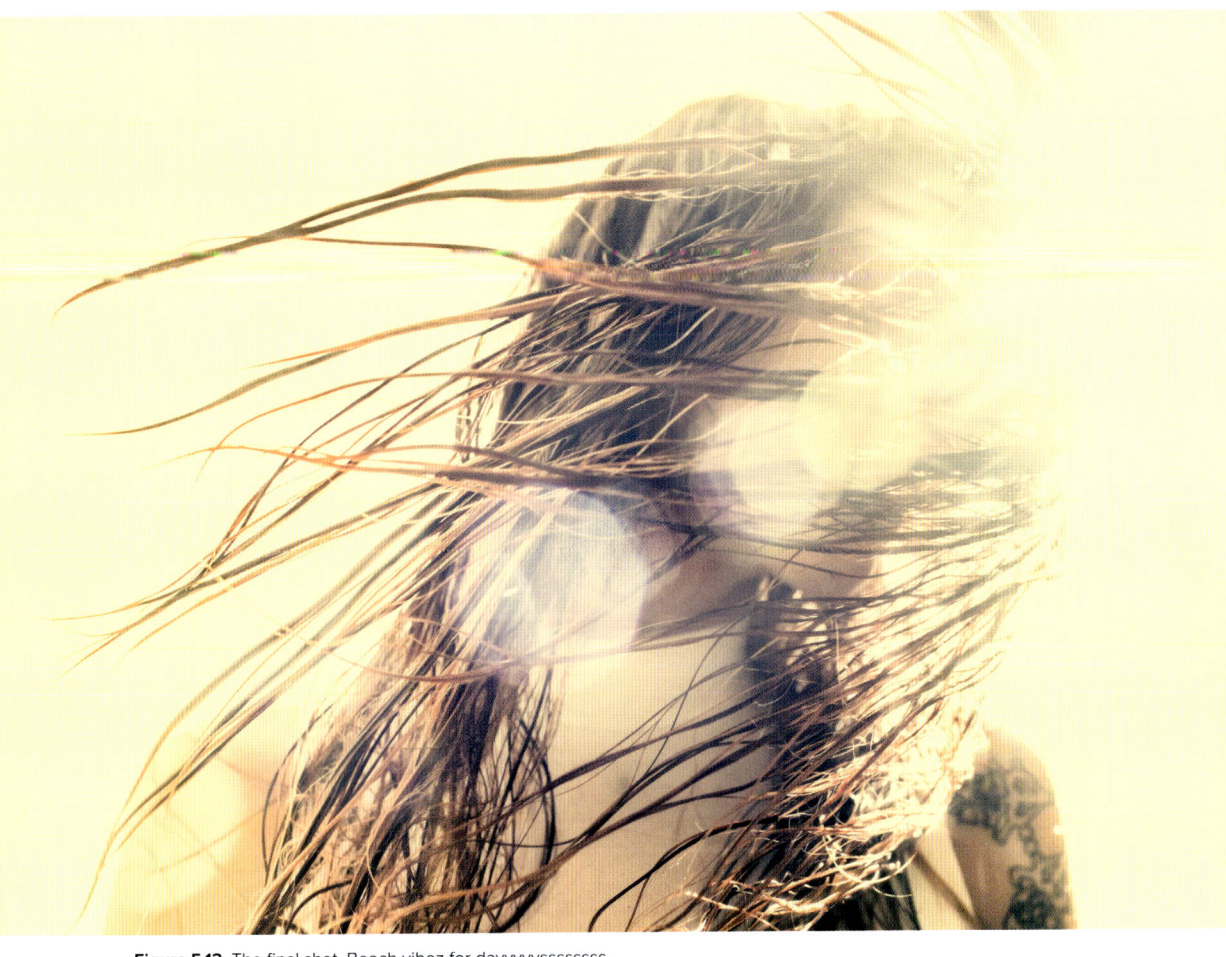

Figure 5.13 The final shot. Beach vibez for dayyyyysssssss.

The proverbial cherry on top of my fake *sun*dae was adding warm tones to the highlights in Lightroom (**Figure 5.12**). Besides maxing out the Contrast and increasing the Vibrance slider, I also lowered the highlight point in the Blue channel of the Tone Curve panel quite a bit, giving the image a golden wash. I used the Dehaze a bit and reduced the magenta glow in the shadows with the Camera Calibration panel. The final shot (**Figure 5.13**) is looking so cinematic that it's just one post-rock song short of becoming an episode of *Friday Night Lights*.

MAXIMIZING ONE LIGHT

This scenario is another one of those aberrations where I talk about soft light for a moment. The lighting setup (**Figure 5.14**) is similar to the previous indoor beach scene in that the light is once again behind and aimed back at the model, but this time I added an umbrella to soften the light. You'll notice that I am not aiming my camera back toward the light either. The thing that makes this technique noteworthy is that it only uses just one flash to light the subject from all sides, but it also works great with reflective surfaces (her sunglasses).

If you've ever photographed a reflective surface you know that it's not only a feat to photograph it without getting your reflection in the shot, but it's also a whole other beast when it comes to lighting. A small light source, such as a single flash, won't fill out a reflective surface of an object. If you've tried doing this, you know that simply aiming a flash at a pair of sunglasses will get you a reflection of the flash being fired, rather than a large gradient of light across the lenses, which is ideal. What you need to do the job is either a large modifier, such as a large softbox, or a large, blank surface you can use to bounce light, such as a white v-flat. Because I was shooting on location in a cramped hair salon, I didn't bring a large light modifier with me, so I used the white side of a piece of poster board, which I clamped to a light stand in front of the model (**Figure 5.15**). Now she was well lit, complete with a nice gradated reflection in her sunglasses (**Figure 5.16**).

Figure 5.14 The setup. The light is once again behind the model, aimed back toward her, but this time I added an umbrella to soften the light.

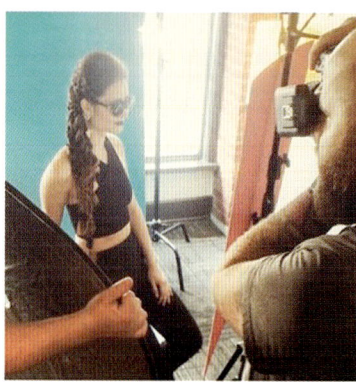

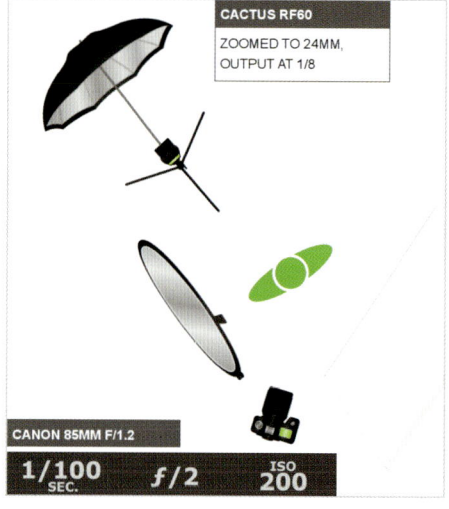

CACTUS RF60

ZOOMED TO 24MM, OUTPUT AT 1/8

CANON 85MM F/1.2

1/100 SEC.   f/2   ISO 200

Figure 5.15 The lighting diagram. I used a reflector and a sheet of white poster board to bounce the backlight on to the model.

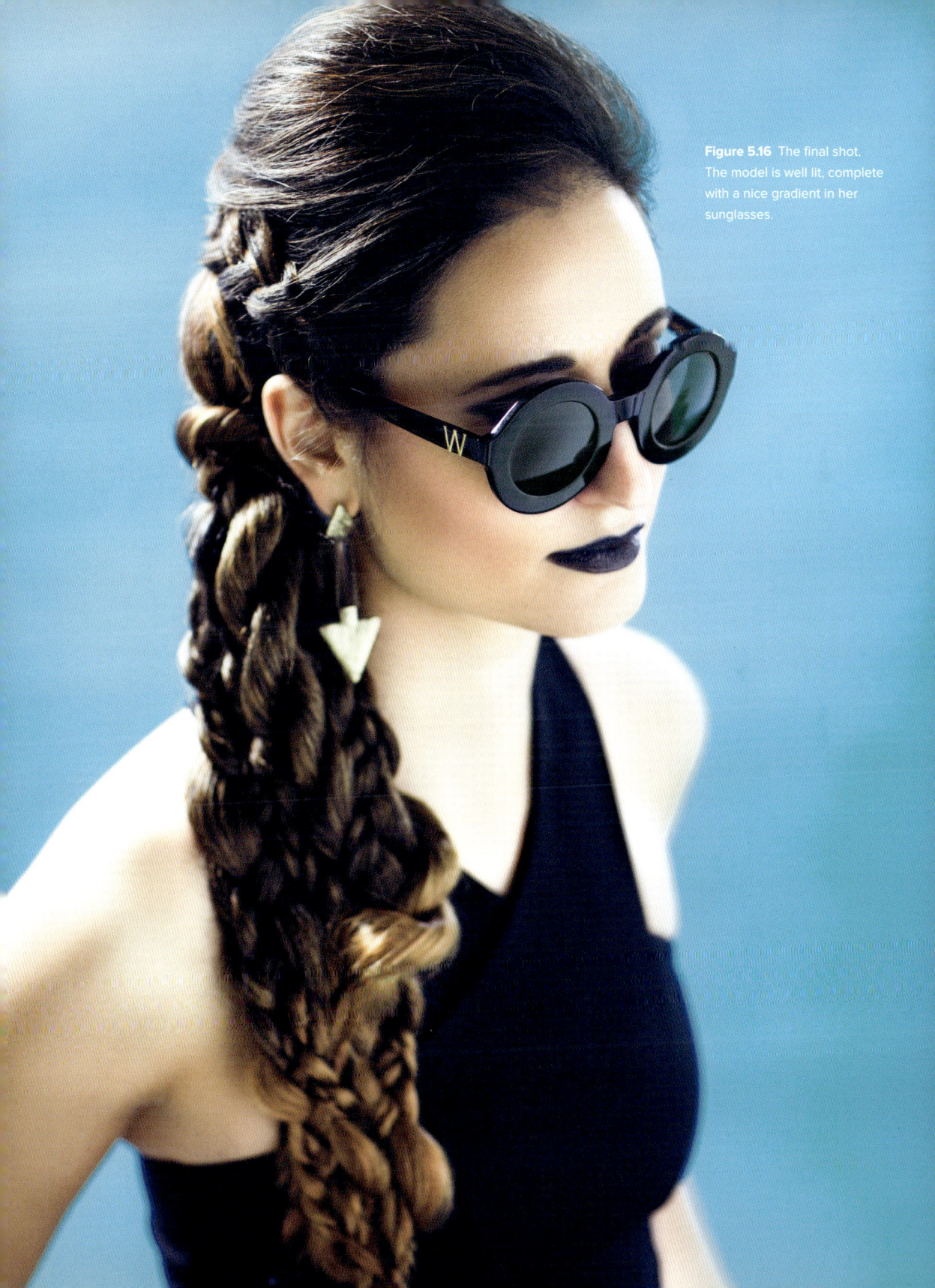

Figure 5.16 The final shot. The model is well lit, complete with a nice gradient in her sunglasses.

NEITHER RAIN, NOR SNOW...

This next technique is one to pull out when it's overcast, raining, or dark—basically Ohio nine months of the year. As you can see in **Figure 5.17**, we are once again doing a scenario where the light is placed behind the subject, aiming back toward the camera. It's actually just like the lens flare scenario, except that I am using a hacked reflector for fill and shooting outdoors. Essentially, we are doing what filmmakers do on Hollywood soundstages, except on a much smaller scale: we are manufacturing light in a location where sunlight is typically found—outside. The one thing to keep in mind when composing your shot with this technique is that any element in your background that isn't also lit with the strobe may give away the charade. In other words, even if your model is perfectly lit, and it looks exactly like sunlight, but the shot's background is a gloomy, overcast scene, your mind will have a harder time believing that the light in the shot was naturally occurring. Your options are then to completely blow out your background with a small depth of field or compose your shot with a background that is easier to control, such as the façade of a building. I used the building for **Figure 5.18**. One other thing to keep an eye on when using this technique is the model's hair. Any flyaways will be especially apparent in the model's glowing mane.

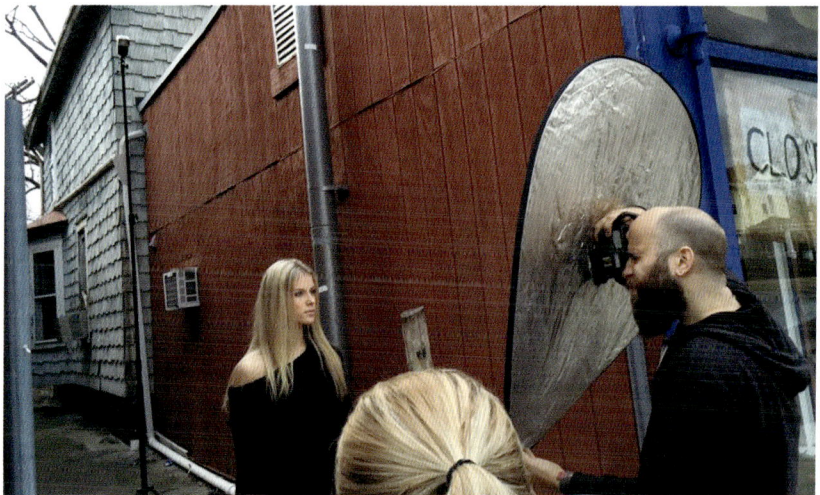

Figure 5.17 The setup. Once again, my light is behind the model, aimed back at the camera, except that this time we are outside on a dark day, in front of a brick wall. *Photo by Emily Burbacher.*

Figure 5.18 The final shot. Make sure your background is completely lit and keep an eye out for flyaway hair when using this technique.

Figure 5.19 The
setup. I've even tried
faking the sun while
it was literally raining,
as seen here.

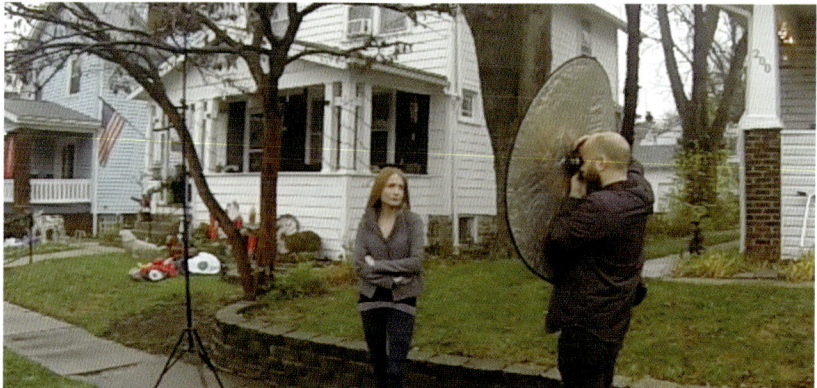

I've even pulled off this technique when shooting in the rain (**Figure 5.19**).
Granted it wasn't pouring outside (I wouldn't subject my model or my gear
to that), but it was raining enough for the rain to be visible in the shot
(**Figure 5.20**). But once I removed the rain spots, using the Healing Brush in
Photoshop (Lightroom's healing tool still isn't up to snuff), and I warmed up the
tones just like I did in Figure 5.13, the fake sunlight was looking pretty damn
believable, if I say so myself (**Figure 5.21**).

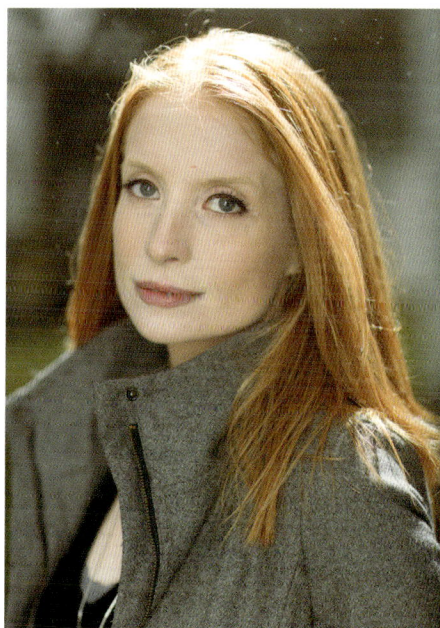

Figure 5.20 The raw file. Before anyone
believes that this shot was taken on a sunny
day, those raindrops need to be removed.

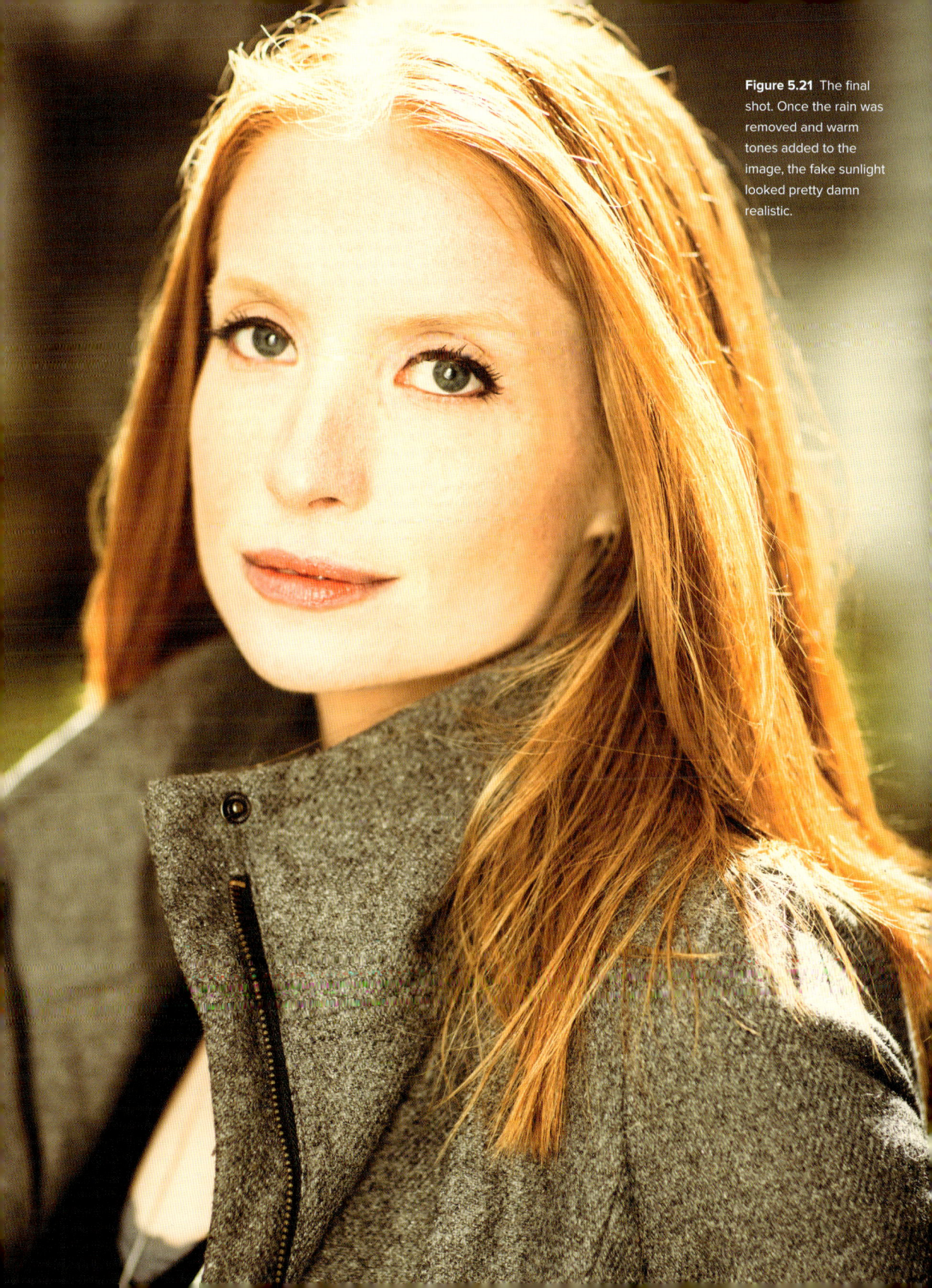

Figure 5.21 The final shot. Once the rain was removed and warm tones added to the image, the fake sunlight looked pretty damn realistic.

FINDING INSPIRATION

When I graduated from Ohio State in 2005, I was excited to launch my career as a photographer. I was one of the top in my class and was certain I would crush any of my competition, because I had the advantage of a fine art background. Hell, I shot *film*. But then I discovered Flickr—specifically the "Explore" page. Literally every image on there was better than anything I had shot or even knew how to shoot. I was overwhelmed by the beauty, but not in a good way. It made me feel tiny. Like I knew nothing. I started down the rabbit trail, clicking on random profiles and digging through portfolio after portfolio, determined to find the end of the good photos so I could fully understand what I was up against. It was on par with trying to find the edge of the Earth. It was not possible. The fact was, and is, that there is so much talent in this world. And this isn't a bad thing. It's awesome that so many people out there are creating amazing work. But that means that I really have my work cut out for me if I want to stand out above the rest. I can't succeed just because the others are worse than me. I have to be better than the already great. However, my growth process didn't begin with technique. The technique came later. It began, rather, with inspiration.

Inspiration comes from a number of places, and each artist is inspired by different things. For me, inspiration has always come from movies, music, and fashion editorials. A note that a singer's voice hits in a song may trigger an emotion in me that conjures up a memory of the past. At the same time, maybe I had been thinking about a film I had recently watched that especially moved me. Then the next day I may be flipping through the latest issue of *Interview* magazine (which is my go-to spot for finding amazing editorials) and come upon an especially breathtaking editorial where the photographer was using a lighting technique that I hadn't seen before.

These series of events, though unrelated, all work together to push me to create. It's a drive in me. If I'm not creating new work everyday, I feel empty. Honestly, maybe I just need to up my meds, but it nonetheless fuels me to keep pushing myself. I also learned early on not to pay attention to the competition around me—meaning the other photographers in Columbus. If I am looking at what only my peers are doing, I will always be a step behind them. Instead, I look at what the best of the best in the world are doing, and I try to reverse engineer their lighting by studying their images. Then I set up test shoots with subjects and models where I try out these methods. This is how I learn and grow.

This process of experimentation and discovery has helped me to learn more than I ever did at a university. As I said earlier, everyone is different. People learn using a variety of methods and are inspired by a variety of things. The trick is to find out what inspires you and pushes you to create, and then to surround yourself with these things. Most importantly, don't get crushed by it all.

You may have heard the Charles Bukowski quote, "Find what you love and let it kill you." I both agree and disagree with this sentiment. I think that what you love—what you find inspiring or beautiful—should maim you. It should stop you in your tracks, make you weep. But the end result should be inspiration rather than death. Death comes through shame—those thoughts of self-doubt that creep in when you experience an especially beautiful piece of art, as I felt with the artists on Flickr. Don't let what you love kill your need to create. Let it feed it.

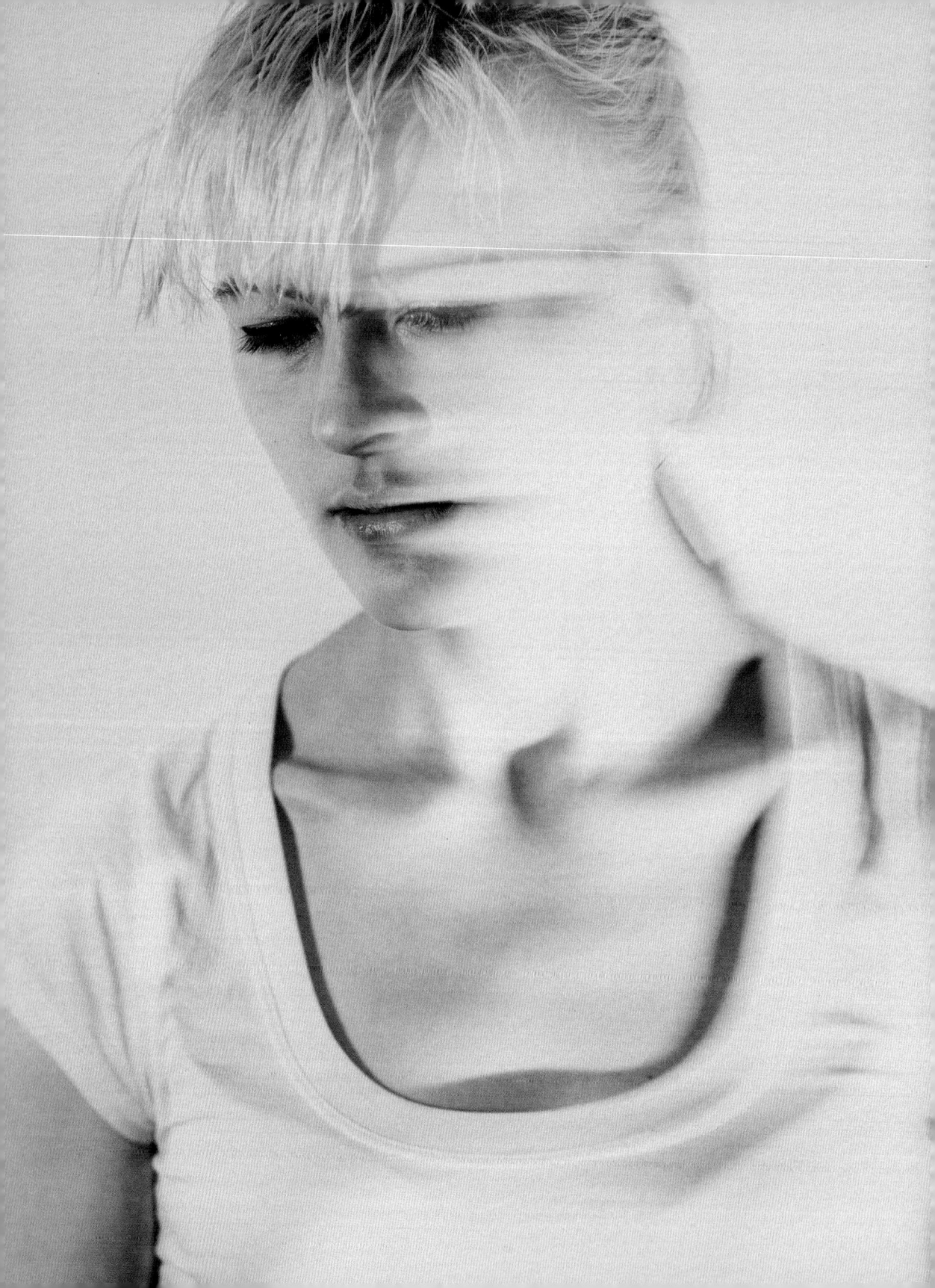

CHAPTER 6

LONG EXPOSURES

Long-exposure photography is an art form. It brings a bit of unpredictability back to photography which, since its switch from film to digital, has become rather predictable. Long exposures allow you to do a range of things, such as painting with light, which results in streaky light, reminiscent of brush strokes. You can also make multiple flash exposures, which results in multiple, perfectly defined captures within a single frame. Or you can do a combination of frozen and blurred subjects.

These techniques of capturing artistic blurring with shutter drag and even using multiple flash exposures to freeze motion date all the way back to the creation of strobe light with Harold Eugene Edgerton's experiments and the motion studies of Eadweard Muybridge. I will go into both techniques in this chapter

PERCUSSIVE LIGHT

Long-exposure photography is a tricky beast. At least it is for me. It took me a long time to wrap my head around understanding strobe light versus ambient light and how to control them individually and together. So when you go and throw in long exposure, which is yet again something that is beyond what the naked eye can see, you have a hell of a technical shot on your hands.

My client was Ohio State University. The point of the shoot was to create content for the dance and music department in promotion of its annual collaborative show, Drums Downtown. At our initial meeting, where we discussed concepts for the show, we talked about a darker, moodier set of images that also managed to unify the movement in the percussionists with the dancers. I immediately thought of Edgerton's strobe experiments (thank you Photo History class). When I showed the director the images, he was sold.

I felt confident going into the shoot that I could pull off this technique, but I knew that it'd be tricky. I didn't realize the full breadth of what I was getting into until we were already shooting. I anticipated shooting in a dark room, so I brought a tripod and a flash with me to the shoot. As you can see in **Figure 6.1**, my exposure was five seconds long, and this wasn't because I needed the ambient light to fill in the exposure. In fact, there was no ambient light. At all. The reason for the long exposure was that I needed enough time to fire off a sequence of light bursts in order to capture the percussionist's moving arms at varying heights.

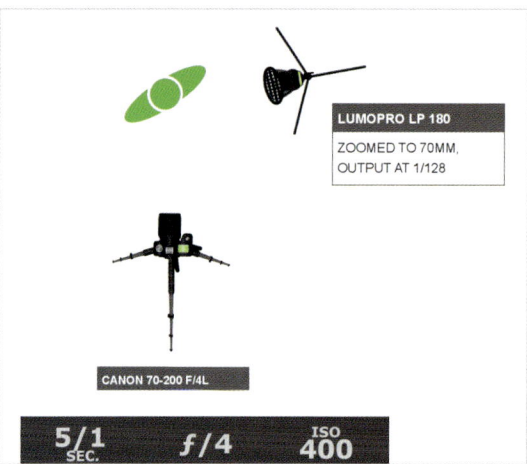

Figure 6.1 The lighting diagram. The long exposure was not used to gain a proper ambient exposure but rather to allow enough time to fire the strobe a number of times.

I set up a gridded, unmodified flash beside the subject, raised to about eight or nine feet. I aimed the flash so that the light fell mainly on his arms and hands. When I clicked the shutter, the flash fired as expected. I then used the remaining exposure time to manually fire off the flash by hitting the test button on my trigger. I had my flash set to the lowest output, which allowed for a fast recycle time. If I had to guess, I'd say that I fired off eight to ten flashes during the exposure.

The technique went swimmingly. His arm movements were captured crisply and the shot was dramatic (**Figure 6.2**). What I had failed to anticipate, however, was that his torso and head would also be slightly moving as he drummed, resulting in his face appearing blurry. Once I realized why this was happening, I knew how I could fix it. Rather than trying to have him attempt to drum without moving his upper torso, I had him hold position and I took a single exposure with the flash at a slightly higher output of 1/16 power to get a properly exposed (because I was firing the flash only once instead of eight to ten times) and frozen image of the percussionist (**Figure 6.3**).

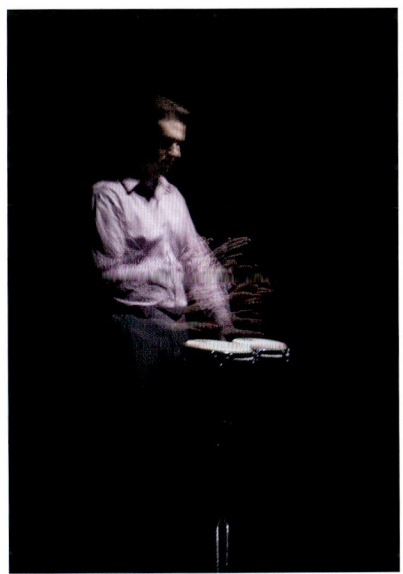

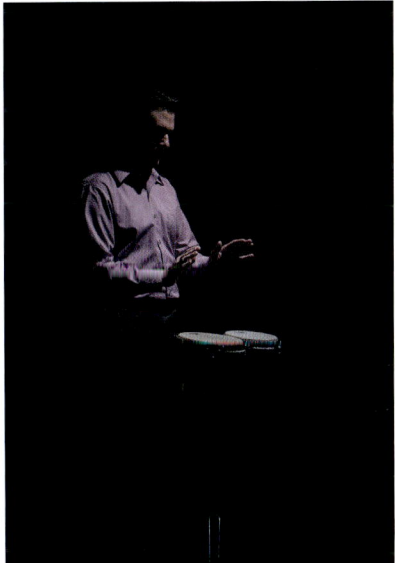

Figure 6.2 The raw file. Although the series of flashes captured the drummer's movement in the way I wanted, I hadn't anticipated the blurring in his face.

Figure 6.3 The second raw file. I needed to make a second exposure for which the flash was fired only once in order to freeze the percussionist's upper torso and head. I needed to increase the output of the flash to 1/16 power, because I wasn't triggering the flash eight to ten times in this shot.

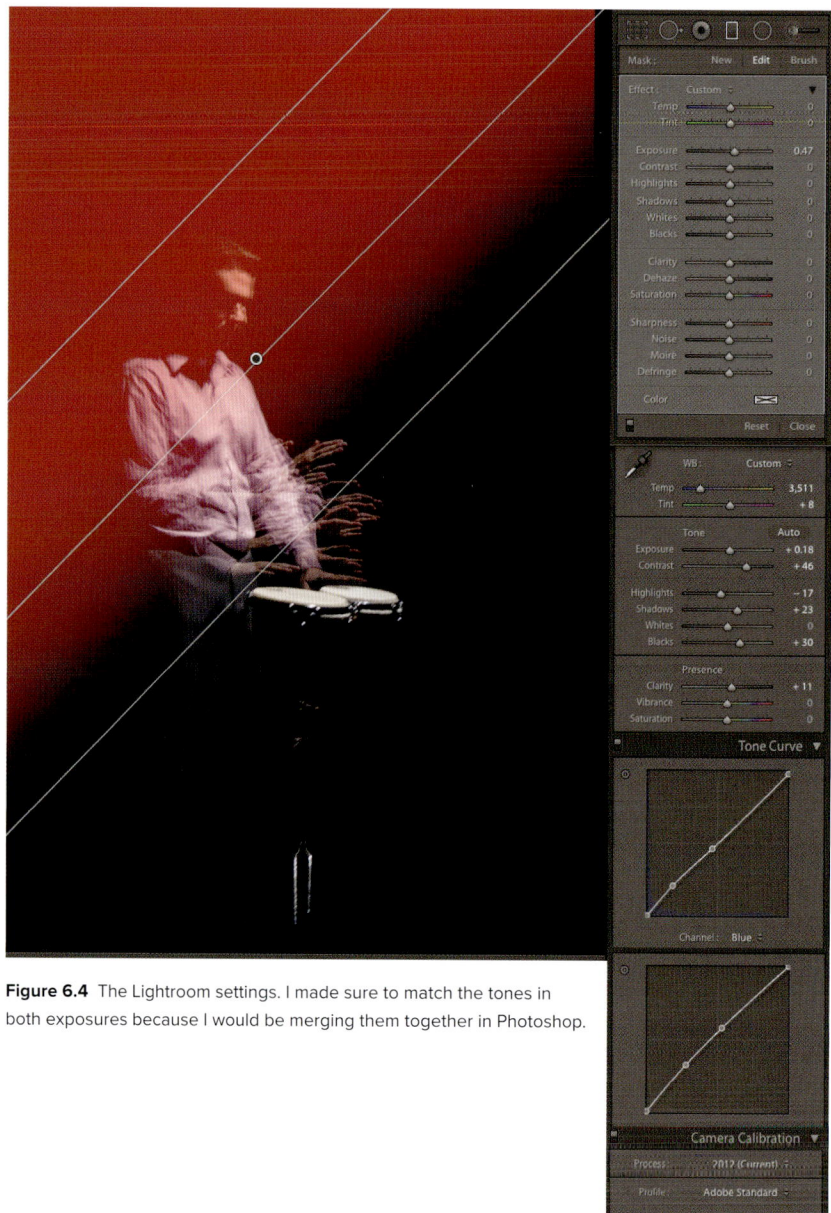

Figure 6.4 The Lightroom settings. I made sure to match the tones in both exposures because I would be merging them together in Photoshop.

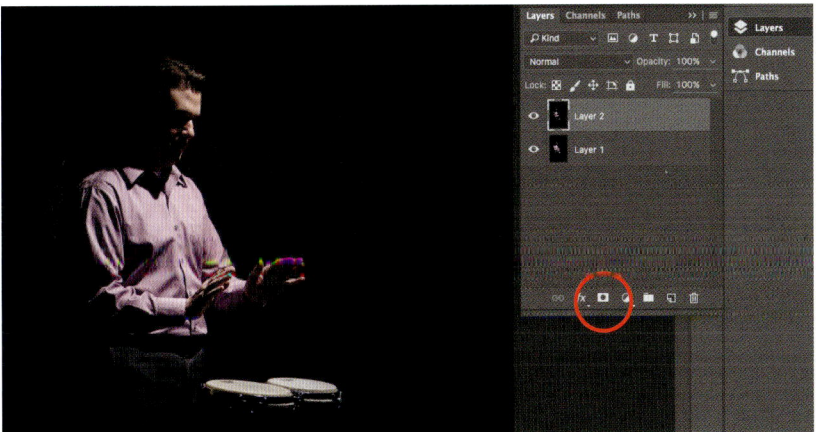

Figure 6.5 I placed the frozen image in a layer on top of the blurred image and then created a layer mask (seen in red).

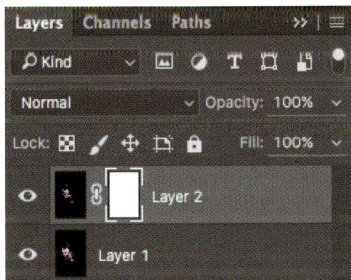

Figure 6.6 Here is my layer mask.

Now all I needed to do was combine the two images into one. Although it may sound tricky, it's actually super simple to do using layers in Photoshop. In **Figure 6.4** you can see my Lightroom settings. I basically needed to align the tones in the two exposures so that blending them together in Photoshop would be easier. Once the files looked good, I opened them in Photoshop. Once in Photoshop, I took the image where the percussionist's face was frozen and put it in a layer on top of the blurred image (**Figure 6.5**). Then I created a layer mask (**Figure 6.6**). Then I selected the Brush tool and set the Flow at 3% (**Figure 6.7**). This allowed me to blend in my brush strokes, creating a smooth transition from the top layer to the bottom layer. Sometimes I'll even take it a step further by making a "box blur" on the layer mask, after I've painted away the area to smooth out the brush strokes.

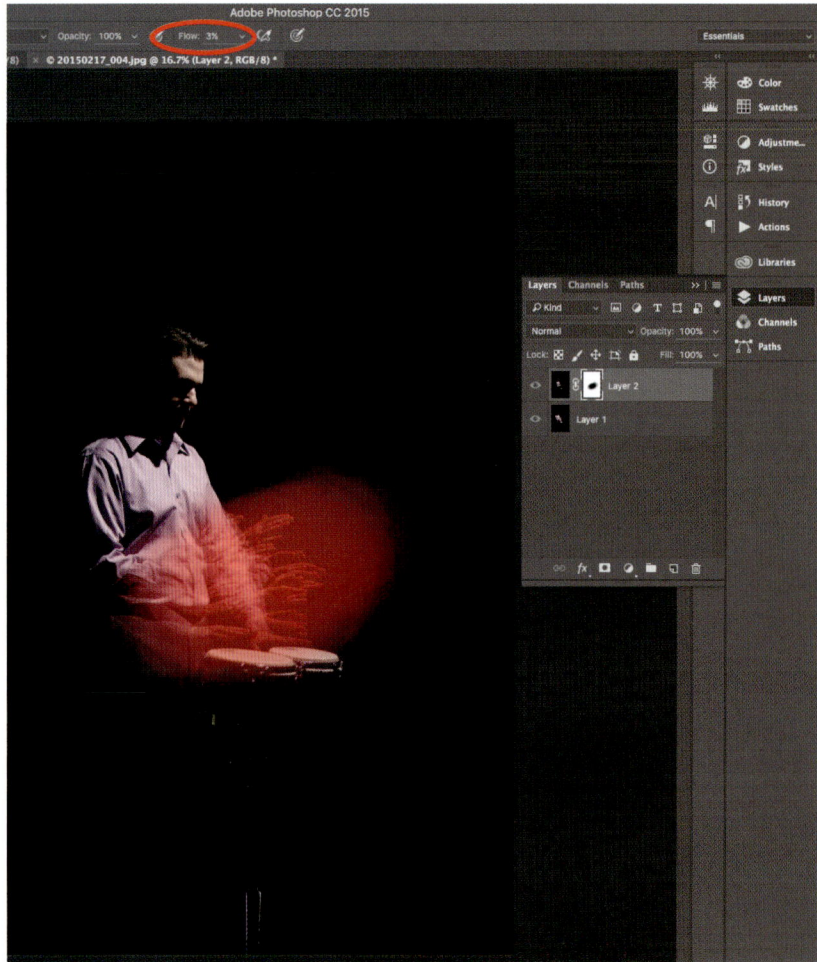

Figure 6.7 I selected the Brush tool, setting the Flow to 3%, and then painted away the top layer from his arm and hand area, leaving a smooth transitional window to the bottom layer.

Note, this technique of laying a static image over a moving image is based on the same idea that's behind the cinemagraphs that have been trending these last couple of years. In **Figure 6.8** you can see the final shot. That ain't stage fright causing the percussionist to freeze up. That's all technique, dawg.

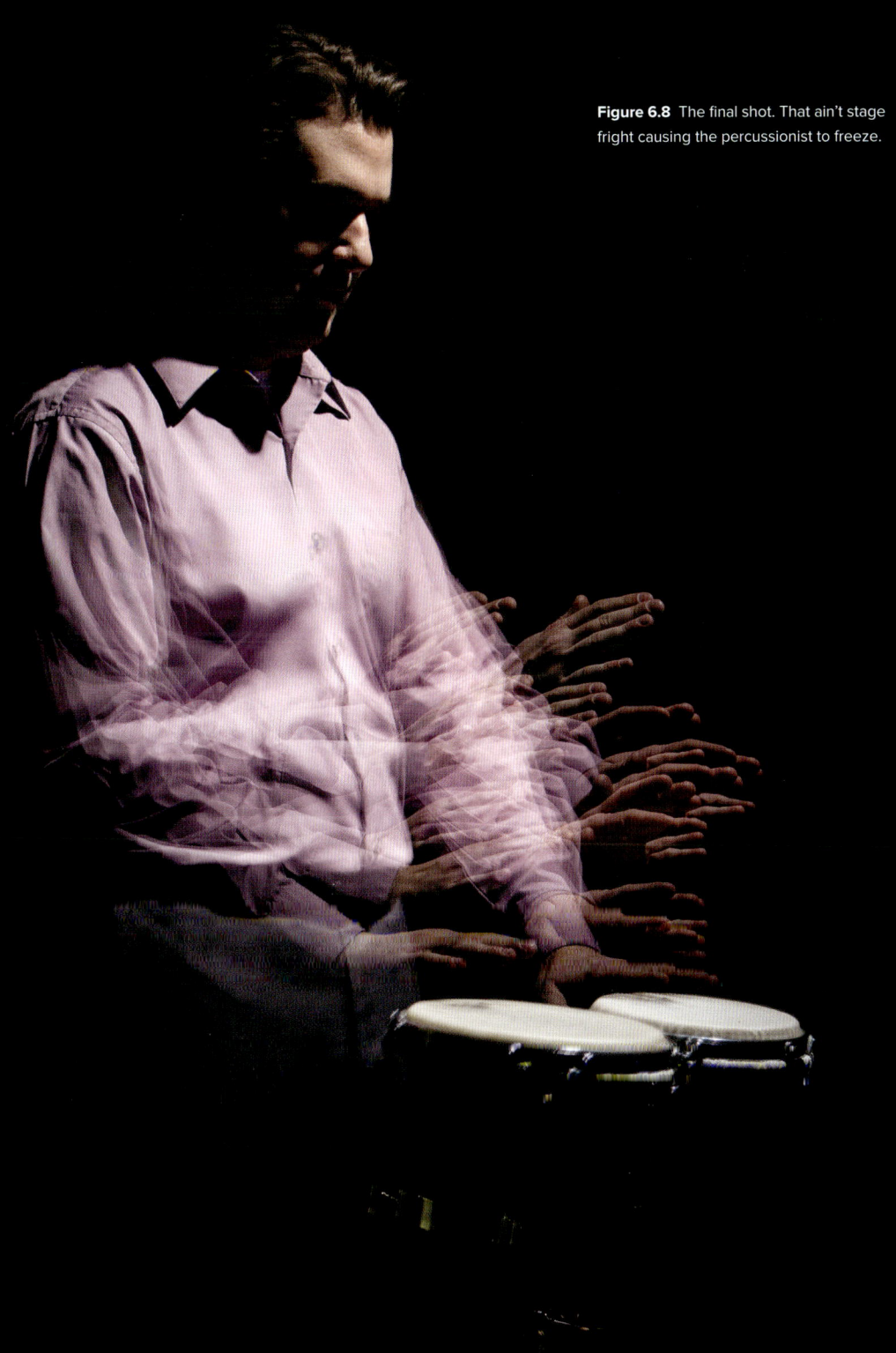

Figure 6.8 The final shot. That ain't stage fright causing the percussionist to freeze.

PAINTERLY LIGHT

The Ohio State shoot was for a collaboration between the percussion and dance departments. With the percussion half finished, let me explain how I handled the dance portion of the shoot. The camera and flash settings were nearly identical to the first setup (**Figure 6.9**). The only difference was that I moved the flash into a forward-facing position and removed the grid, which allowed more light to come from the flash. As a result, my ISO was a bit lower.

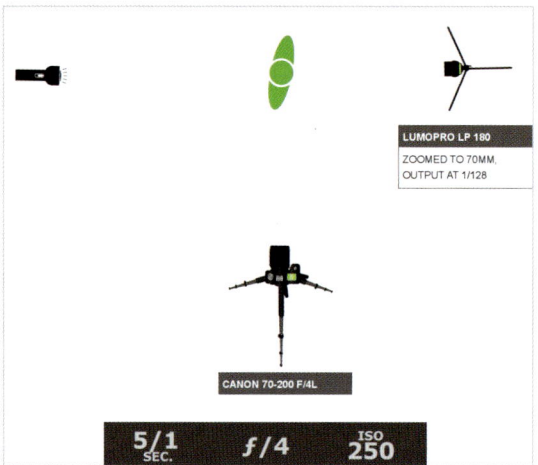

Figure 6.9 The lighting diagram. The settings are nearly identical to the previous setup. Because my grid was removed, I had a higher flash output, which caused me to lower my ISO a bit.

For the dance scenario, I wanted a trail of blurred movement to follow the dancer through the frame. This meant that I needed a second, constant light source to accompany my strobe. At first I tried using a floodlight, but no matter how much I flagged the light, there was still light spill on the black curtains, which were 20 to 30 feet behind the dancers. I finally settled on having the percussion professor hold my flashlight and move it up and down throughout the exposure, "painting" in the light on the moving dancer.

Because my camera was on a tripod and I was in a fixed position, and because it was so dark that I couldn't really see to focus or compose the shot, I turned on the house lights and locked in my exposure. Note: to keep the camera from attempting to refocus once the lights go out, you can either switch the lens over to manual focus once focus is attained, or you can use back-button focus, which is what I use.

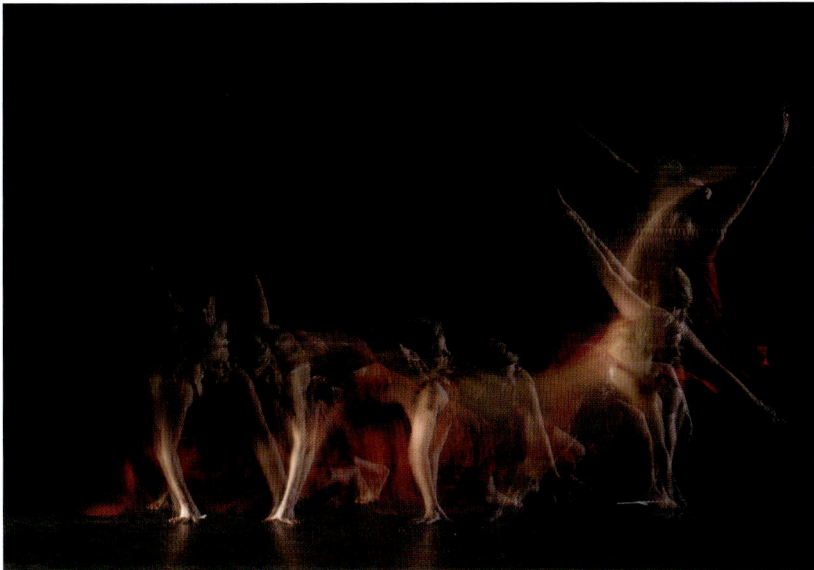

Figure 6.10 The raw file. To get the blurry light trail to follow the dancer, I had someone "paint" in the ambient light with a flashlight.

Once I locked in my focus, I had the dancer get in position at the edge of my frame on the left and I marked this starting position with a strip of white gaff tape on the floor. She then moved to the edge of the frame on the right, where I marked the ending point. Now the lights could go off and the dancer had the tape to give her a reference for her movement. After several exposures, I decided that I wanted her to start in a low, crouched position and to transition to a standing position as she moved through the frame. It made for a super rad light trail (**Figure 6.10**).

Although I had done my best to minimize light from spilling onto the ground or the curtains in the background in order to retain a dark mood, some light spillage had occurred. To remedy this, I made a gradient adjustment in Lightroom, lowering the Exposure and Shadows sliders (**Figure 6.11**). After I removed the white tape markers from the floor, the shot was good to go (**Figure 6.12**).

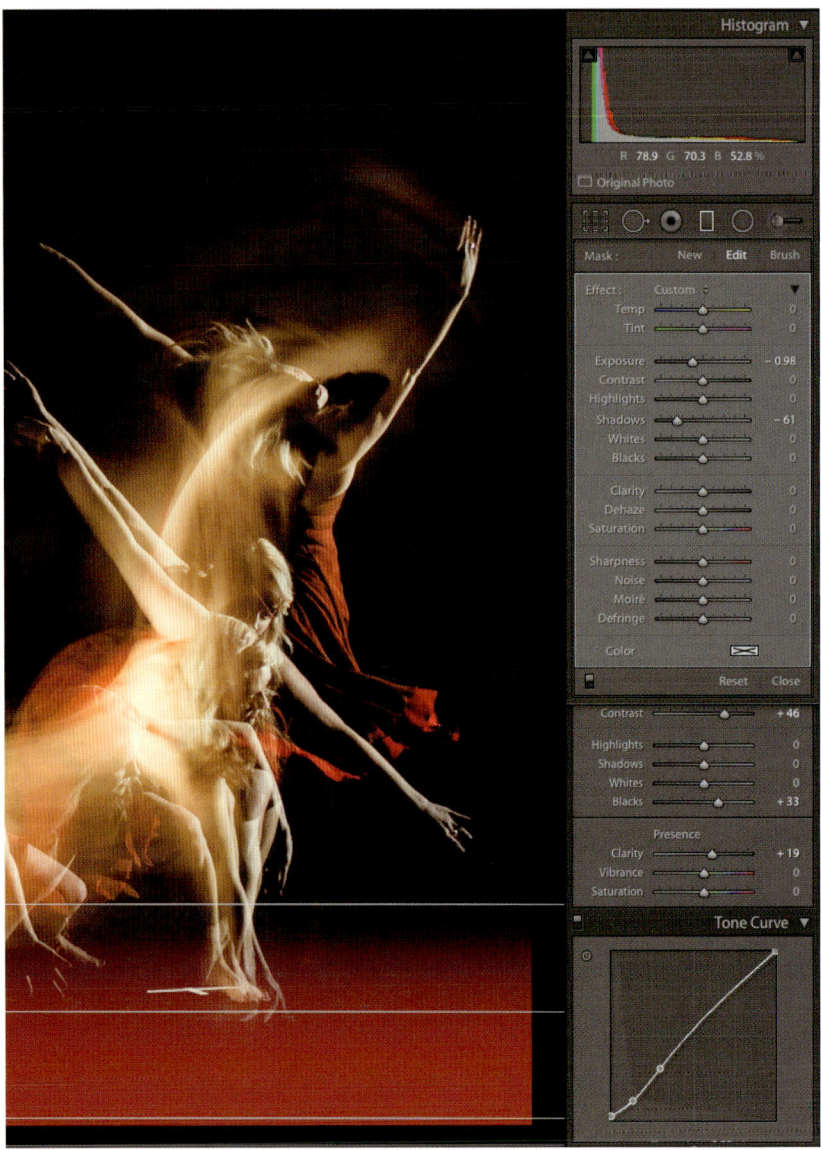

Figure 6.11 The Lightroom settings. To minimize some of the light spill on the floor, I made a gradient adjustment, lowering the Exposure and Shadows sliders.

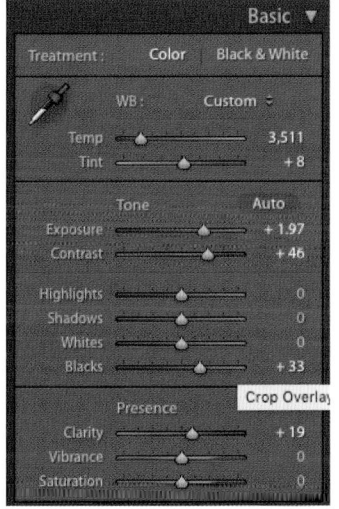

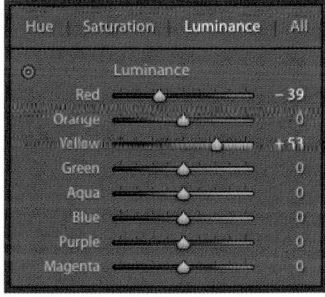

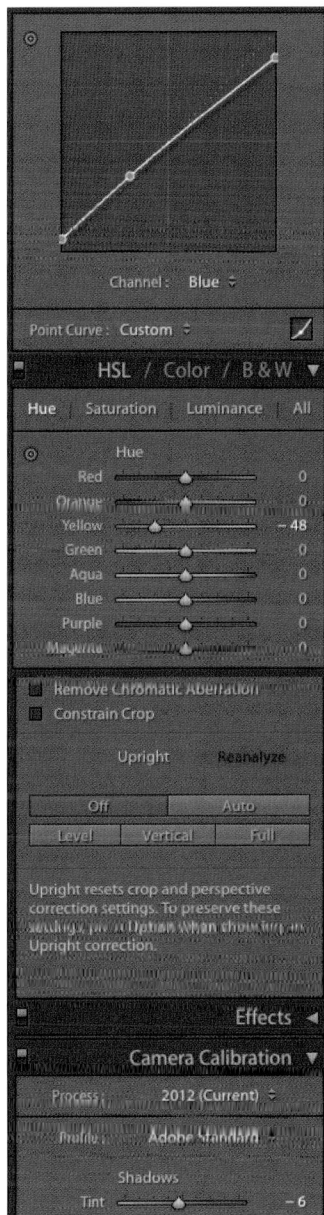

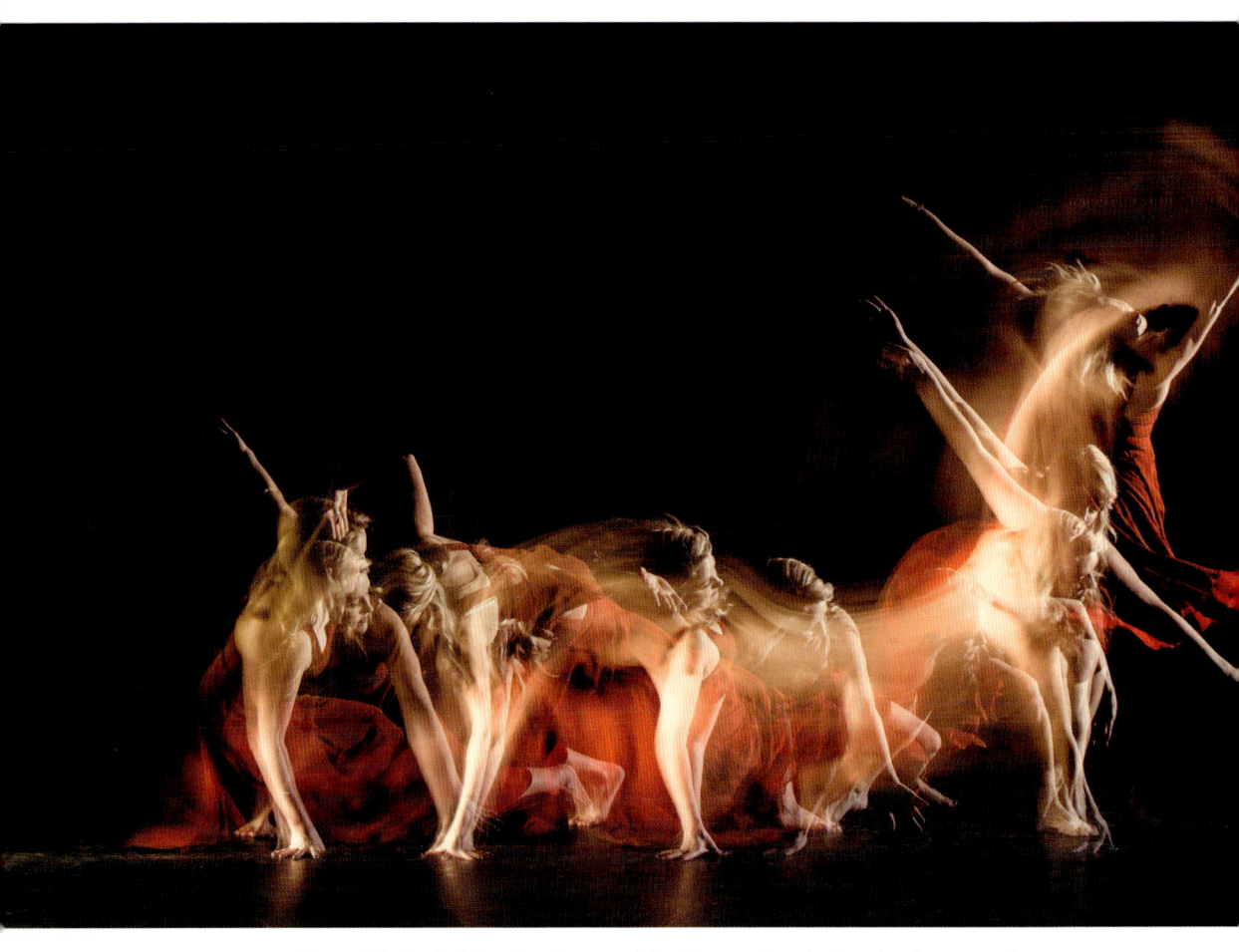

Figure 6.12 The final shot. Once I removed the white tape from the floor, the shot was ready to go.

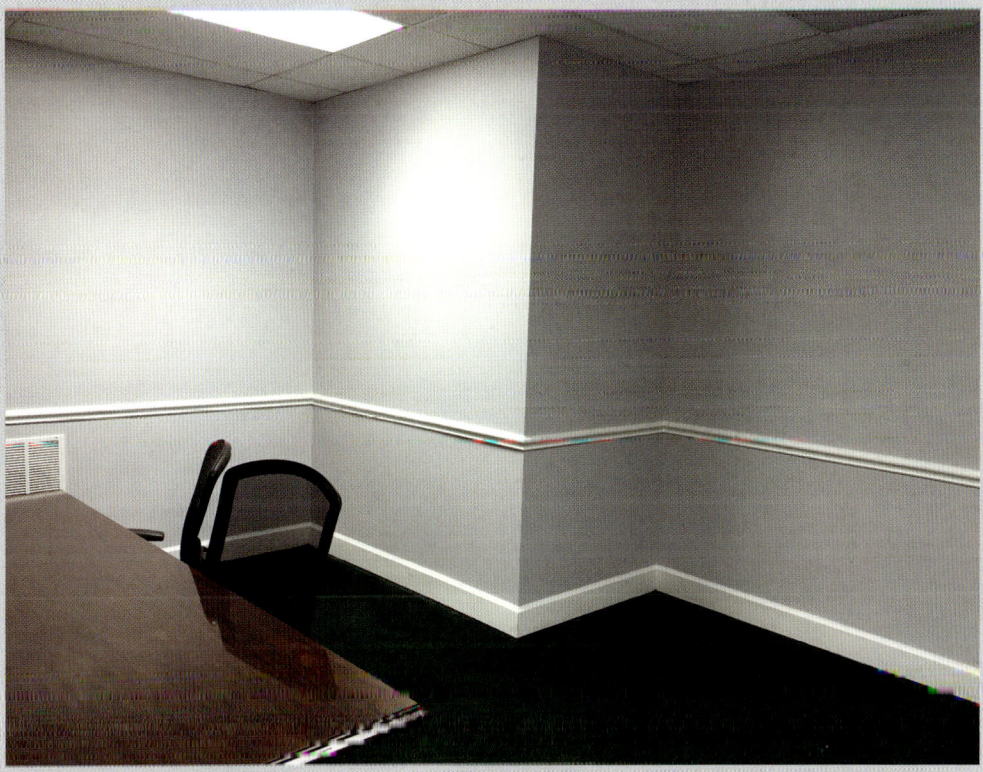

Figure S.3 This is what I had to work with at the shoot location. Where might I place my subject and my light (or lights) to get an airy portrait on a pure white background? Flip to the back of the book to see where I placed them.

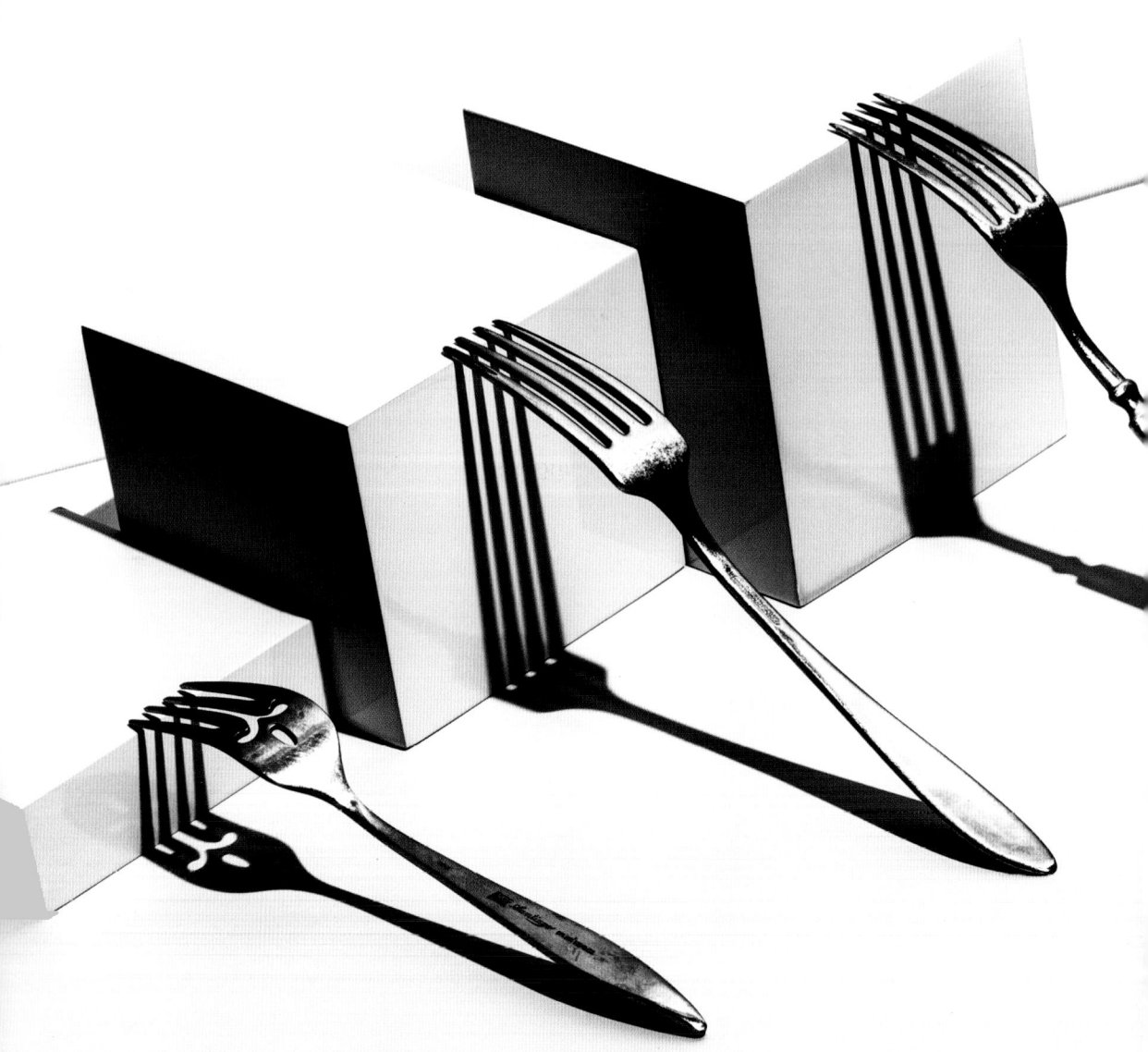

CHAPTER 7

PAINTING WITH SHADOW

In the previous chapter, we discussed the technique of "painting" with light, wherein during a long exposure, ambient light can be burned into the exposure with flashlights, glow sticks, or other constant light sources. Well, it turns out that shadows can also be manipulated in creative ways. By changing the relation of the light source(s) to the subject, you can soften, harden, lengthen, or shorten shadows accordingly. By knowing how light direction and distance affect shadow quality, you can adjust the lights to shape the precise type of shadow that you desire. This chapter goes over these methods, setting you up to essentially "paint" with shadow.

SHOOT THE FORK UP

We touched on controlling shadow length and direction back in Chapter 2, with the ice cream shots. I want to go a bit more in depth regarding how you can use the skill of shadow control to your creative advantage. Take a look at **Figure 7.1**. As you can see, my light is raised quite high (about eight feet) and is close to the silverware (about three feet away), which helps give the silverware a short shadow (**Figure 7.2**).

Note: when you're lighting and shooting from overhead, it's a balancing act to avoid getting your own shadow in the frame. This will be a no-brainer for some of you, but if you have a longer focal length lens as well as a wide angle, use your long lens, so you can back out of the way of the light, or even cheat your angle a bit to the side. As it is, you can see the edge of my transmitter on the right side of the frame in Figure 7.2.

Regarding light height, the greater the distance of the light to the product, the more even the spread is by the time it reaches the product (inverse square law). As long as the product is close to the surface or background, the shadows

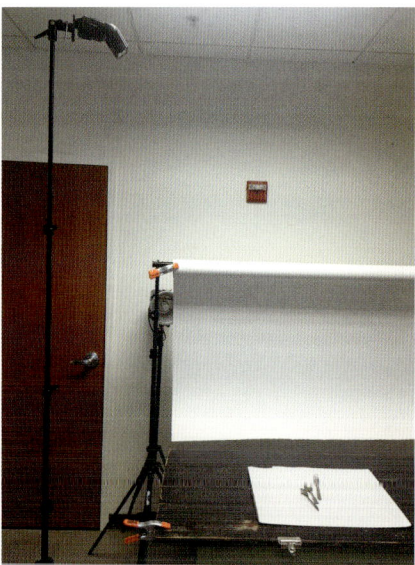

Figure 7.1 My light is raised to about eight feet and is about three feet from the silverware.

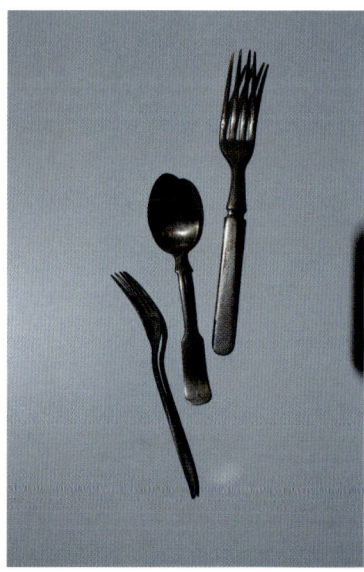

Figure 7.2 The elevated height and close proximity of the flash produces a short, crisp shadow.

produced will be well defined; it's on par with looking at your shadow on the sidewalk at noon on a sunny day. I have the flash zoomed out to 24mm, which allows the flash spread to cover the image frame. Also, as you'll recall from the introduction, a Speedlite creates a more defined shadow than a larger studio strobe.

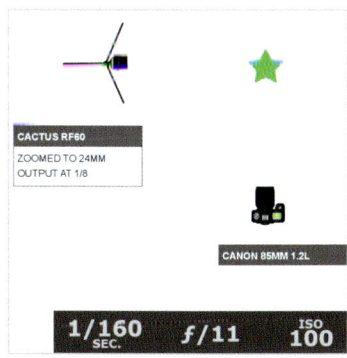

Figure 7.3 The lighting diagram. My flash and camera settings were the same in every shot.

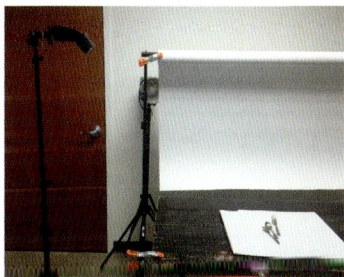

Figure 7.4 All the settings and the distance of the light are the same as for the previous scenario, except this time my light has been lowered to five feet.

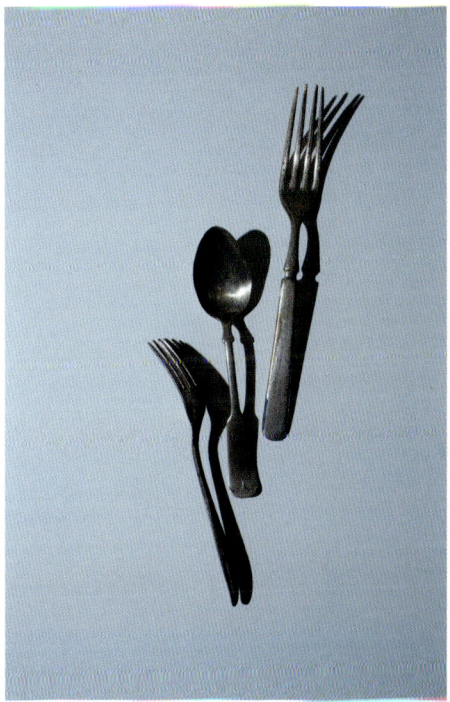

Figure 7.5 The shadows are starting to get longer, revealing more of the curvature of the silverware.

If I were to keep everything the same—same light output, camera settings (**Figure 7.3**), and distance of the light to the silverware—but I lowered my light height (**Figure 7.4**), can you guess what would happen? The shadows start to get longer, as you can see in **Figure 7.5**. Again, think about the sun. Shadows begin to get longer as the sun starts going down. The cool thing that starts to happen as the light height is lowered is that more of the qualities of the silverware shape are revealed in the shadow. For example, you can see the curve of the spoon and fork now, where it wasn't obvious in the first setup.

Finally, if I were to lower my light as low as I could without my setup going to total darkness (**Figure 7.6**), the shadows would be so long that they would begin to overlap (**Figure 7.7**). If you look closely at these shadows, you will notice that the shadows soften at certain points. These softer shadows are cast by the parts of the silverware that are further from the paper backdrop. The parts that are actually touching the paper make crisp shadows.

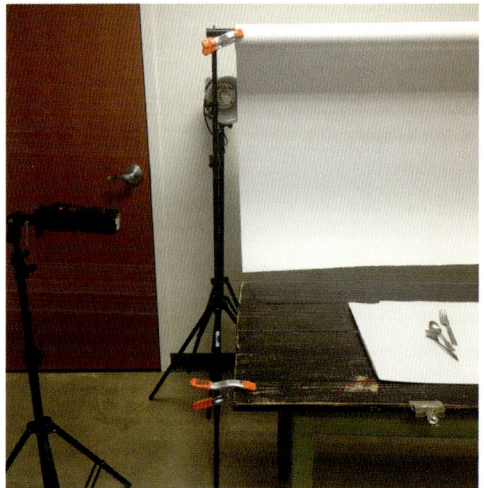

Figure 7.6 For the next shot, I lowered my light as low as I could, short of leaving my setup in darkness.

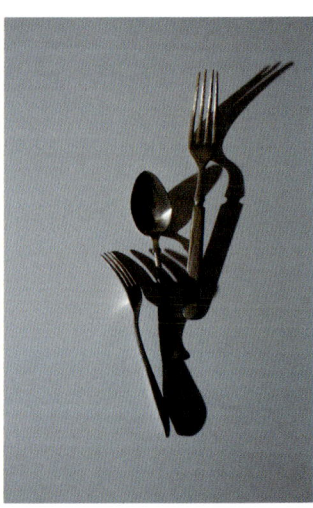

Figure 7.7 The shadows are now so long that they are starting to overlap.

As you can see, the SOOC files aren't too pretty to look at. Because I am showcasing the shadows only, however, I can get away with murder when it comes to my color grading (**Figure 7.8**). Contrast? All the way over. Clarity? That too. Highlights up, Shadows down. Only the blackest blacks and the whitest whites for these light and shadow studies. It works for these images, as you can see in **Figure 7.9**. It wouldn't work as well when working with a person, however, as you'll see in the next section.

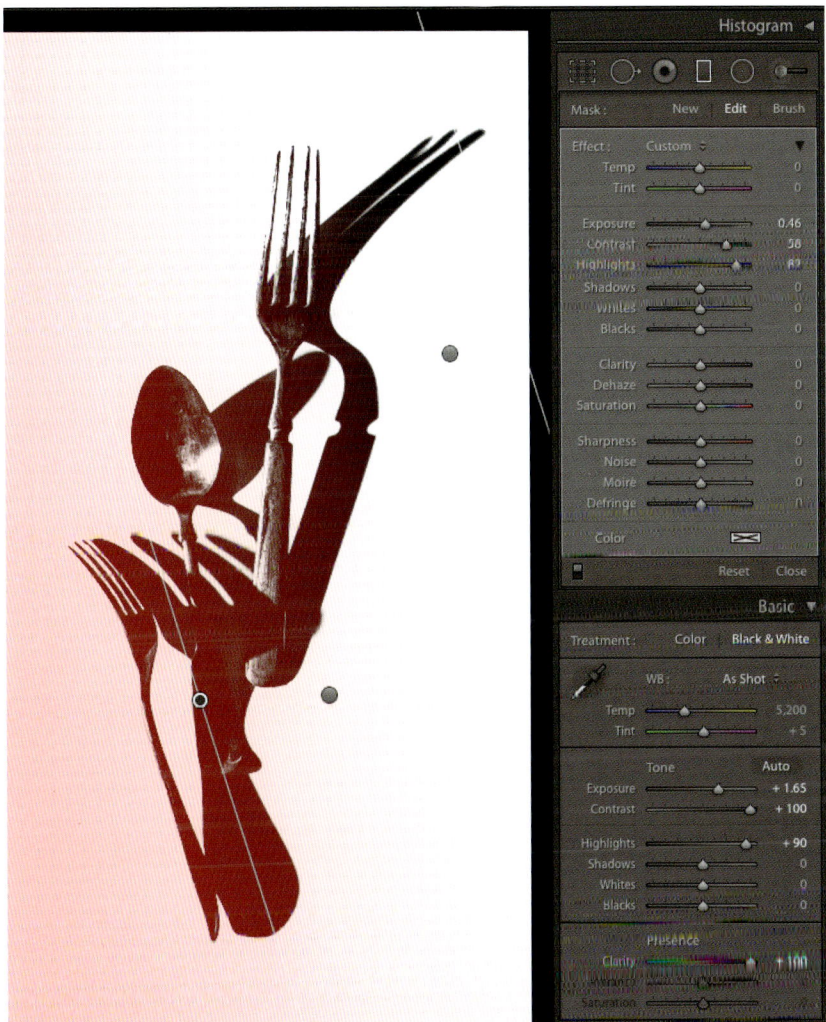

Figure 7.8 The Lightroom settings. These images are about the shadows, so I was able to crank up the contrast without losing important details.

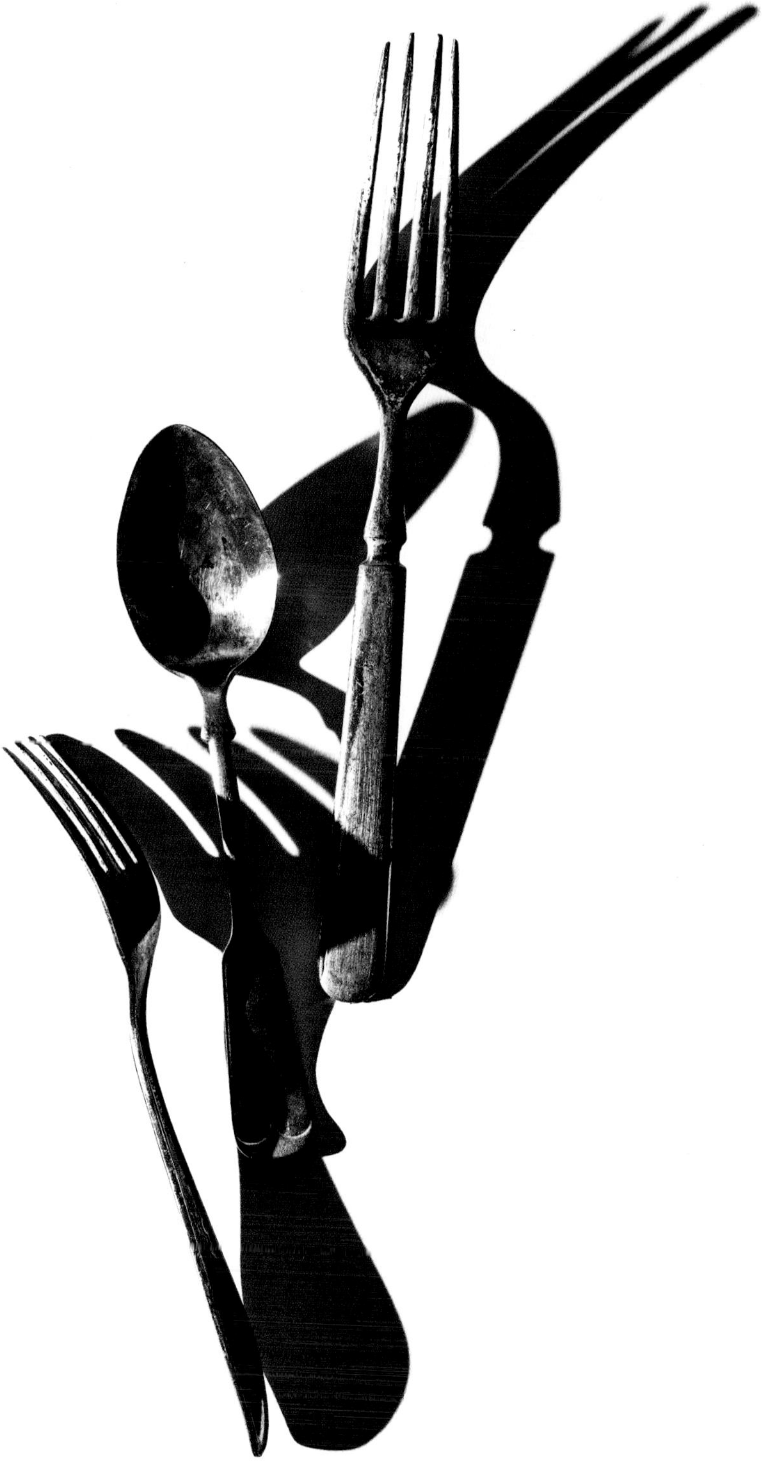

Figure 7.9 The final shot.
Looks beautiful as fork, no?

MULTIPLE SHADOWS

As I mentioned earlier in Chapter 5's *Finding Inspiration* section, I try to sur-round myself with photographers who are doing what I want to do and are the masters of the field, with *Interview* magazine being one of my main sources of inspiration. There I found Sølve Sundsbø's photographs of *Game of Thrones* actor Michiel Huisman, which were inspiring to say the least. One of my favorite photographers, Sundsbø had created an amazing triple shadow in one of the shots and a quad shadow in another. I had never seen anyone light like that before. Still, it wasn't hard to reverse engineer his lighting setup by studying the light and shadow qualities in the images. All that remained was finding a model available within the next hour so I could try out this technique *immediately*.

Lucky for me, art student/cosplay model extraordinaire Stephanie Flor was willing to give me 30 minutes before her class to try out this technique. I met her on campus and staged the shoot in the hallway outside her classroom—all I needed was a blank wall and a bit of space (**Figure 7.10**). I set up my three flashes, staggered in a diagonal line to Stephanie, raised to chest-level height; the lower height gives the shadows an elevated angle (**Figure 7.11**). Again, note the distance of the flashes to the subject. The closest one to her is still a good five feet away. I need to allow enough space for the flash to spread evenly across the frame. I also needed her right against the wall to get a crisp shadow (**Figure 7.12**).

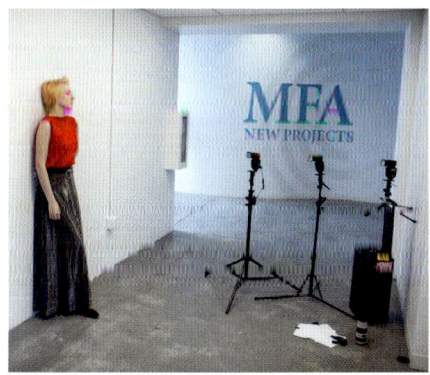

Figure 7.10 The setup. I staged the shoot in the hallway outside the model's class. All I needed was a blank wall.

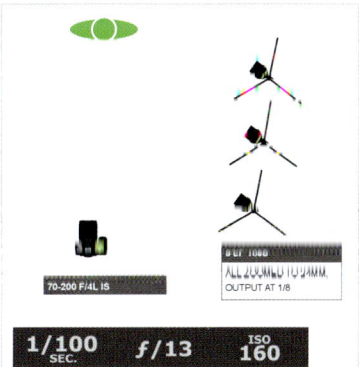

Figure 7.11 The lighting diagram. I staggered three flashes in a diagonal line to the subject, whose back was against a white wall.

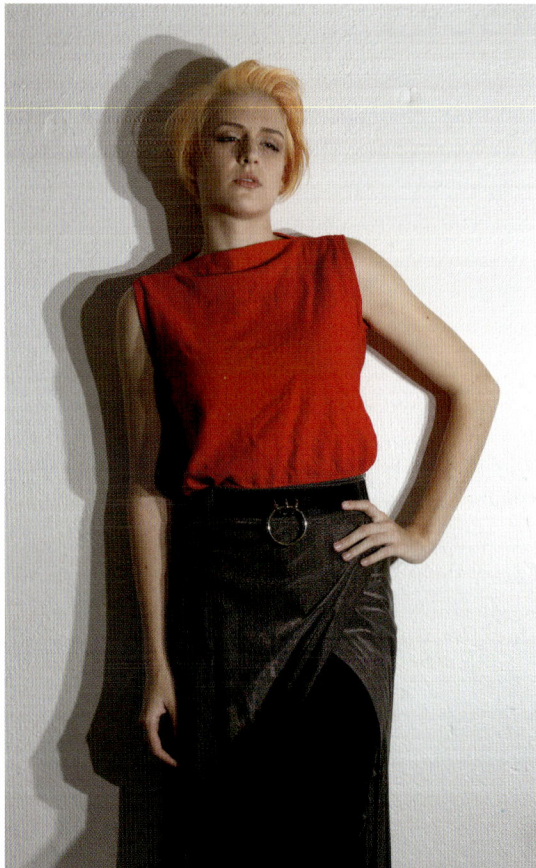

Figure 7.12 The raw file. Stephanie's close proximity to the wall helped create crisp shadows.

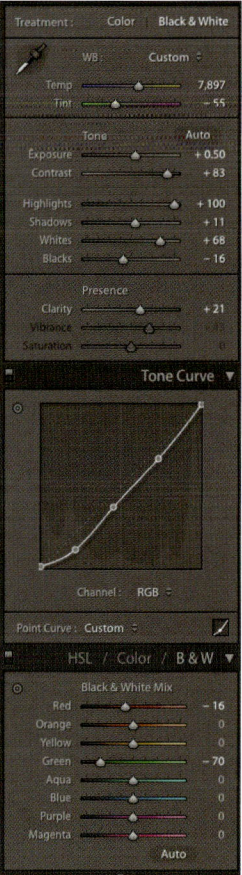

Figure 7.13 The Lightroom settings are similar to the way I processed the silverware shots, just less extreme.

When it came to color grading the image, I once again added a great deal of Contrast, in addition to raising the Highlights and Whites and lowering the Blacks (**Figure 7.13**). Because Stephanie is a human and not a spoon or a fork, I had to go easy on the Clarity setting, which gets far too harsh with overuse. I also brought up some shadow detail in the Tone Curve.

Although I was happy with my results (**Figure 7.14**), I wasn't done experimenting with the technique. This exercise really opened up my mind to thinking about light in a whole new way. It whet my appetite, and I was hungry to keep exploring.

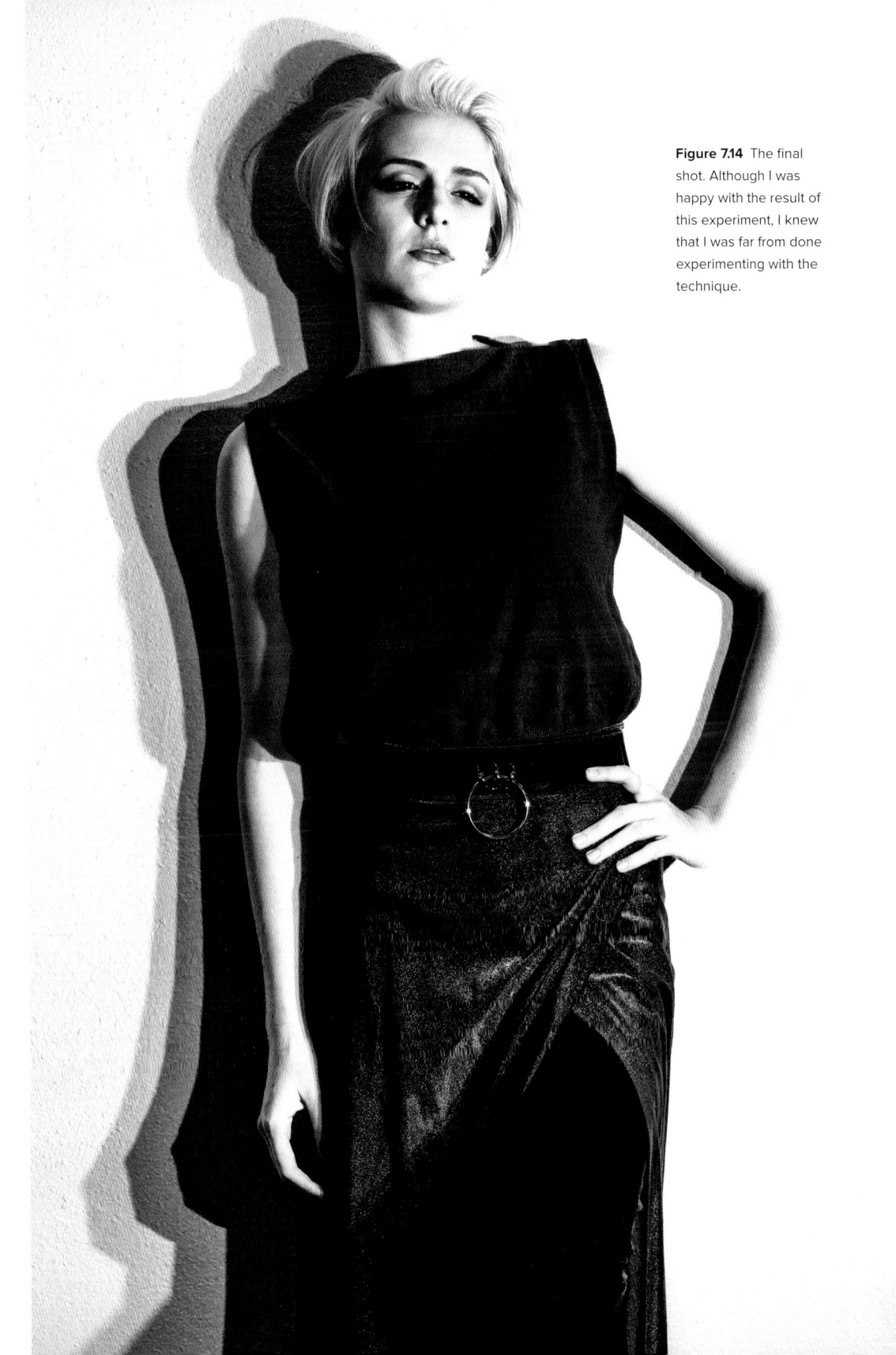

Figure 7.14 The final shot. Although I was happy with the result of this experiment, I knew that I was far from done experimenting with the technique.

When I graduated from college with a degree in photography, I was hungry for a job (read: *any* job) in my field. Because I lived in Columbus, Ohio, studio photography jobs were scarce. Hell, any photo jobs were few and far between. I was ready to take a job photographing babies, weddings, you name it—anything to get out of working retail. After receiving a ton of encouragement on how good my work was and how well I would succeed doing my own thing, I eventually decided to become an LLC (Limited Liability Corporation) and quit my part-time job at Starbucks, though I didn't really have any photo gigs lined up at all.

Needless to say, I didn't fare well. I spent most days alternating between checking the Creative Gigs section on Craigslist, laughing at the jobs posted in said section, and crying in the shower. Aside from picking up a couple of wedding gigs, I couldn't find anything. My failure to launch was a result of poor planning on my part. I decided to get my job back at Starbucks, which at least covered health insurance for me and my wife, and continue to hustle for photo gigs in my spare time.

After a couple of years of slinging lattes in the morning, shooting random, one-off gigs in the afternoons, and photographing weddings on the weekend, I started to gain some traction. I got to the point where I was too busy to work at Starbucks any longer. Throughout this time, I was also doing as many test shoots and self-assignments as I could—mainly musicians, models, and dancers—in order to build a portfolio that matched the kind of work that I'd like to be hired to create.

I did mainly weddings for the next three years, all the while keeping my ear to the ground for any studio hiring a commercial, portrait, or fashion photographer. Although I didn't mind shooting weddings, they weren't the reason I got into photography in the first place. My first passion was editorial portraiture and fashion.

Finally, in 2011, four years after I had launched my LLC and two since I had quit Starbucks, my train came in. JackThreads was a new, local company, featuring men's fashion, and the creative director wanted me to shoot for the company, full-time. Me! Shooting fashion! Full-time! It was a dream come true. (You know how the company's creative director found me? I had shot his wedding a few years prior. Never take any gig for granted, because you never know where it could lead.)

As we started discussing time commitments versus compensation, I realized that I would be taking a significant loss in income if I were to go full time and totally cut out the wedding and smattering of random photo gigs that I was now bringing in. Remember, just three years ago, I would've killed for an in-house gig, and now I was weighing the pros and cons. I decided to counter the offer. What if, I suggested, I committed to five half-days a week at an hourly rate, as a freelancer, keeping my mornings (and weekends) open for other freelance work? That way, JackThreads wouldn't need to pay for employee benefits and I would have the benefit of having regular income coupled with the freedom to bring in more freelance work on the side. After all, I was finally gaining some momentum in bringing in my own repeat clients, and I wouldn't want to lose any momentum.

The creative director went for it, and I was ecstatic. I shot for JackThreads for 14 months, until the company announced that it was moving to Brooklyn and invited me to go along too. Talk about a dream job; shooting fashion in New York City. But seven years had now passed since I graduated from OSU. I had two kids and a mortgage. NYC was not in the cards for me. Again, if 2007 Nick could've heard me turning down that offer, he would've beat my ass. But now I knew for certain that freelance life was the life for me. Although the risks are higher, like not having benefits or a regular income, the payoff is also higher. And I still go through slow seasons, where I need to borrow money or open a credit card for a period of time. There are ebbs and flows. But the flows can sometimes be raging rivers. Some gigs, even after usage is factored in, have paid me the equivalent of three to four months' wage had I been at a salary job. Those are the times that make the risks worthwhile.

In the time that's passed since JackThreads moved to NYC, I have worked as an in-house freelance photographer for three other companies, and I have no regrets, making an hourly rate at each place. At my newest part-time gig, which is at Jeni's Splendid Ice Creams, I decided to switch to a reduced day rate instead of hourly. I work very quickly, and found at my last gig that I was wrapping up my shot list several hours earlier than expected, but since I was hourly, I was actually getting paid less. I was essentially being penalized for being efficient. So rather than trying to dumb down my process and work slower so I could get paid the agreed-on amount, I opted to switch to a flat half-day or full-day rate that is significantly lower than my normal day rate, since this was a semi-permanent gig.

This arrangement is still mutually beneficial because I can book gigs the other three days of the week, and they get a senior level photographer at the rate of a junior level photographer, since they only need to pay me for two days. The reason why our arrangement works is because I am doing a week's worth of work in two days—they just have to organize their shot lists so that I can get all their weekly photo needs knocked out in two days, which not every company can do.

If you are just launching your photo career, don't put too much pressure on yourself. Don't rush the process. The photographers you look up to have been doing this a lot longer than you. You have time to catch up. Focus on test shooting, building your portfolio with diverse, quality images that reflect your passion and skills. Clients don't know that you're capable of creating a certain type of image unless they see it in your portfolio. Although shooting food was no harder for me than shooting a person, I didn't start getting food photography gigs until clients saw food photography on my website. So if your portfolio is lacking in an area where you want to be booking jobs, set up those types of shoots in your free time to fill those gaps. Meanwhile, take any photo gig you can land that pays the bills. Just don't blog it if it's not the kind of work you want to keep getting.

Finally, if you are lucky enough to have a full-time photo gig or get an offer to go in-house, consider all your options and see what the best fit is for your situation. Maybe you would prefer the less stressful pace of a studio staff position. I can only speak for myself, and now that I've had a taste of the freedom that comes with doing my own thing, I wouldn't have it any other way.

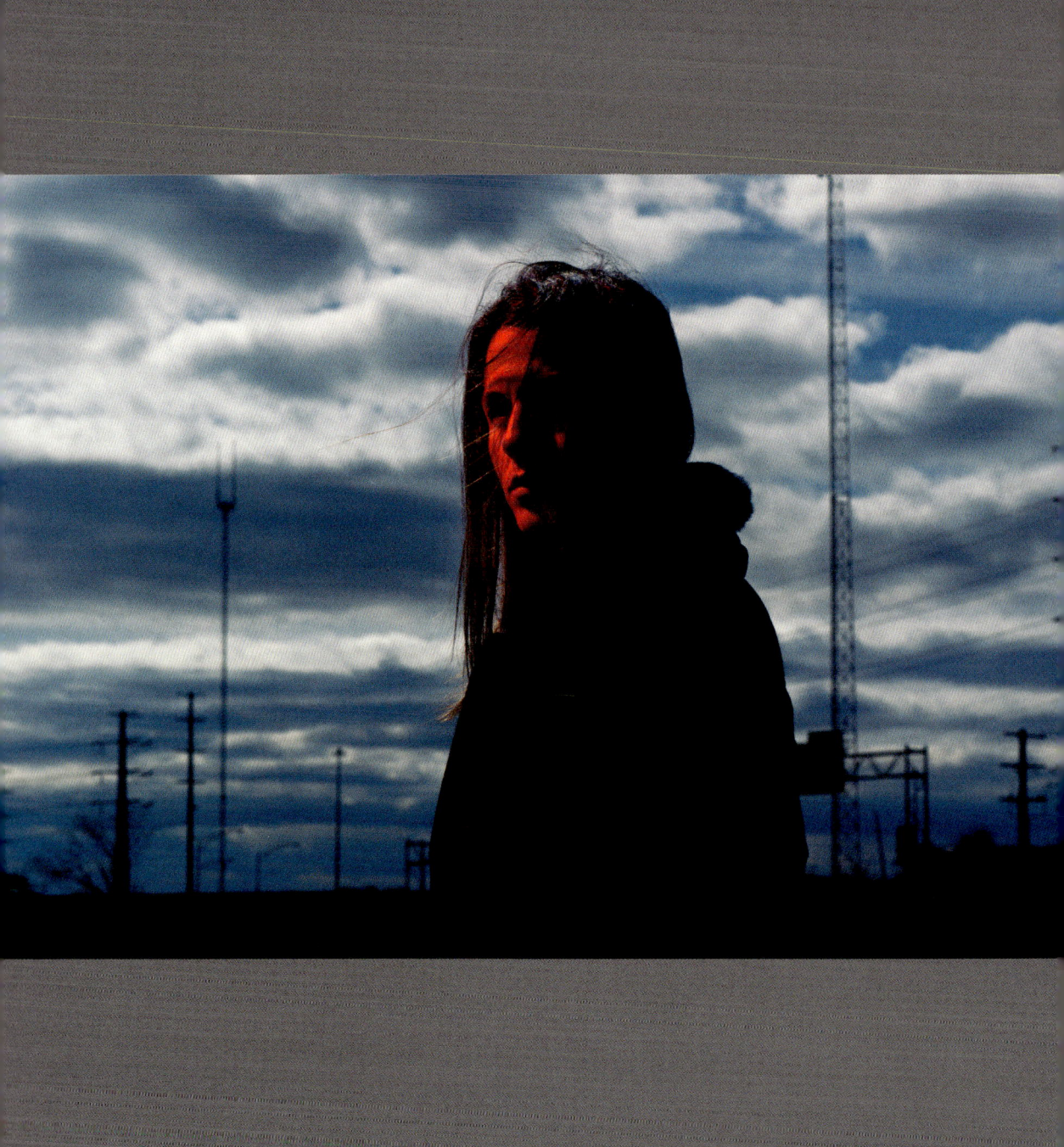

CHAPTER 8

COLORED GELS

Colored gels are the smallest, simplest, cheapest, and yet most powerful light modifiers. With a single one of these small pieces of acetate, you can transform the entire mood of a portrait. Gels are most commonly used for color correction, such as when you need to reduce the orange glow in a tungsten-lit room. In the previous *Studio Anywhere* book, I also discussed how to use the situationally opposite corrective gel to push ambient colors to your liking. This chapter on colored gels will go more into color theory and how to stack colored light to get stylized results. Although I most often use gels in a studio-like setting, I also love using them to introduce a pop of color in outdoor scenarios, as seen on the opposite page.

COLOR THEORY

One of my favorite courses in college was actually not even a photography class; it was a color theory class. I was not only fascinated to learn about complementary color combinations and how different color wheels worked (yes, there are more than one kind), but I was also really into learning about the science behind color. I studied this stuff for ten weeks and by no means mastered it, so forgive my brief, troglodytic overview of it.

Subtractive color (**Figure 8.1**) covers the mixing of colored pigments in paint. When these colors are mixed together, black is the end result. This always confused me when I was a kid; I was taught that white was the combination of every color. All I knew was that when I mixed all of my paints together I got a brownish-black. The truth of it is that in order to get white by combining colors, you need to be combining colored *light* rather than pigment (**Figure 8.2**). This is known as *additive* color, which is what we photographers use. It starts with red, green, and blue light. Green and red light overlap to create *yellow* (grab that gel and set it aside). Red and blue light mixed make *magenta* (grab that one too). Finally, blue and green make *cyan* when combined (that's the final gel you'll need). Now if you take three flashes and gel them—one cyan, one magenta, and one yellow—and aim them at your subject, "white" or colorless light is created at their intersection.

The other really important (and super cool) takeaway from my color theory course was the idea of neighboring colors and complementary colors. To quote painter Marc Chagall, "All colors are the friends of their neighbors and lovers

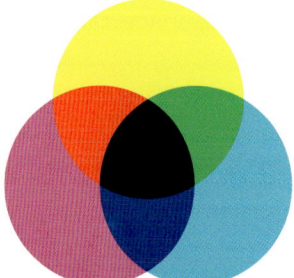

Figure 8.1 A subtractive color wheel, which encompasses mixing paint pigments. When the colors are combined, black is created.

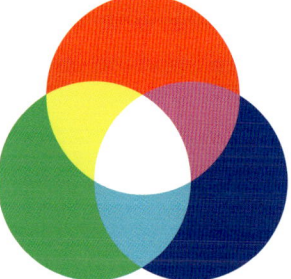

Figure 8.2 An additive color wheel, which encompasses mixing light (what we'll be doing). When the colors are combined, white light results.

of their opposites." A neighboring color is a color that sits on either side of a color on a traditional color wheel. For example, the neighbors of magenta are violet and red. On the other hand, complementary colors sit opposite each other on the color wheel. Try it out. Look up a photo of a traditional color wheel and locate the color red. What color sits across from it? Green. That means that green is red's opposite. To boot, when two complementary colors are combined, they cancel each other out, making a neutral tone. For example, red plus green equals a brownish grey color. Orange plus blue? Samo. Purple plus yellow? Yep. Opposites really do attract. It's poetic, really.

A while ago I did a shoot for a collaboration between The Atlantic and IBM. They wanted to produce a series of portraits that were all lit with two different colors. The images needed to work on their own and as a series. This proved to be a lot more challenging than I had initially anticipated. It's easy enough to select a color on the color wheel and find its opposite. It's a whole other task to find a color that works on a certain person's skin tone. I was photographing a couple Caucasians, an Asian, and an African-American, and each skin tone reacted to the colors differently. Purple proved to be too strong of a color on a white person, but it looked great on the black subject. I eventually stopped trying to strictly follow color theory and just started pairing different cool colors with warm ones until something worked (**Figure 8.3**).

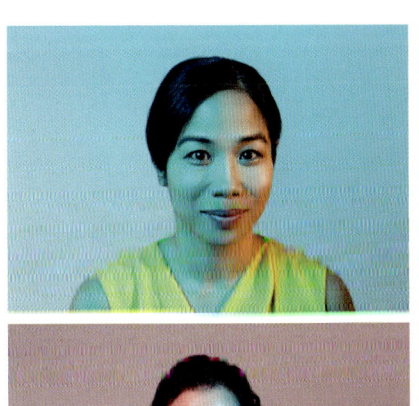
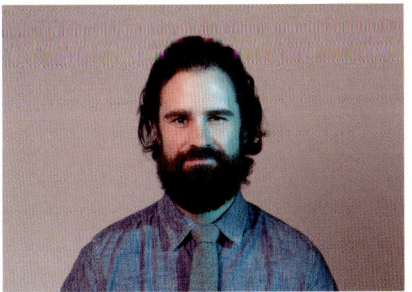
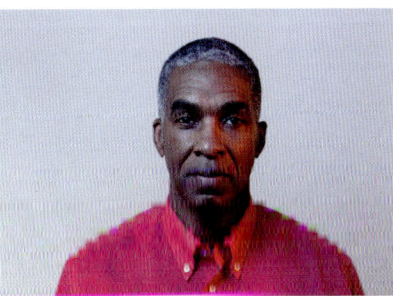
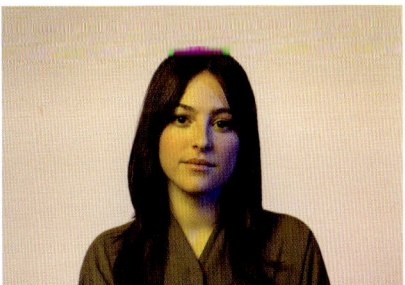

Figure 8.3 This series of portraits, shot for IBM, needed to incorporate a range of complementary colors that worked together as a series as well as stand-alone images.

ANAGLYPH 3D

Last fall I was in NYC to visit my buds at JackThreads as well as do a bit of shooting, as I do once a year or so. While I was in town, I made sure to line up a few test shoots with models because NYC models.... One such is Halle Sobiech, an Ohio girl who made good. After graduating high school, she moved to New York and has since blown up. Now that she's signed with IMG, she goes back and forth between New York and Milan, killing every shoot in her path. Before her big break I'd worked with her a few times, and lucky for me on this trip, she had a day off and was still willing to work with a bottom feeder like me. The only problem was that I was coming up short when it came to finding a spot to shoot.

At the time, Halle was staying at an agency dorm and wasn't allowed to have visitors in the building, so we couldn't shoot there. I was staying in a cramped hostel in Williamsburg, which, for lack of other options, would have to work as a shoot location. I had white walls, which was a bonus, but not much space (about ten feet from one wall to another). I didn't want Halle to be positioned against a wall, because I wanted a shadowless image, so the best I could do was to sit her in a chair about two feet in front of the wall (**Figure 8.4**).

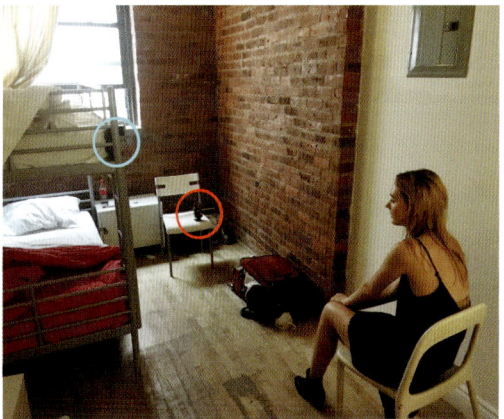

Figure 8.4 The setup. My cramped hostel room ended up being the only spot where we could do our test shoot. The main light was gelled cyan and and the accent light was gelled red.

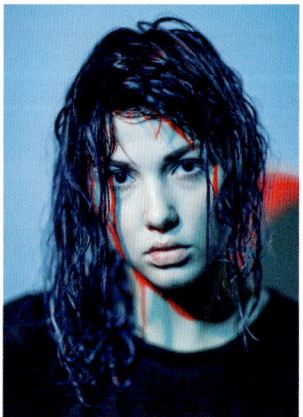

Figure 8.5 My favorite colors to experiment with are cyan and red, which are the colors that make up anaglyph 3D. In this shot I overlapped the colors, creating colored shadows.

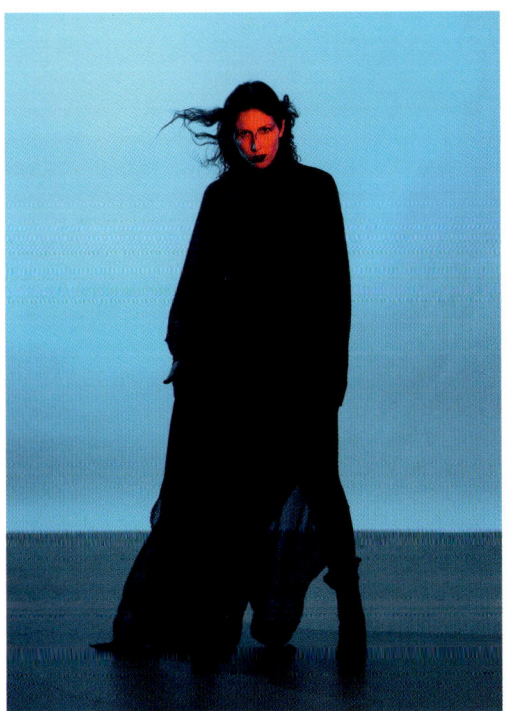

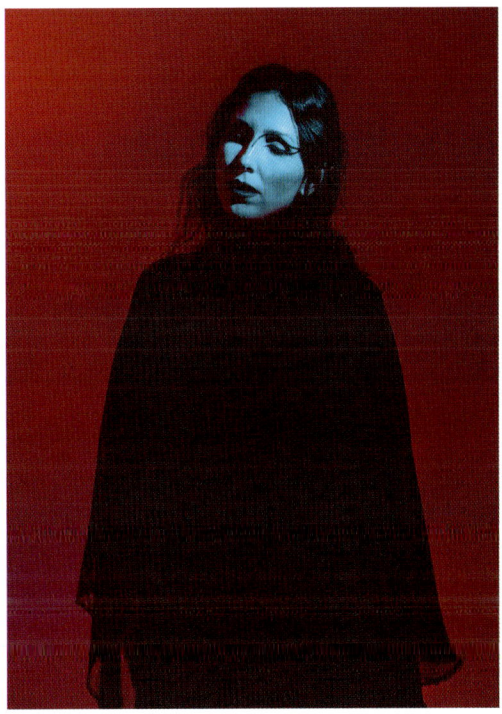

Figure 8.6 In this shot, the main light was gelled red, barn doors attached, with a cyan background light.

Figure 8.7 In this shot, the main light was gelled cyan, barn doors attached, with a red background light.

I had a few ideas that I wanted to play with regarding lighting as I went into the shoot, beginning with the colors cyan and red. Cyan and red is the color combination that makes up the anaglyph 3D effect—you know, the old movie glasses! I love experimenting with this color combination more than any other. Depending on how you place the gels in relation to each other and based on how each light is powered, you can achieve a number of very different results. For example, by placing a cyan light next to a red light with the cyan powered at a slightly higher output than the red light, I achieved the image in **Figure 8.6**. The black shadows that are created by the cyan light are filled in by the red-gelled sidelight, creating blue light with red shadows. I also love seeing how much an image changes just by swapping the red and cyan gels between the main light and the accent light; compare **Figures 8.6** and **8.7** to see what I mean.

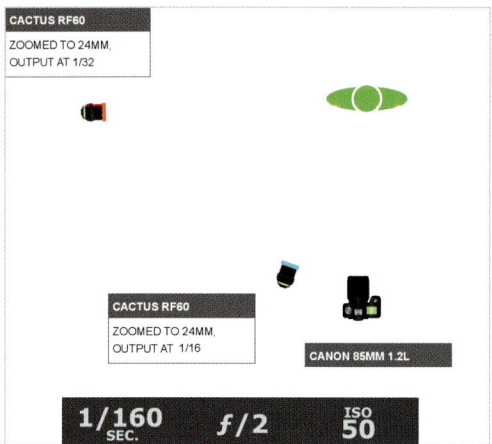

Figure 8.8 The lighting diagram. The cyan light was powered a bit higher than the red so that it overpowered the red, creating an overall blue image.

As you can see, my red light is placed off to the side and my cyan light is just left of center (**Figure 8.8**). The other wall was just out of the frame to the left, and I had my back pressed against it; this is one of those rare times when I could've used a lens other than my 35 or 85mm, such as a 50mm. My cyan light was powered a bit higher than the red light in order to outweigh or overpower the red, avoiding a red cast to her face. If you are trying out this technique and too much red is showing through on your subject's face, increase the difference between the outputs of the two flashes (lower the red output or increase the cyan). And this may go without saying, but if you're getting colored shadows in your background and don't want shadow, move your lights and subject further from the background. You can see just the edge of a shadow on the right side of the raw file (**Figure 8.9**). Had I had a bit more space, I would've moved Halle off the wall a bit more, but as it stood, I easily cropped out that area of the image without compromising the composition.

There is one thing I want to mention when it comes to shooting an image that has no neutral-colored area: Set your white balance to anything other than Auto. I typically use the Sun/Daylight setting. The last thing you want is the white balance shifting from shot to shot. This will make your color grading a special kind of hell. The goal is to have the most consistency possible as you move from shot to shot so that you can color grade one image and sync the rest, save for a few minor crops or tweaks, and be done with your editing in an hour or less.

Speaking of color grading, it can get a bit tricky when it comes time to correct a color-gelled image (**Figure 8.10**). For example, the red in my image isn't as

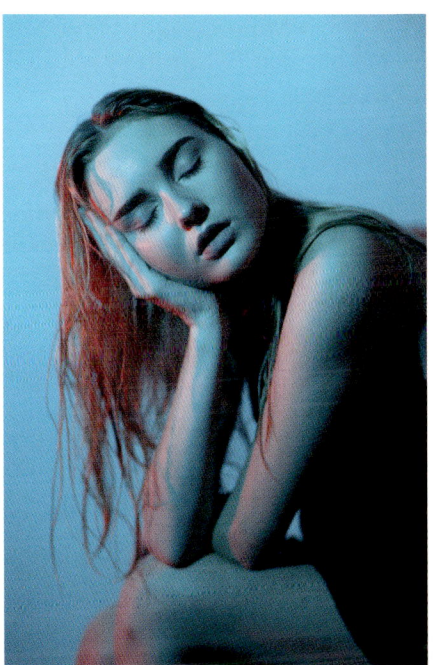

Figure 8.9 The raw file. The image has the mood I was going for and is nearly shadowless, save for the spot on the right side of the frame.

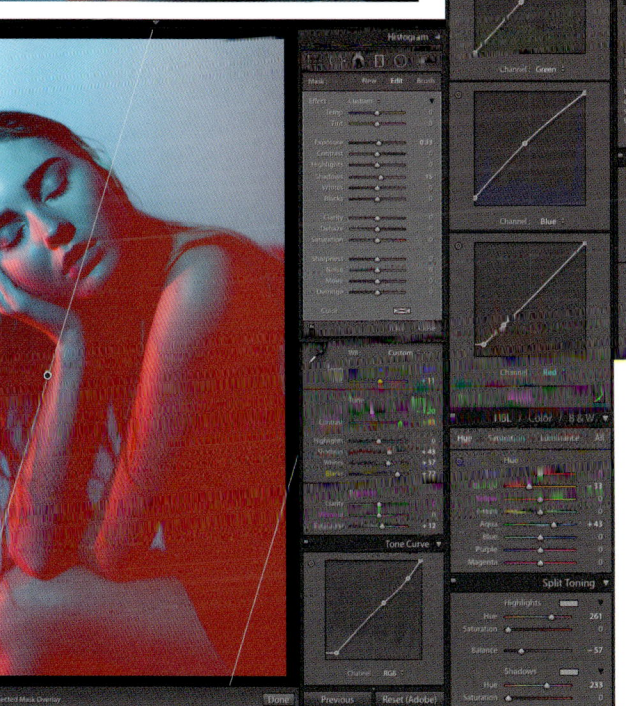

Figure 8.10 The Lightroom settings. When it comes to color grading color-gelled images, it can get a bit tricky. I start by setting the White Balance and then proceed to adjust the Hue sliders as needed.

saturated as I would like, but fixing it isn't as simple as increasing the Saturation slider. As a starting point, I set the Temp and Tint sliders in the White Balance panel to get the overall colors as close as I can to desirable. Then I go into the HSL panel and tweak the Hue sliders in the necessary color channels; in this case it's the Orange and Aqua channels. To bring it home, I add a subtle magenta tone by raising the shadow points in the Red and Blue Tone Curves and raising the midtones in the Blue and Green Curves. Given the circumstances, I am more than happy with the resulting image (**Figure 8.11**).

Figure 8.11 The final shot. Given the tiny space I had to work with, I am more than happy with the resulting image.

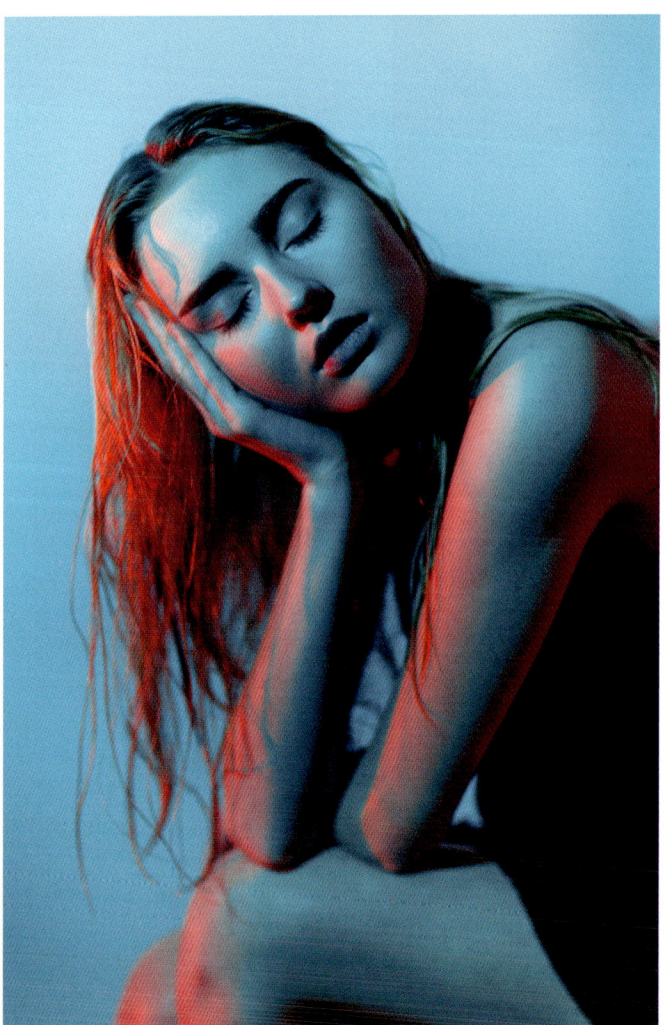

ADDITIVE COLOR

This next technique was the main inspiration behind me writing a sequel to *Studio Anywhere*. Not too long after I wrapped writing that book, I was sitting in my basement studio, bored, trying to figure out what to do next. I had just recently been experimenting with using three staggered flashes to make a triple shadow, inspiration coming from a recent issue of *Interview* magazine (remember the last chapter?). I can't say what exactly motivated me to go upstairs and grab the vase of flowers and set them up below three gelled and staggered lights (**Figure 8.12**). I just had an idea pop into my head: What would happen if I staggered the three colors that overlap to create white light? Would it actually work for me? Could cyan, magenta, and yellow light overlap to make pure, colorless light? Not only did it work (**Figure 8.13**), the unintentional results—multi-colored shadows—were the best part. I noticed that there were colored shadows in certain areas, where one of the colored flashes couldn't light. This meant that some spots were only lit with yellow and magenta light or cyan and yellow or magenta and cyan. When these obstructions and overlaps occurred, magic resulted. Now, to find a model immediately so I could explore the technique on a moving subject.

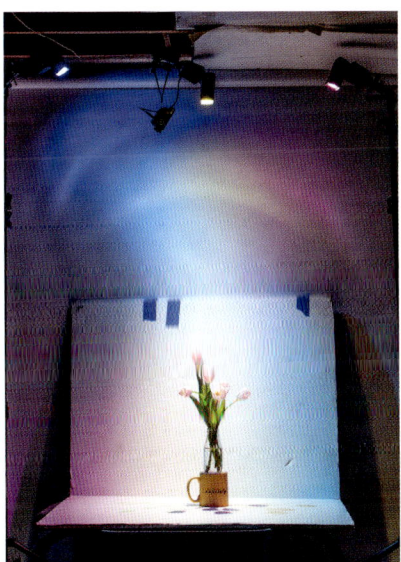

Figure 8.12 After experimenting with triple shadows in the previous chapter, I had the idea to gel the three lights cyan, magenta, and yellow so that the overlapping light was colorless.

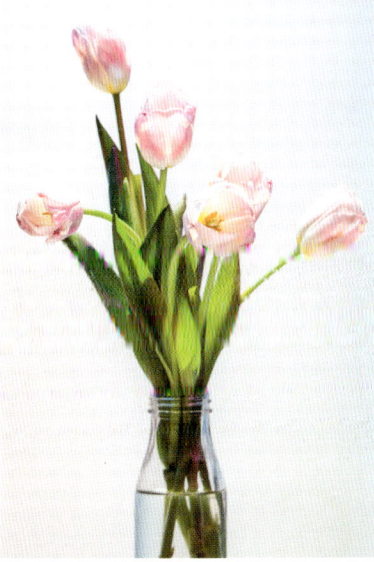

Figure 8.13 Not only did the science behind the technique work (imagine that), the experiment also got my mind working in new ways. Now I had to try it out on a model.

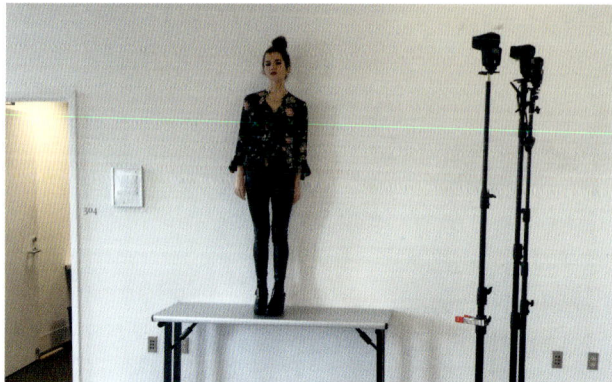

Once again, an art student, this time Alaina Aylward, came to my rescue. She was able to give me a small window of time to try out this technique, amidst her busy schedule. I met her at her school and quickly set up my three lights (**Figure 8.14**). Since this was the first time I tried the technique, I wasn't sure how much space should be between the lights or if the orders of the colors made a difference. Once I started placing them side by side, I realized how cumbersome it was to have three separate stands, with the legs all tangled together. (Mental note: Buy or make a bracket to hold three lights, spaced 18 inches apart.)

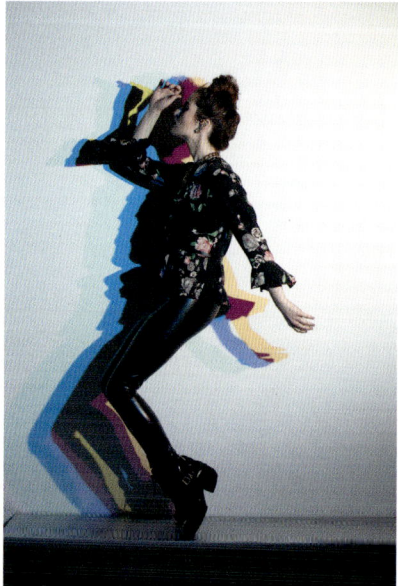

Figure 8.15 The raw file. After giving Alaina a bit of movement direction, she started coming up with cool moves on her own, this one being my favorite.

After snapping a few frames, after I was sure that the technique was still working for me, I asked her to start moving. The part that I was the most excited about was seeing what kind of random colors and shadows started to appear as she moved. I enjoyed introducing a bit of chaos into a world of relative predictability. "Turn to the right. Nice. Now to the left. Try arching your back. Maybe a hand on the hip?" After a bit of direction, she really started to move on her own. She made this Michael Jackson, tiptoe move, that I really liked, so I asked her to do that five to ten times. **Figure 8.15** ended up being the money shot.

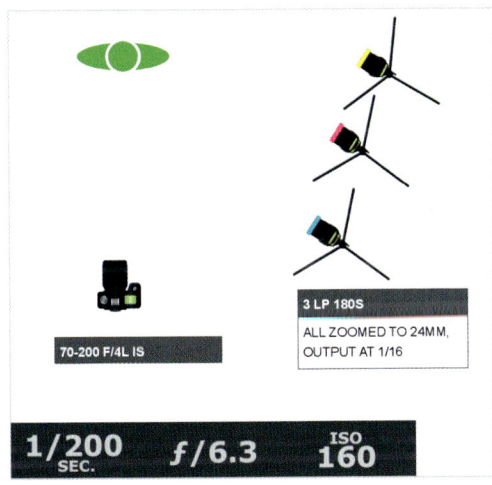

Figure 8.16 The lighting diagram. The three lights were all spaced about a foot apart with the same zoom and output.

The one foot of space that I allowed between each light was sufficient to allow for each colored shadow to appear. The closer the colored lights are to each other, the less tri-shadow you have (then you have only black shadow, which is no fun). However, you could space them further apart, if you like, allowing more space between the colors. The main thing to keep in mind is that you need an area where all three colors overlap that is large enough to cover the subject. Otherwise, the subject won't be lit with colorless light and will appear more yellow or magenta or cyan. Also note that the lights are all at the same zoom and output (**Figure 8.16**). You want a wide light spread to avoid a vignette. Finally, don't forget that the closer your subject is to the background, the sharper the shadow will be, with flashguns being sharper than studio strobes.

In Lightroom, you will once again need to tweak the quality of the colors to get them optimal (**Figure 8.17**). This time, I mainly needed to adjust the Luminance of certain colors, specifically the Yellow, Aqua, and Blue. Other than Luminance, my usual Tone Curve tweaks and a significant increase of contrast, my image was pretty similar to what it looked like in camera (**Figure 8.18**).

Figure 8.17 The Lightroom settings. Other than the normal adjustments, I also needed to adjust the Luminance in the Yellow, Aqua, and Blue channels to get the colors I wanted.

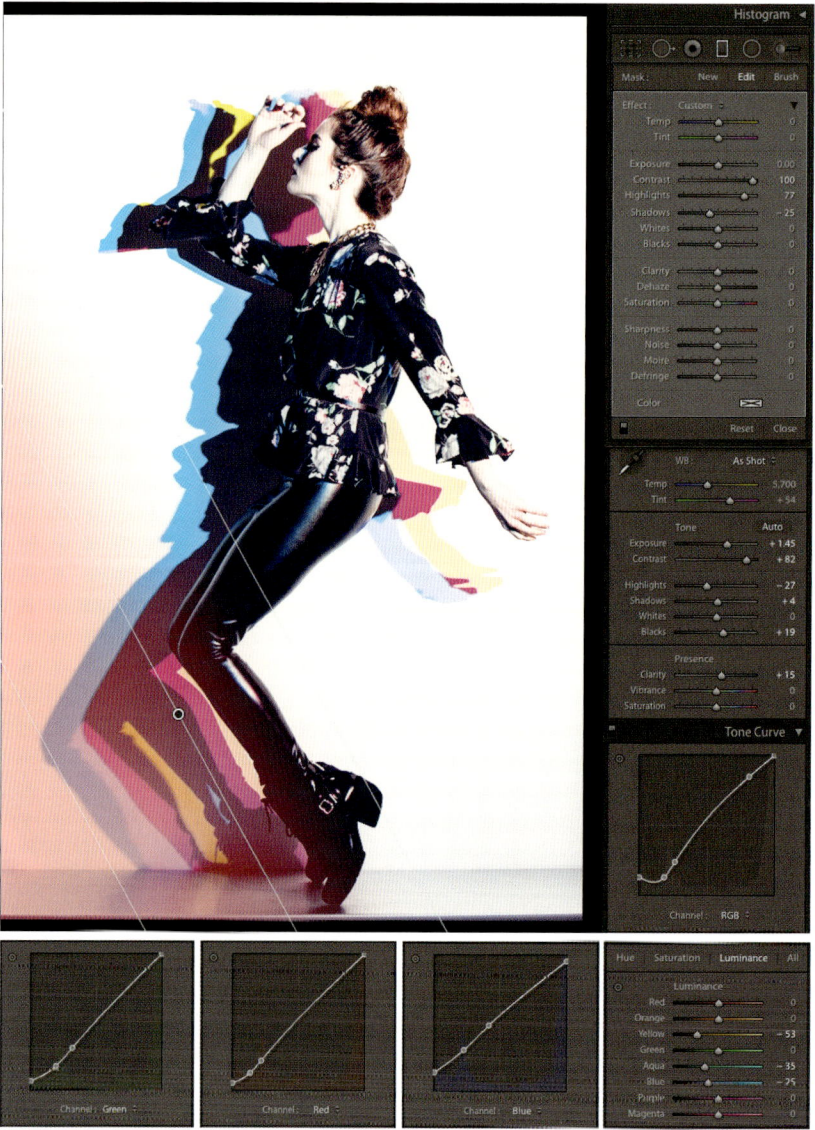

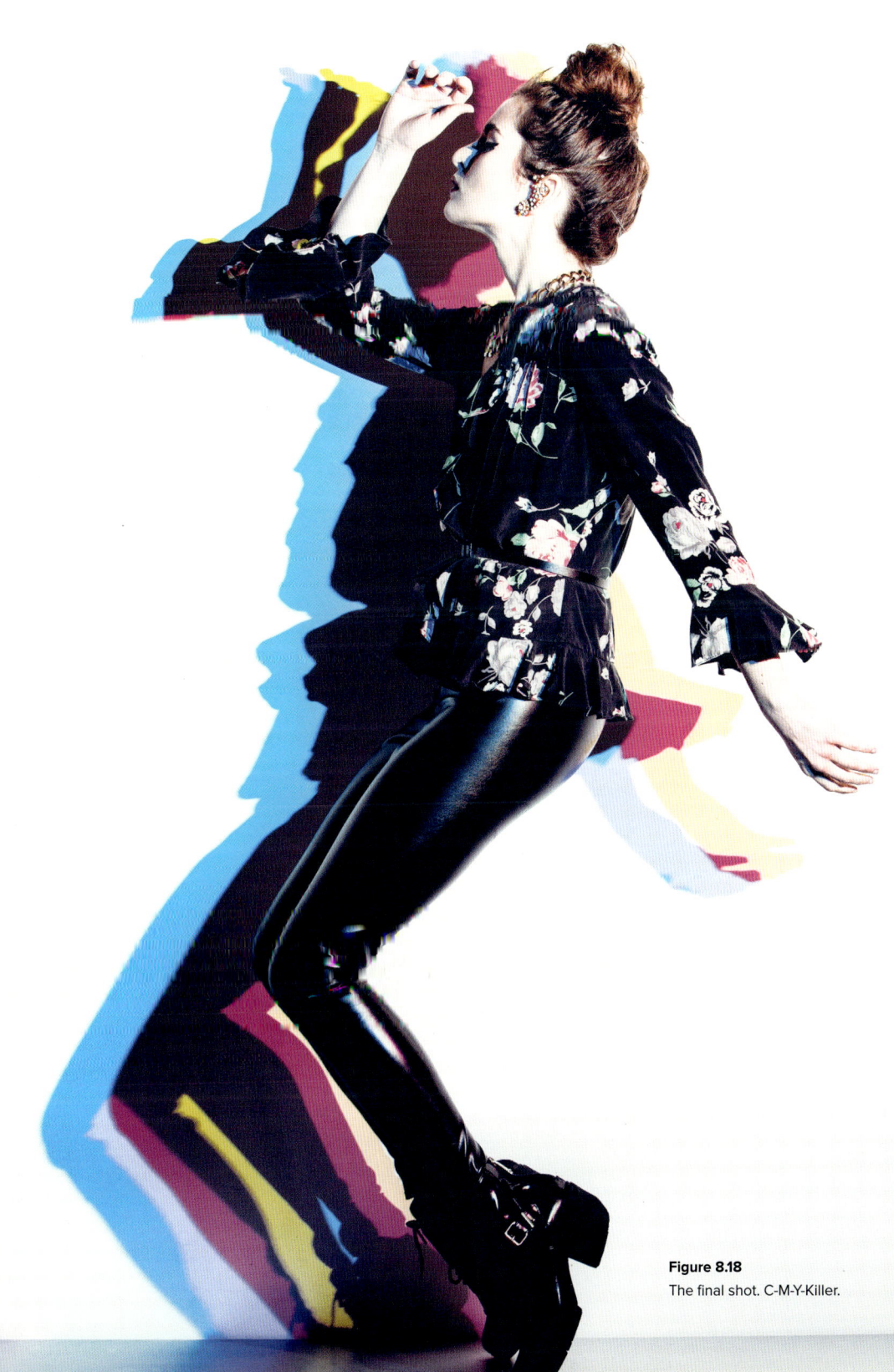

Figure 8.18
The final shot. C-M-Y-Killer.

Over the past year, I've since perfected the technique a bit. I now use a 16-inch cold shoe extension rail to hold my three flashes on one stand (**Figure 8.19**). Although I'd prefer to have at least a foot of space between each flash (meaning I'd need a 25-inch rail), the technique still works; the colored shadows are just closer together (**Figure 8.20**). I've also played around with the order of the colors to see if there is one configuration that I prefer over another (**Figure 8.21**).

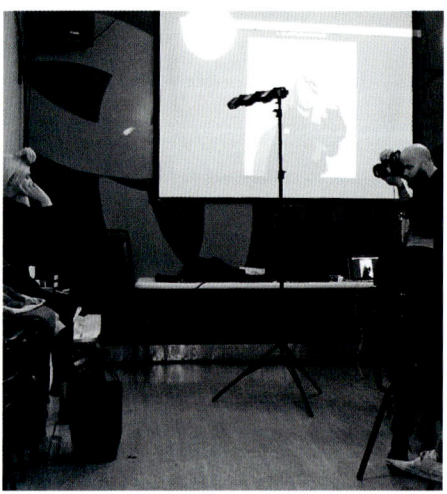

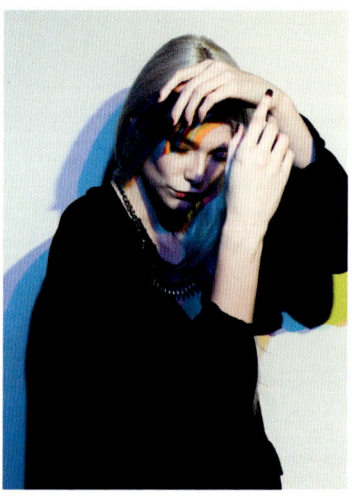

Figure 8.19 I've since switched to using a 16-inch cold shoe extension rail to hold three flashes on one stand. *Photo by Kelly Prescott.*

Figure 8.20 The colored shadows are a bit closer together when I use the 16-inch rail.

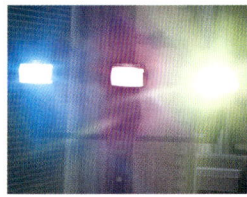
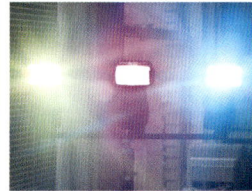
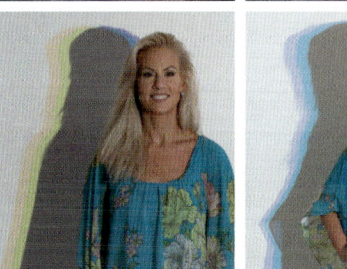

Figure 8.21 The order of the colors actually does matter. See how dramatically the shadows shift when the Cyan and Yellow flashes are swapped.

MAKING A SCENE

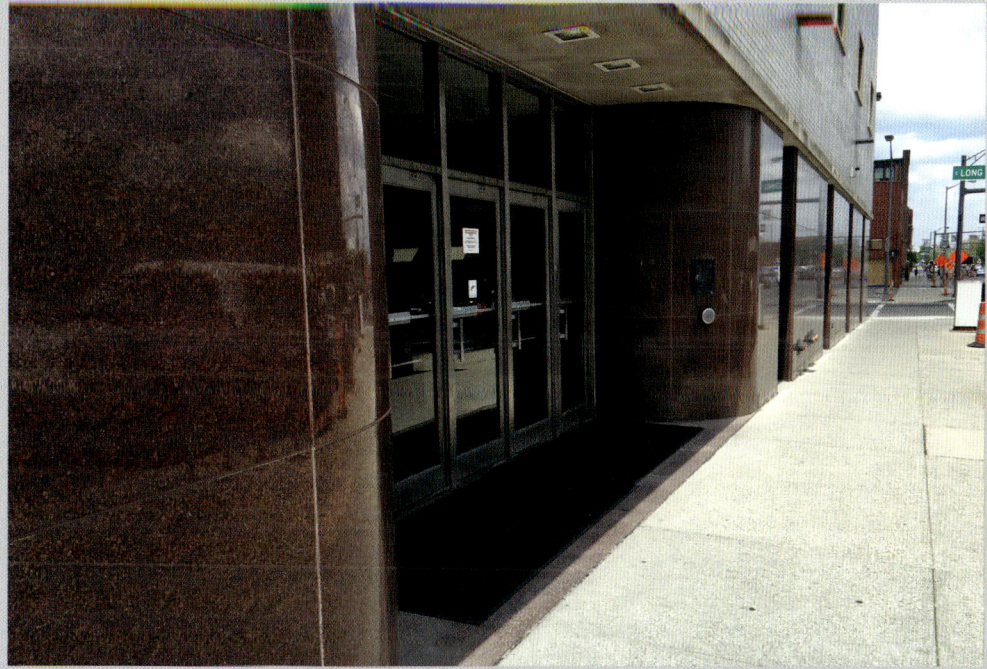

Figure S.4 This is what I had to work with at the shoot location. Where might I place my subject to get a dark, moody portrait using only natural light? Flip to the back of the book to see what I did.

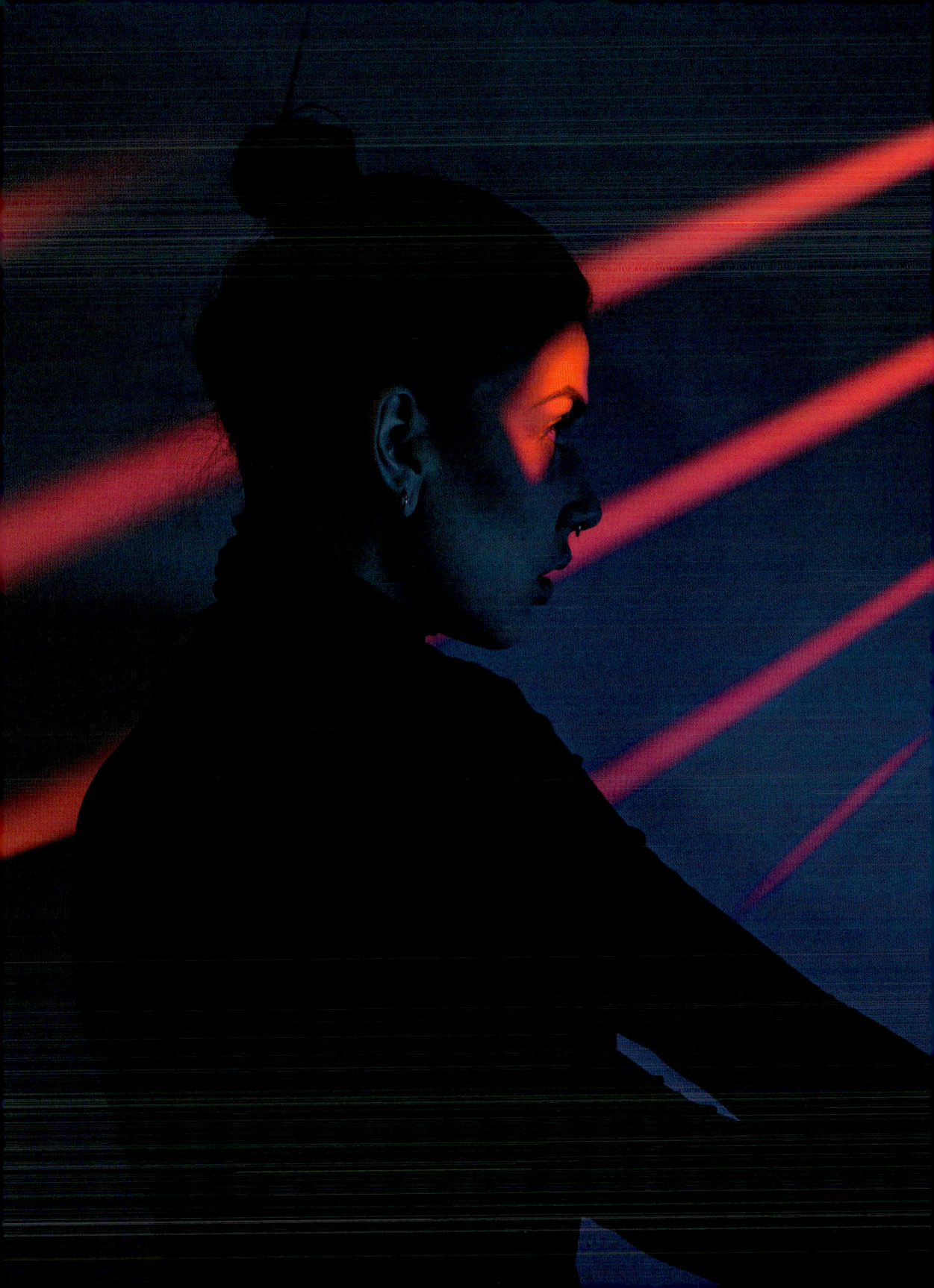

CHAPTER 9

GOBOS

So far we've discussed how to shape and control light by using snoots, grids, and barn doors. We've also talked about how the distance of the light to the subject and of the subject to the background affects the clarity of a shadow. What's next? A different kind of modifier. A shaper of light that comes in so many shapes and sizes that, quite honestly, anything can be one. This magical light modifier is a gobo. The term is derived from the phrase "go between," referring to anything that goes between a light source and the subject. After you train this final, mysterious, shade-throwing beast, your training will be complete.

MAKING A GOBO

Typically, the term "gobo" is reserved for the lens filters and patterns that are affixed to theater lights. The terms "flag" or "cucoloris/cookie" are actually more accurate for what we're going to be using in this chapter, referring to an object placed between the light and the subject, but not attached to it. For the sake of simplicity, however, I'll use the term "gobo" to encompass all such modifiers. So, what can you use to make a gobo? Here are some ideas.

CINEFOIL

As I said, gobos can be quite literally anything that stands between your light and your subject. To block or shape light or create stylized shadows, you use an opaque gobo. Although you can use pretty much any non-transparent material, such as cardboard, foam core, or poster board, cinefoil is the easiest to mold. If you aren't familiar with it, cinefoil is essentially a slightly thicker, black aluminum foil. It's lightweight and easy to cut and shape, which is both a blessing and a curse. You can quickly mold it into any shape you need, and because it's super lightweight to work with, you can easily hang it with nothing more than gaff tape. The down side of working with a super thin, lightweight material like cinefoil is that your gobos will be fairly temporary. Any shapes that you cut into it can easily spread or tear, so you pretty much need to make a new one each time you use one.

As you can see in **Figure 9.1**, my gobo is hanging by strips of gaff tape from the low ceiling while Sydney is reclining on my weight bench (which never gets used) in a beautiful gown and black socks. You will learn just how invaluable mobility is when you start working with gobos and realize how precise the placement needs to be. I'm often moving the gobo two inches forward, back, to the right, or to the left in order to get it in proper position, so a lightweight modifier that's held in place with tape makes the adjusting process an easy one.

When working with gobos, you will need to call on your knowledge of light spread and shadow quality. Remember that the closer an object or person is to a background, the more crisp the shadow that's created. This info is doubly important when using a gobo because not only are you factoring in the shadows being cast on the background but now you're also factoring in shadows being cast on the subject. As you can see in the lighting diagram (**Figure 9.2**) the light is about three feet from the gobo, which is about three feet from the subject, who is right in front of the background. Still with me? This distance,

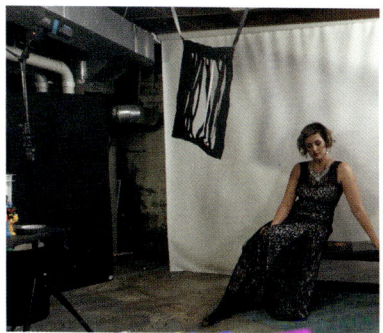

Figure 9.1 The setup. This gobo was made out of cinefoil, a thin, lightweight, black foil that you can easily shape and use in a number of ways.

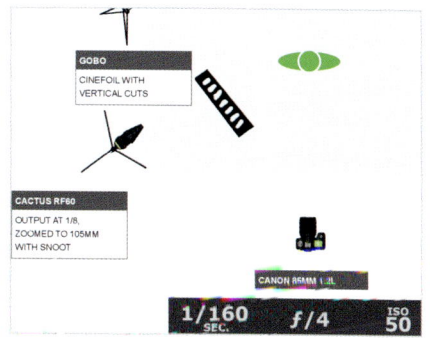

Figure 9.2 The lighting diagram. The light is roughly three feet from the gobo, which is roughly three feet from the subject, who is right against the backdrop. The close proximity creates more defined shadows.

which is rather close, allows for more defined shadows (less feathering). Also note that my light is not only zoomed in to 105mm, to create a narrow light stream, but I even added a snoot to further contain the light. If I had failed to properly constrain my light, it would spill to the left or right of the gobo, resulting in harsh light directly hitting the model and the background.

To further complicate things, you can dramatically change the quality of a gobo just by positioning it at an angle to your light, rather than placing it straight on. For example, look at the gobo shape in Figure 9.1. There are a number of similarly sized vertical strips removed from the cinefoil. If I shift the angle of the gobo so one side is closer to the light and one farther away, the gaps closest to the light will let more light through than the strips that are now positioned farther away and at an angle. To boot, now the thinner gaps that are farther from the light will be more defined, while the closer gaps, which are now appearing larger, will be more feathered by the time they reach the subject. If your mind isn't twisted by now, I'm thoroughly impressed. Don't get frustrated if you don't understand gobos right away. The learning curve is much steeper. You really just need to experiment with them to fully grasp all the variances.

Moving on to the raw file, take a look at the shadows on the left side of the frame in **Figure 9.3**. Notice that they appear more defined than the shadows on the right. This is because the gobo was closer to the background on the left than on the right. Meanwhile, her shadow on the background, seen on the far right, is very crisp, because she's only a foot away from the sweep.

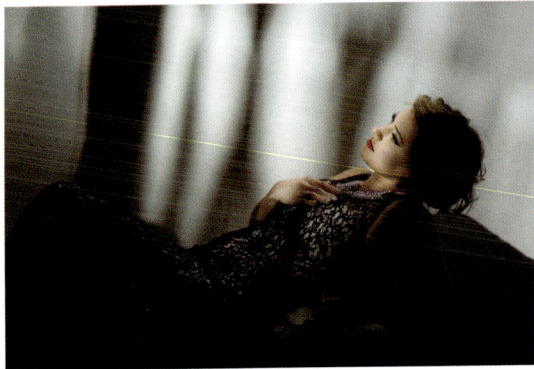

Figure 9.3 The raw file. Note that the shadows created on the left side (where the gobo was closer to the background) are more defined than the shadows on the right.

Because this was a film noir–inspired shoot, I converted the file to black and white in Lightroom and added some grain (**Figure 9.4**). Aside from my normal adjustments to the tone curves I also used the Dehaze feature a bit, to pull down some of the extra light glow, bringing more detail back to the highlights.

Figure 9.4 The Lightroom settings. Because this was a film noir–inspired shoot, I converted the file to black and white, adding grain and using the Dehaze feature to restore highlight detail.

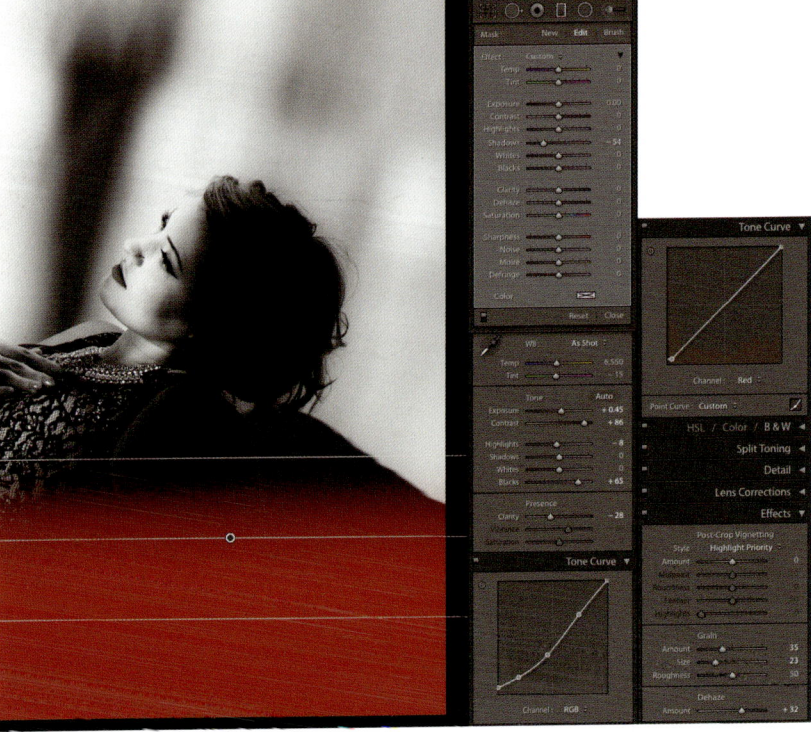

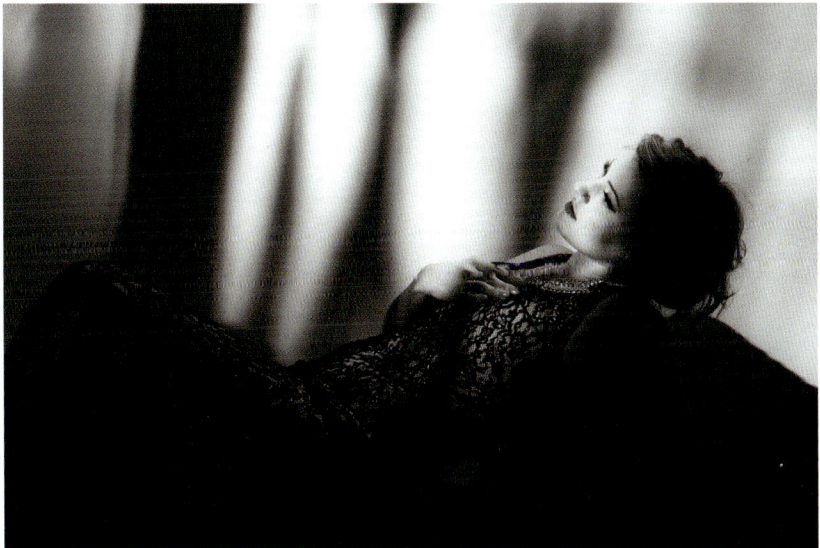

Figure 9.5 The final shot. Sydney is looking even more glamorous now that her black socks and the workout bench are gone.

Finally, I made a gradient adjustment to the bottom portion of the frame, pulling the bench she was reclining on into shadow. No more weight bench or black socks to be seen. Shadow can hide a multitude of sins (**Figure 9.5**).

PRISMS

Prisms are really fun to play with. They are also really unpredictable. Depending on the size, shape, and distance of the prism(s) to your light, the effects you create can differ dramatically. However, prisms are also more difficult to work with because they are often heavy and oddly shaped. This makes rigging them up in front of a flash a bit tricky. In **Figure 9.6** you can see I used a C-stand and a couple of spring clamps to dangle a custom prism rig in front of my light. For this shot, I zoomed my flash in to 105mm and placed it right against the prism, which worked in throwing some beautiful, dappled light on my subject, reminiscent of reflected window light (**Figure 9.7**).

I commissioned a photographer I know to glue a handful of long, triangular prisms together into a giant Voltron prism. This beautiful monstrosity throws more light than Zeus (**Figure 9.8**). As you can see, the light quality changes dramatically as you move the light away from the prism. I wouldn't recommend experimenting with prism gobos until you have a pretty firm grasp on shaping light. They can be endlessly maddening to work with, because of how quickly they change the light.

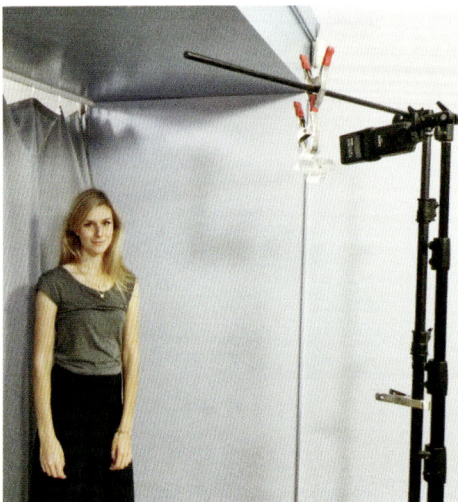 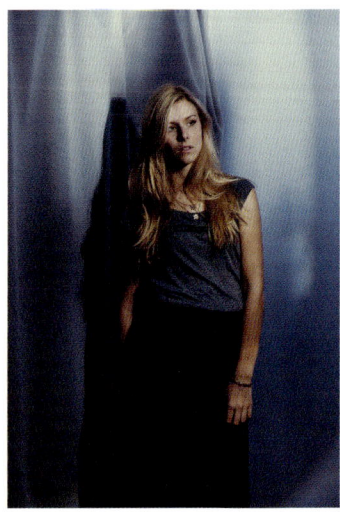

Figure 9.6 The setup. I used spring clamps to hang my prism gobo from a C-stand in front of the light, which was zoomed in to 105mm.

Figure 9.7 The final shot. The dappled light has a nice, natural quality to it.

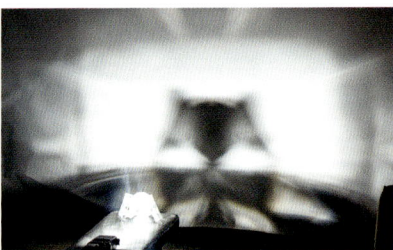 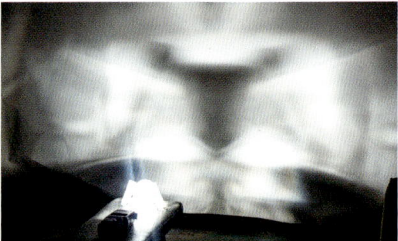

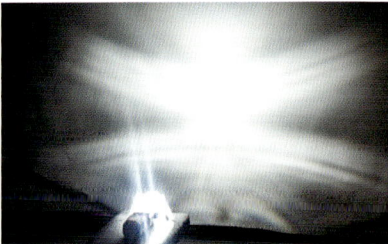

Figure 9.8 The prism gobo. I had this custom prism gobo built for me by a photographer. The distance of the light from the gobo dramatically changes quality of light.

You can also get some fun effects by using more than one gobo in a shot. In **Figure 9.9** you can see a shot that was lit with my prism gobo. I was also using a second light, which was placed behind a door window, firing through a set of blinds (**Figure 9.10**). When I fired both lights together, the effects overlapped (**Figure 9.11**), creating a cool shot (**Figure 9.12**).

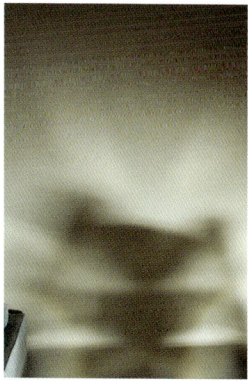

Figure 9.9 This shot was lit by one light firing through the prism gobo.

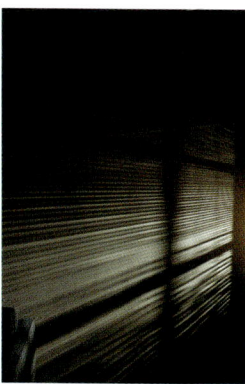

Figure 9.10 This shot was lit by one light firing through window blinds.

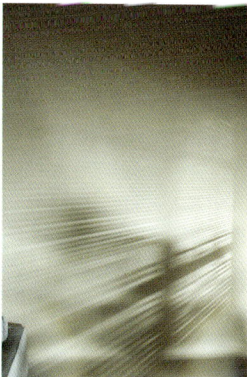

Figure 9.11 This is what it looked like when both lights were fired.

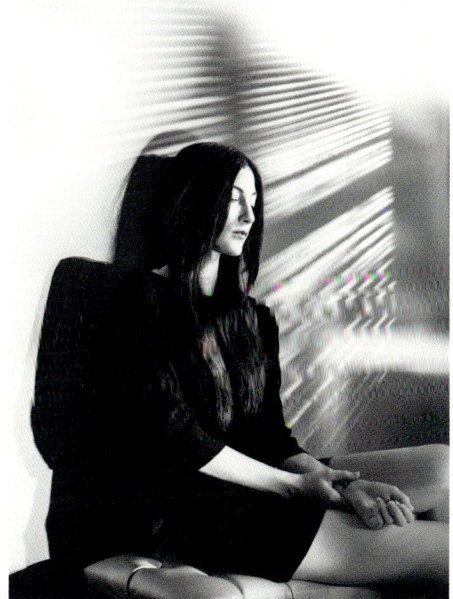

Figure 9.12 The overlapping gobo'd lights make a cool effect.

FABRIC

A white bed sheet can make a great gobo. Sheets are cheap, easy to modify and hang, and more durable than cinefoil. Because they are translucent, they allow some light to pass through, giving a softening effect to the light, similar to a softbox. If you cut some shapes into the fabric, however, you can let some hard light peek through, making for some cool effects. In **Figure 9.13** you can see I am using two lights, one gelled red, aiming through the hole in the fabric, and one gelled cyan, firing through the lower, uncut portion of the fabric. The result, seen in **Figure 9.14**, is soft light falling on the bust (*Michelangelo's David Bowie*, get it?), with a strip of hard, red light on his face. Are you beginning to see the possibilities?

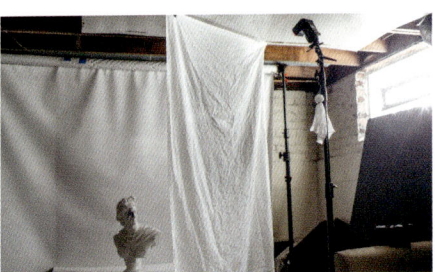

Figure 9.13 The setup. I modified a white bed sheet by cutting a horizontal slit in it, which allowed a bit of hard light to peek through and mix with the otherwise soft light.

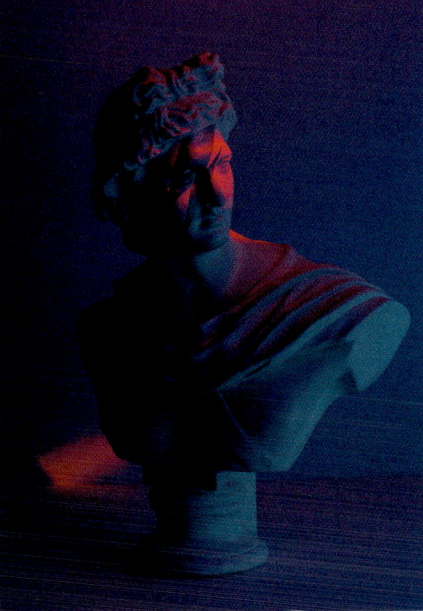

Figure 9.14 The final shot. *Michelangelo's David Bowie* is looking vaporwave as hell. Here I fired a red-gelled light through the gobo hole and I bounced a cyan-gelled light.

FINDING A GOBO

As I already mentioned, because anything that is placed between a light source and a subject is technically a gobo, you can be creative using found objects to shape the quality of light. A chain-link fence, for example, is an easy gobo to set up (**Figure 9.15**). Just make sure to place your light several feet away from the fence with a wide light spread, and place your subject as close as you can to the fence to get crisp shadows (**Figure 9.16**). In **Figure 9.17**, I used a potted plant for a gobo. Where do you think I placed the light? If you guessed several feet away from the plant, you'd be correct. This time, I zoomed in the flash to 105mm to make sure that the direct light didn't hit the subject. I wanted only the light coming through the leaves to reach him.

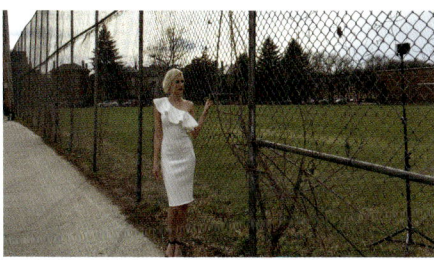

Figure 9.15 The chain-link fence gobo. When placing your light, set it several feet from the fence and place the subject close to it.

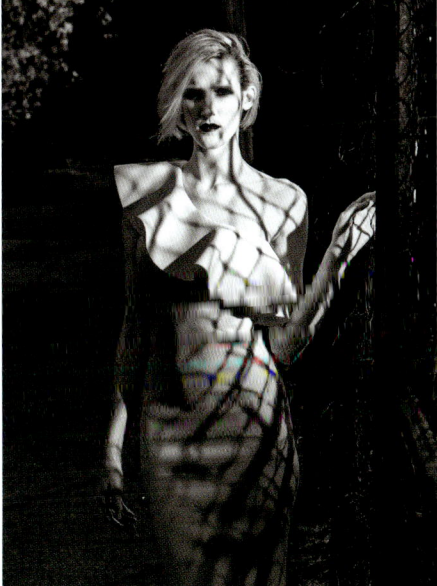

Figure 9.16 The shadows are crisp and create a dramatic effect on the model.

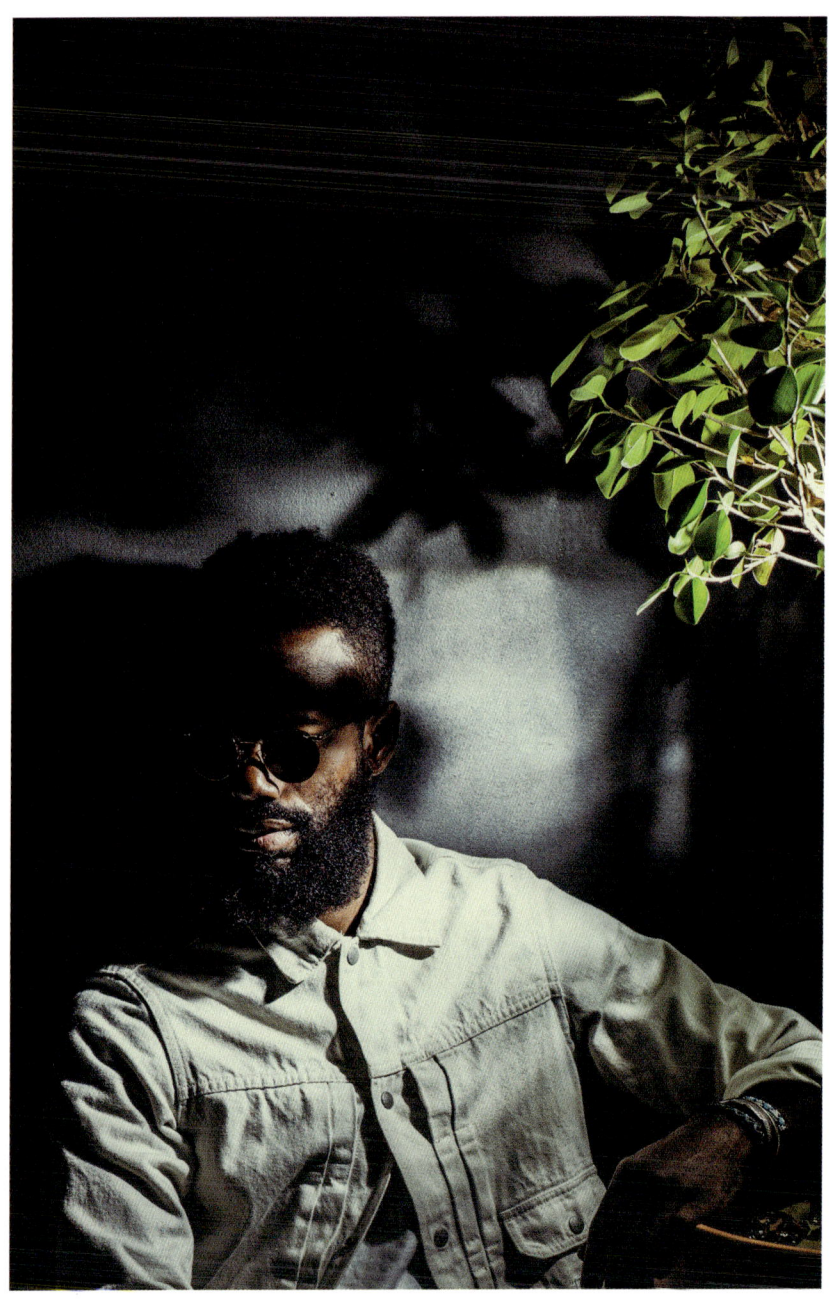

Figure 9.17 The potted plant gobo. Just like the previous setup, place the light several feet away, only this time zoom in the light to 105mm to make a narrow stream of light.

FANS

As I began experimenting with gobos, I started looking at the world around me a bit differently. Everything was a potential gobo. When I met with (amazing) model Clara Buchanan at her Williamsburg apartment, which was serendipitously a block away from my hostel, I immediately spotted the fan and knew I had to try it out as a gobo (**Figure 9.18**). When I began dragging it across her floor, she apologized for the large machine, explaining that she didn't have air conditioning. I assured her that I wasn't trying to get it out of the way but rather wanted to use it to shape my light. There were two things that I learned from working with the fan. The first was that the light hitting the model fluctuated about five stops, depending on how much of a fan blade happened to be blocking the light (**Figure 9.19**). This meant that I needed to shoot relatively rapid fire because every third or fourth shot was drastically underexposed. The super cool, unplanned thing that came from working with a high-powered-fan-as-light-modifier was that it also acted as a hair fan. This meant epic hair and fabric movement in every shot (**Figure 9.20**).

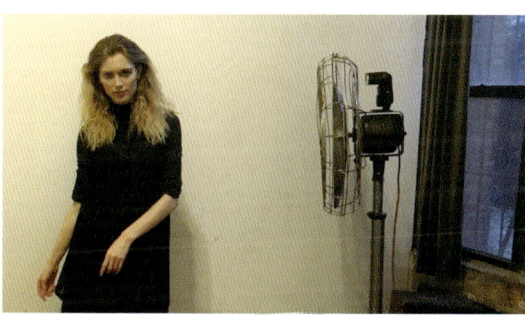

Figure 9.18 The setup. Here I used a pedestal fan for a gobo, placing my flash on the motor.

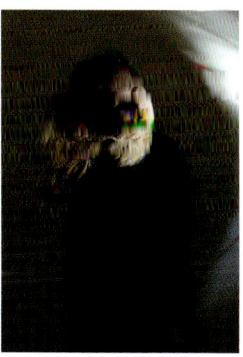 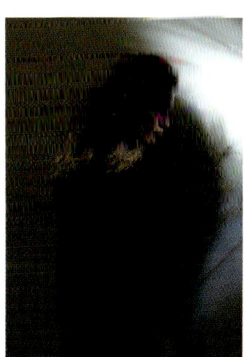 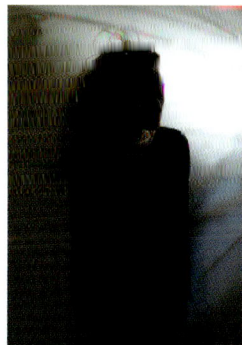

Figure 9.19 I needed to shoot in bursts because every few shots were drastically underexposed if a fan blade happened to be passing in front of the light.

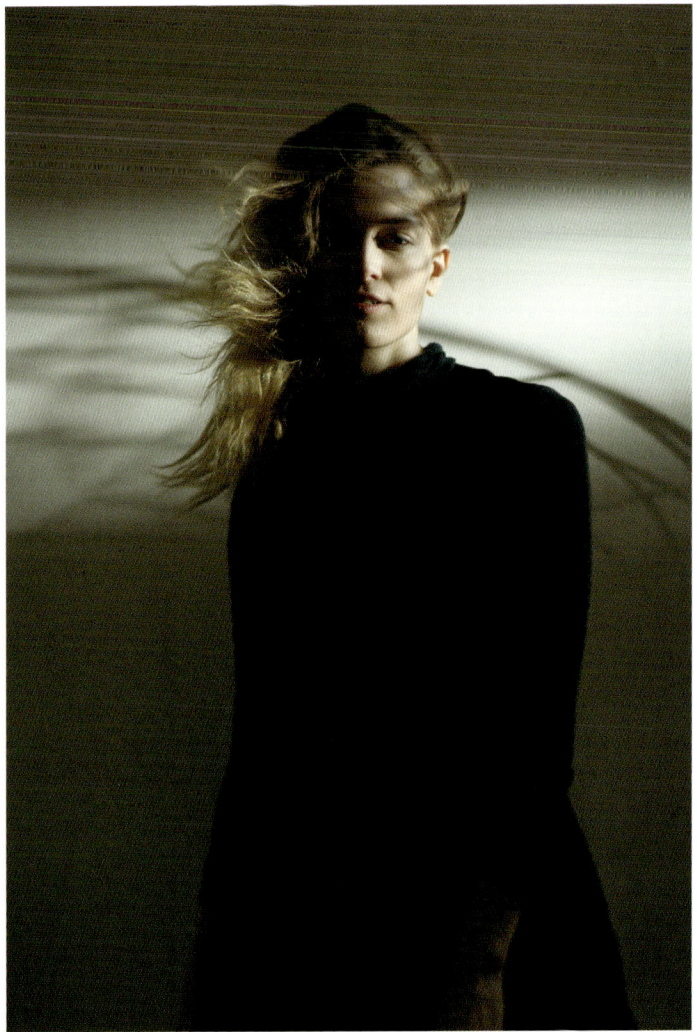

Figure 9.20 The raw file. Having a hair fan built into my gobo made for some rad shots.

Because my light was sitting on the fan's motor, meaning it was right up next to the gobo, the shadows were a bit softer. I also zoomed in the flash to 105mm to ensure that the only light reaching the model had to go through the fan to get there (**Figure 9.21**). Basically, I didn't want a broad spread lighting the whole wall around her. In Lightroom (**Figure 9.22**), I hardly did a thing. Because the light was already so dramatic, if I did anything more than just bump the Contrast setting, the shadows got muddy and the highlights blew out. But as is often said, less is more, more or less.

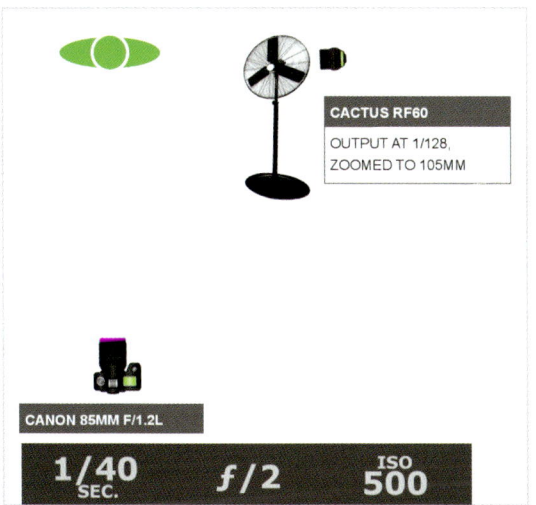

Figure 9.21 The lighting diagram. I also zoomed in the flash to 105mm to keep the light narrow and dramatic.

CACTUS RF60

OUTPUT AT 1/128, ZOOMED TO 105MM

CANON 85MM F/1.2L

1/40 SEC.   f/2   ISO 500

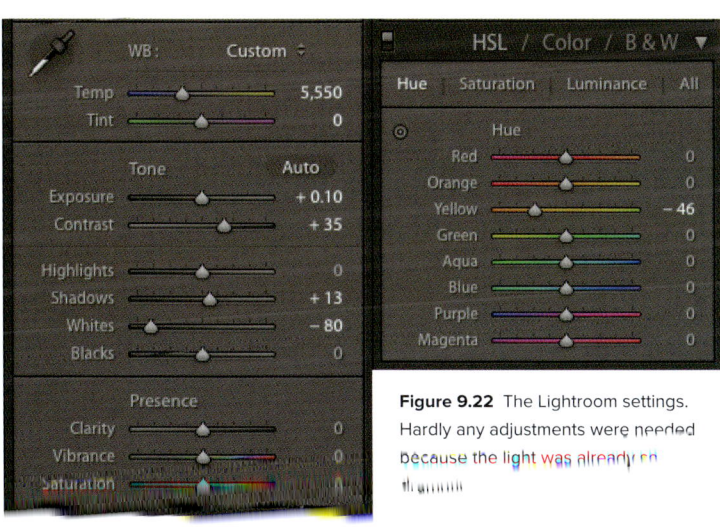

Figure 9.22 The Lightroom settings. Hardly any adjustments were needed because the light was already so dramatic.

I definitely want to experiment some more with fan gobos. I feel like there is a lot more that could be done with them. And having dramatic hair and fabric movement built in is an amazing feature. I guess you could say that I'm a big fan of what this gobo can do (**Figure 9.23**).

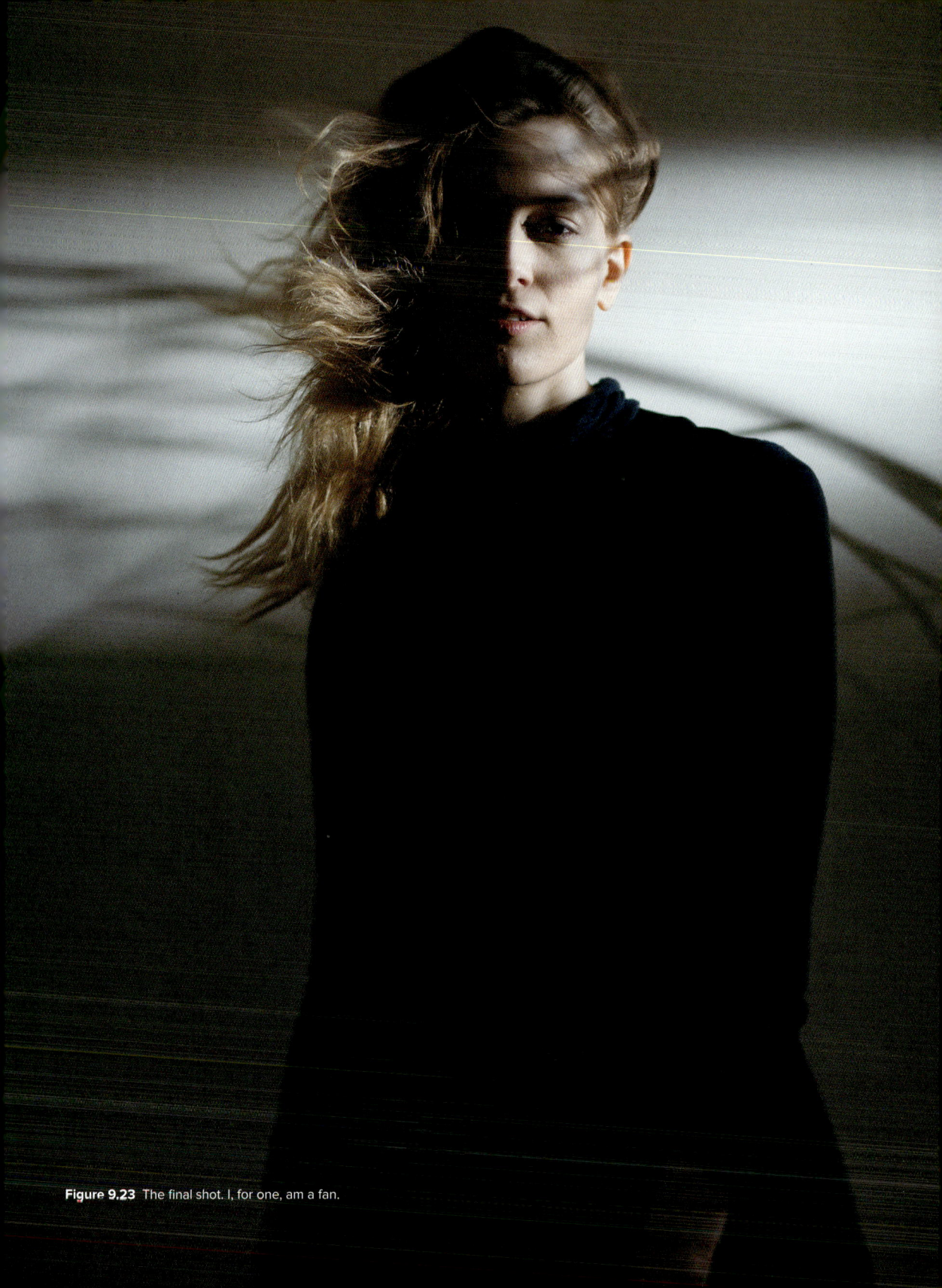

Figure 9.23 The final shot. I, for one, am a fan.

Let me set the scene: It's February in Ohio, which means it's below freezing, cloudy, and icy as hell outside. Perfect time to shoot a travel-themed magazine editorial, no? But that's what the editor of *614 Magazine* was asking for, so that's what I planned on delivering. My options were to shoot in the Franklin Park Conservatory or fake it. I went with the latter.

For some reason I thought of Kanye West's "Bound 2" video, where he and Kim (and then later James Franco and Seth Rogen) are dramatically lit on a prop motorcycle, obviously on some sort of movie set or sound stage in front of a very fake backdrop. Although I generally loathe West's music, I actually loved that video. I loved the disjointed feeling of the scene. It was obviously fake but wasn't trying to hide it. It felt kind of like Old Hollywood, in a way. There is also a fantastic scene in *Pulp Fiction* in which Bruce Willis is talking to a cab driver after a boxing match; the scene seen through the windows is obviously not real, but that complements the scene, adding a detached, surreal vibe. This is what I wanted to bring to the photo shoot.

Still set on finding an indoor setting that could pass as a vacation spot, the stylist chatted with the editor about Columbus's limited options. I chimed in with my idea to shoot in an empty hallway at the magazine office—not what they expected to hear, but eventually they went with it. I then asked the stylist if she could track down a projector for the shoot. Meanwhile, I hopped on Google and searched for a number of exotic scenes. I made sure to use only royalty free images, and I searched for higher resolution files.

The day of the shoot, the stylist brought a janky old projector that she had dug up. This thing was so fidgety that if you unplugged it to move it, it wouldn't turn back on for 15 minutes. It also projected a pretty dim image—the overhead office lights were overpowering the projected image (yeah, that dim). I needed to find a dark hallway, away from the lights.

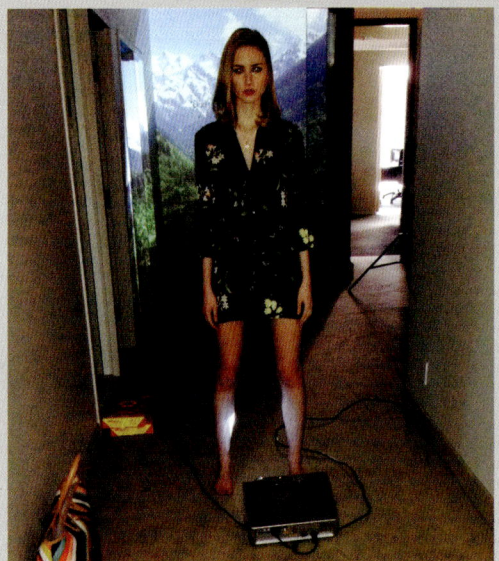

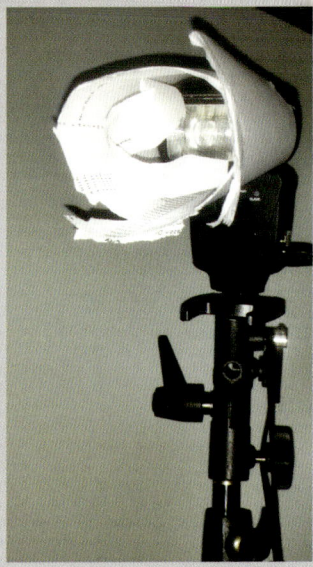

Figure 9.24 The setup. The model is standing over the projector that is displaying the mountain backdrop on the wall behind her. The main light, not pictured, is just out of the frame to the right.

Figure 9.25 The main light. I made a snoot out of printer paper, cutting slits in the edge of the paper with scissors in order to feather the light falloff.

Now that I had a working projector (more or less), images of exotic back-grounds, and a dark, empty hallway to shoot in, I was ready to light a model (**Figure 9.24**). Then I ran into another issue: The wall at the end of the hall was really narrow. I wanted the projected backdrop to go out of focus a bit, so that it looked more real. The long lens that I had with me was a 70–200 f/4L IS. Because the aperture couldn't open up more than f/4, the background was looking too sharp. This meant that to push the background out of focus in camera, I'd need to have the model as far in front of it as possible and then use a longer focal length (which brings lens compression into effect). All that is to say that I was using every inch of the hallway's length. My back was against a wall and Halle, the wonderful model, was standing as close to the background as she could, without blocking the light from the projector—which is why she is standing over it.

Now that the background was ready, it was time to actually light the model. As you may have guessed, my light output needed to be very low so as not to overpower the dim projection. Accordingly, I powered my flashlight all the way down to 1/128, but it was still too bright. I was also getting some light spill from the flash onto the projected background. A snoot would take care of both of these issues. I grabbed some printer paper, taped one side to the top of the flash head, wrapped the paper around to make a tube, and taped the other side. I also made several cuts into the paper in order to feather the light a bit (**Figure 9.25**).

Remember when I said that the projector was dim? It was so dim that my ISO was at 400 and my shutter speed was at 1/10 in order to get a proper exposure (I was really hating my f/4 lens that day). **Figure 9.26** shows the lighting diagram. After all those obstacles had been successfully hurdled, the images looked just how I had hoped. In fact, they almost looked believable (**Figure 9.27**).

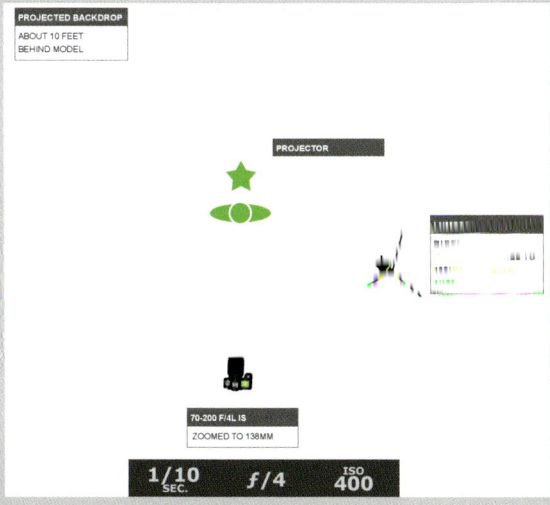

Figure 9.26 The lighting diagram. Because the projector was so dim, I needed to open up my ambient, resulting in an ISO of 400 and a shutter speed of 1/10.

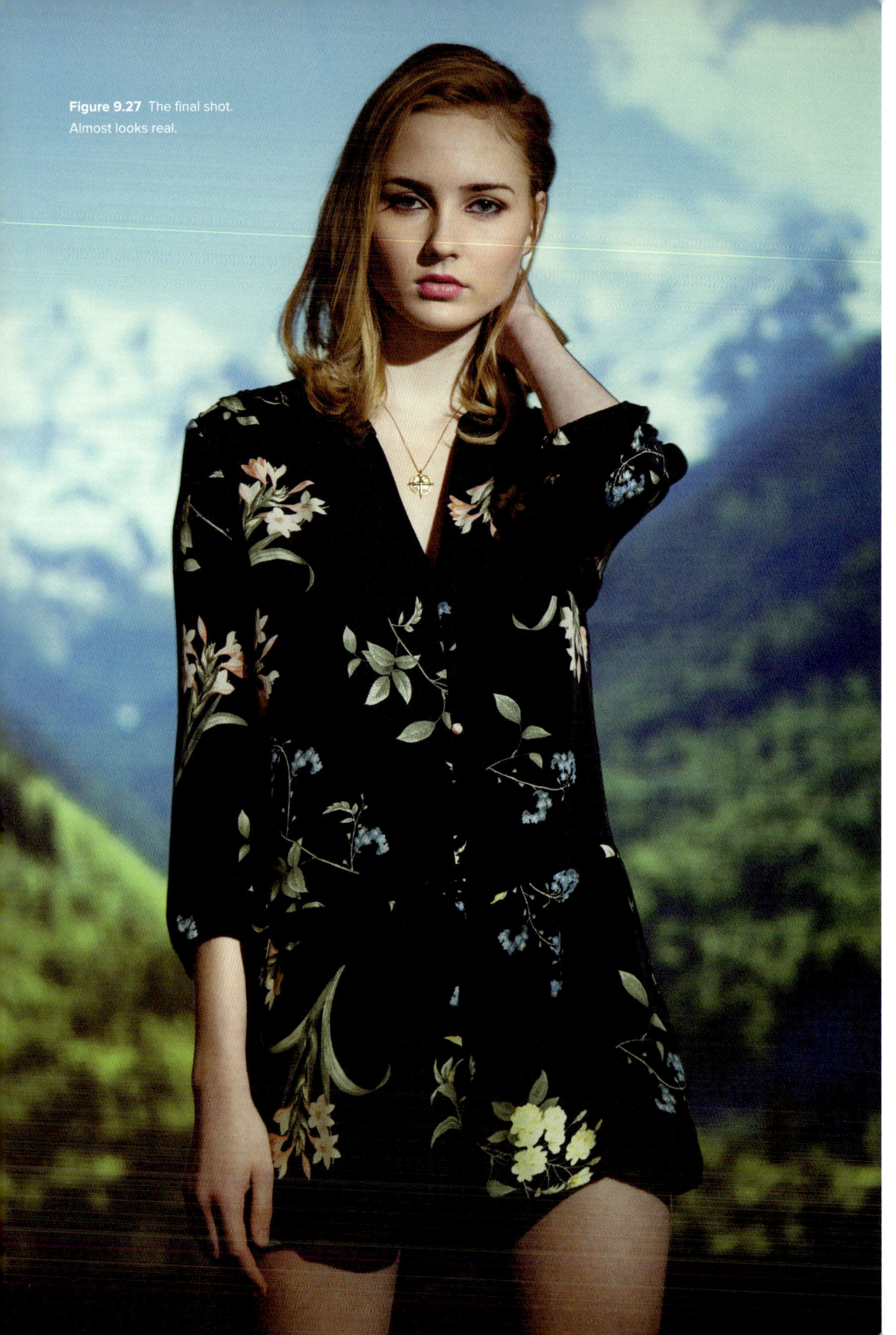

Figure 9.27 The final shot. Almost looks real.

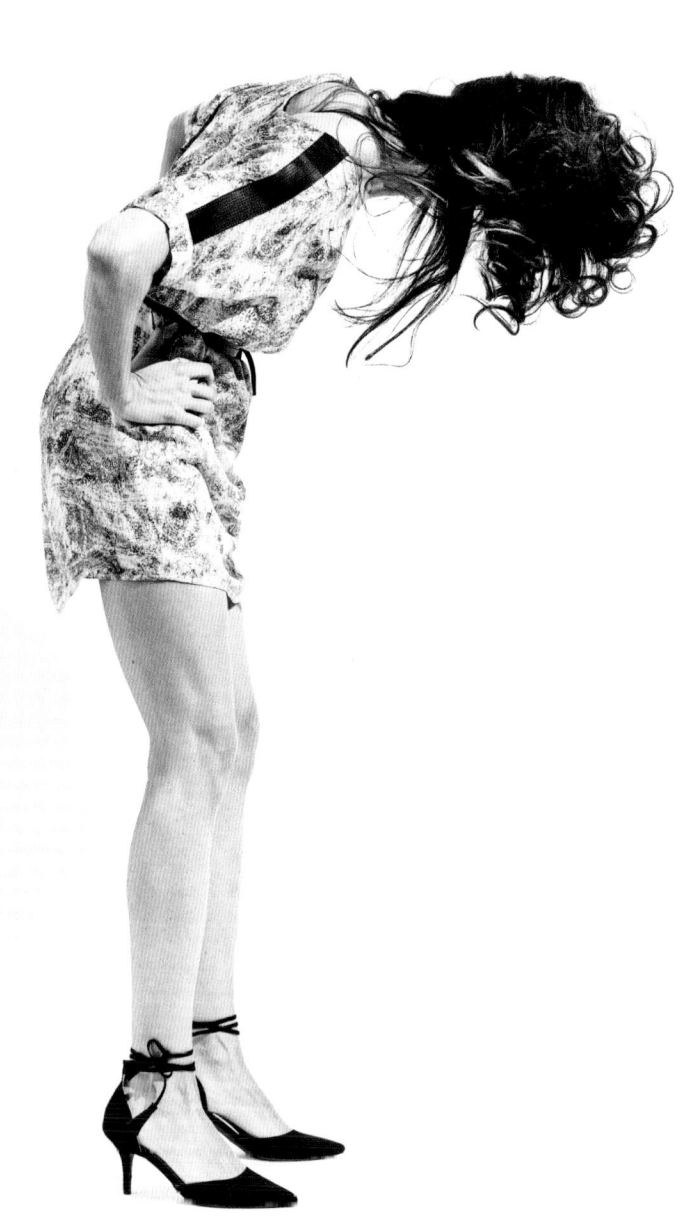

EPILOGUE

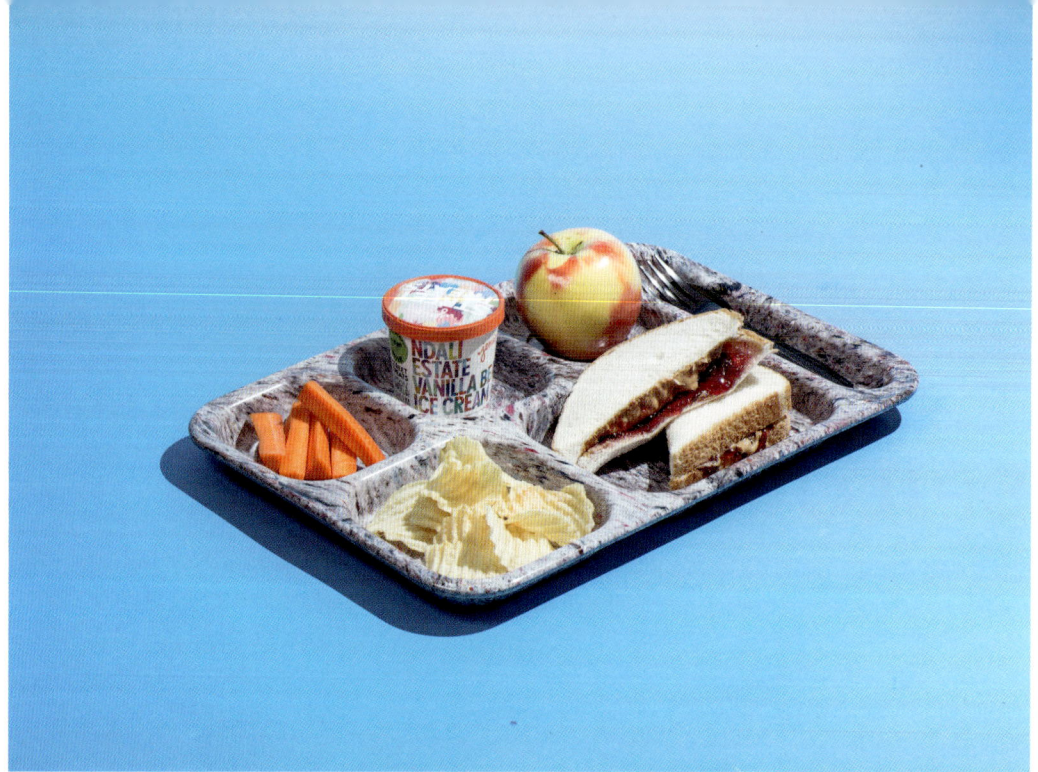

WHAT NOW?

Now that hard light is no longer your enemy, consider how you can integrate it into your everyday use. Hard light actually plays well with others, so consider mixing it in with softer light. And I don't just mean unmodified accent lights, either. Consider overlapping a hard, main light with soft light placed right beside it, as seen above. The hard light creates crisp shadow lines, adding clarity to the image, while the soft light fills in the shadows a bit, adding a subtle warmth, giving the photo accessibility. It brings an excitement to the image that you can't quite put your finger on—something that couldn't be accomplished with a single hard or soft light source.

And while we're on the subject of overlapping light, what would happen if you not only blended hard and light sources, but also gelled them? That's what I did in the image on the opposite page. The main light was gelled cyan and fired through a softbox, while two hard lights, gelled magenta and yellow, were placed to the model's right. Where they overlap, you get neutral light, thanks to our friend, additive color theory. My favorite part, however, is where they don't overlap, and pockets of color remain.

So have fun with your exploration, and share your experiments with me!

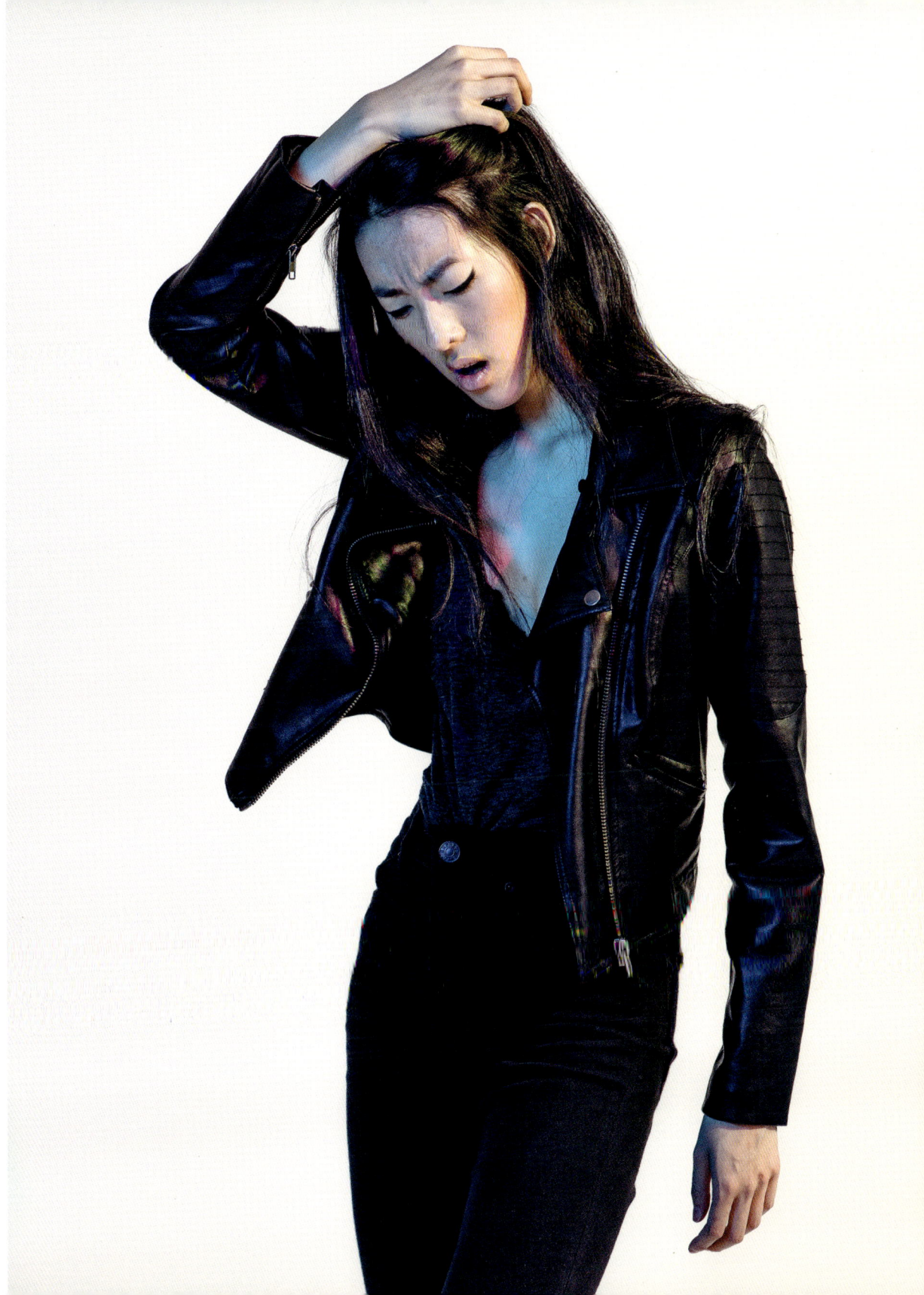

MAKING A SCENE: ANSWERS

My hope is that the techniques that we've worked through in this book have begun to get you thinking about light in a new, well, light. With your new skills of shaping, manipulating, and all-around hacking light, I hope that you can see potential in literally any scenario you encounter. These "Making a Scene" exercises have been meant to jumpstart your new way of viewing potential shoot spots. Your new skills are not unlike those of a trained special agent, one who sizes up any room they enter, immediately recognizing all possible exits and any objects that could be used as a weapon.

Now that you've sized up the scenes from earlier in the book, let me show you how I decided to execute them.

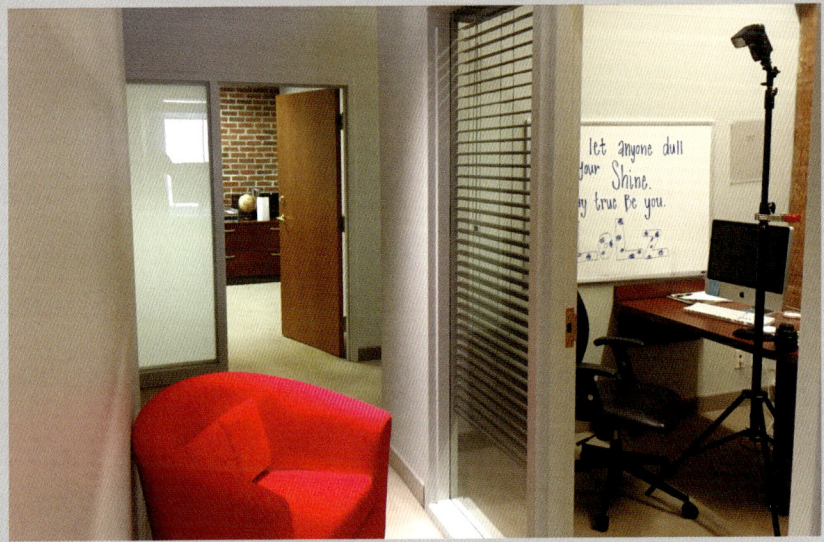

The setup for S.1

My client was *614 Magazine* and my assignment was to take a portrait of *Orange Is the New Black* author Piper Kerman. (If you're unfamiliar with the book, it's Kerman's memoir of her year in prison for money laundering.) Piper was to be photographed at the magazine's office, which I was familiar with. I immediately knew that I wanted to use window blinds as a gobo to make dramatic shadows reminiscent of prison bars. When I arrived at the office, I set up my light several feet behind the blinds in order to have more defined shadows. I found a red chair for her to sit in, thinking that I could shift the red to orange in Lightroom, as a subtle nod to the book (and the hit TV series based on it).

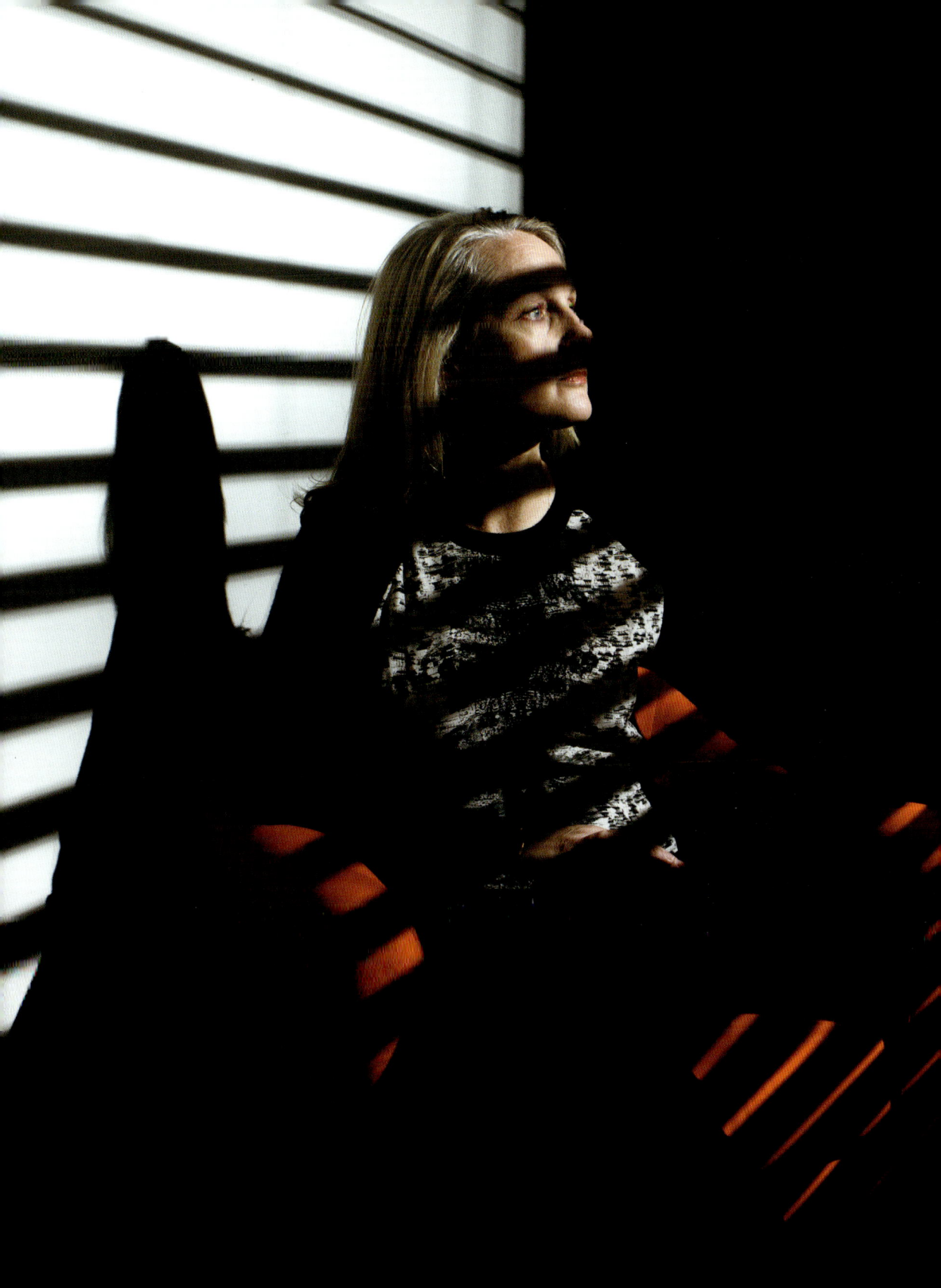

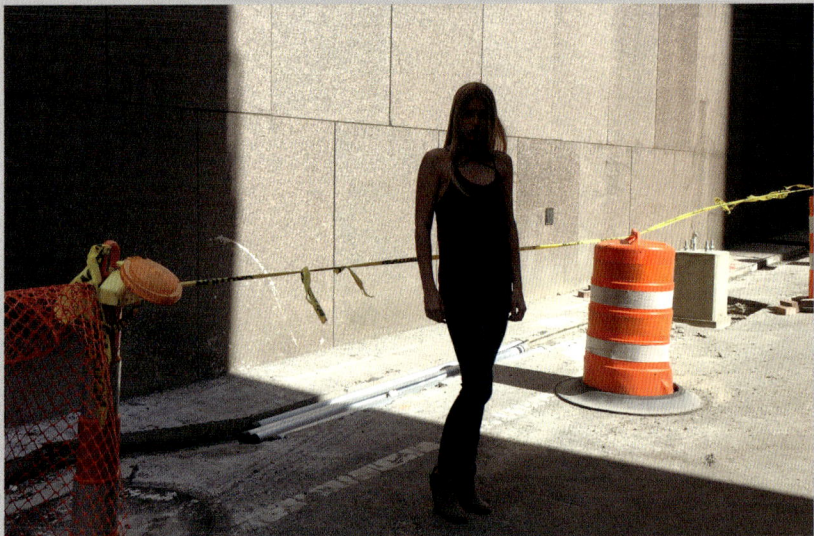

The setup for S.2

In order to get a pure white background without using a single light, you need to find a spot of shade on a bright, sunny day. If you place the subject in the shade and expose for the person's face, the background will blow out white, as long as the background is several stops brighter than the shaded area. The one thing that you need to be aware of is the busyness of the background. I was using a plain building façade, which easily went white. Had there been trees or cars in the shot, they wouldn't have blown out so easily.

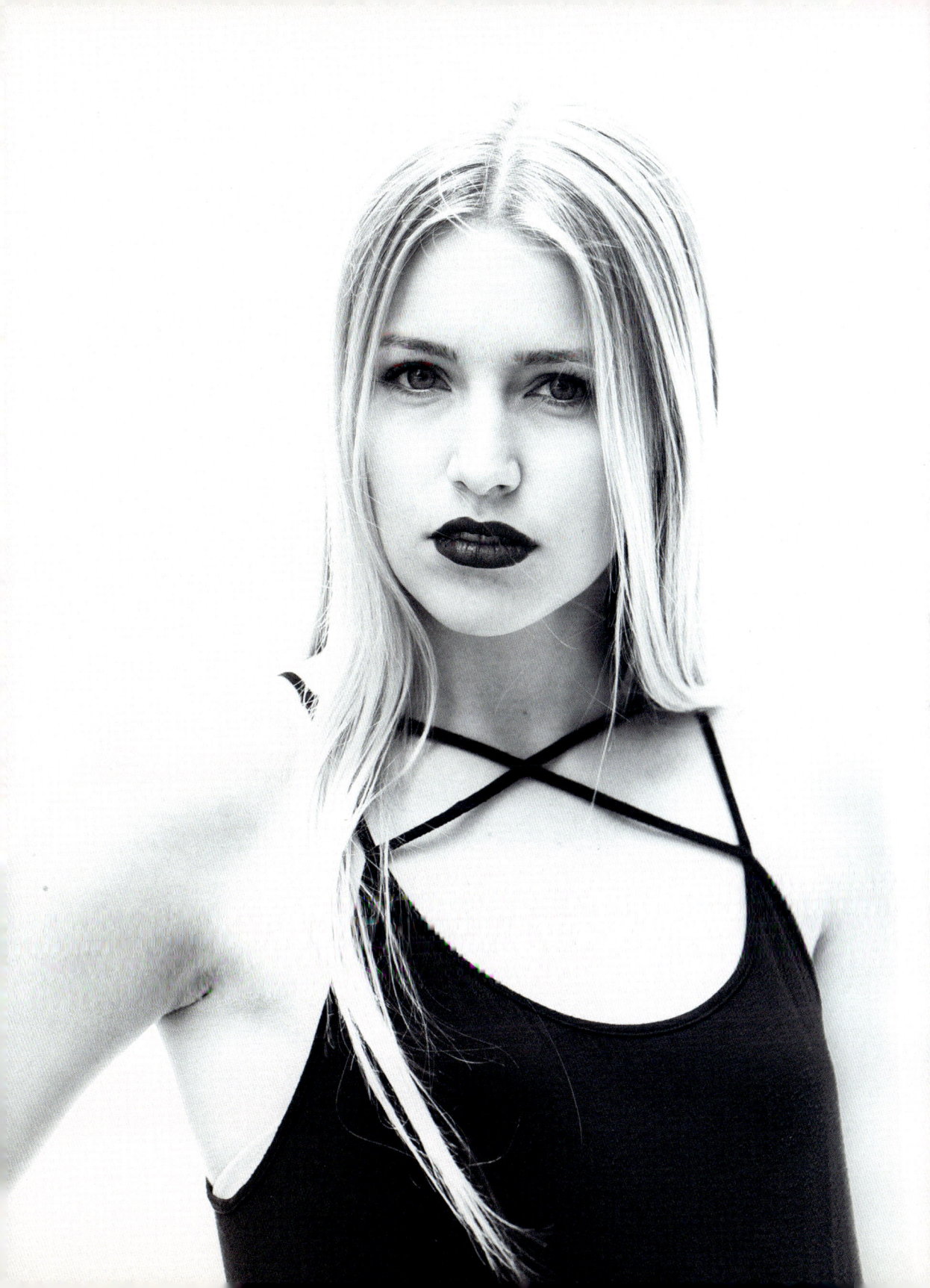

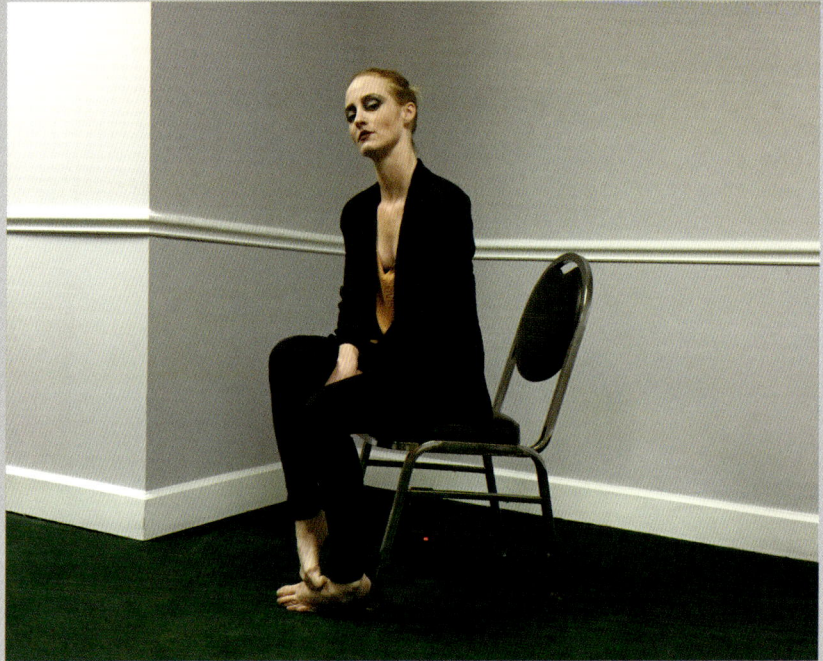

The setup for S.3

Achieving an airy portrait on a pure white background is actually easier than you may realize. As you can see in the setup shot above, I placed my subject about three feet in front of the intersection of two light grey walls. I placed my sole flash next to the back of her chair, aiming at a spot on the wall behind her shoulders. I set the output to 1/4 power and opened my aperture to f/2, at ISO 160. The light bounced off the walls and nine-foot ceiling, wrapping around her. In Lightroom, I utilized the Dehaze feature to reduce the glow on her black jacket.

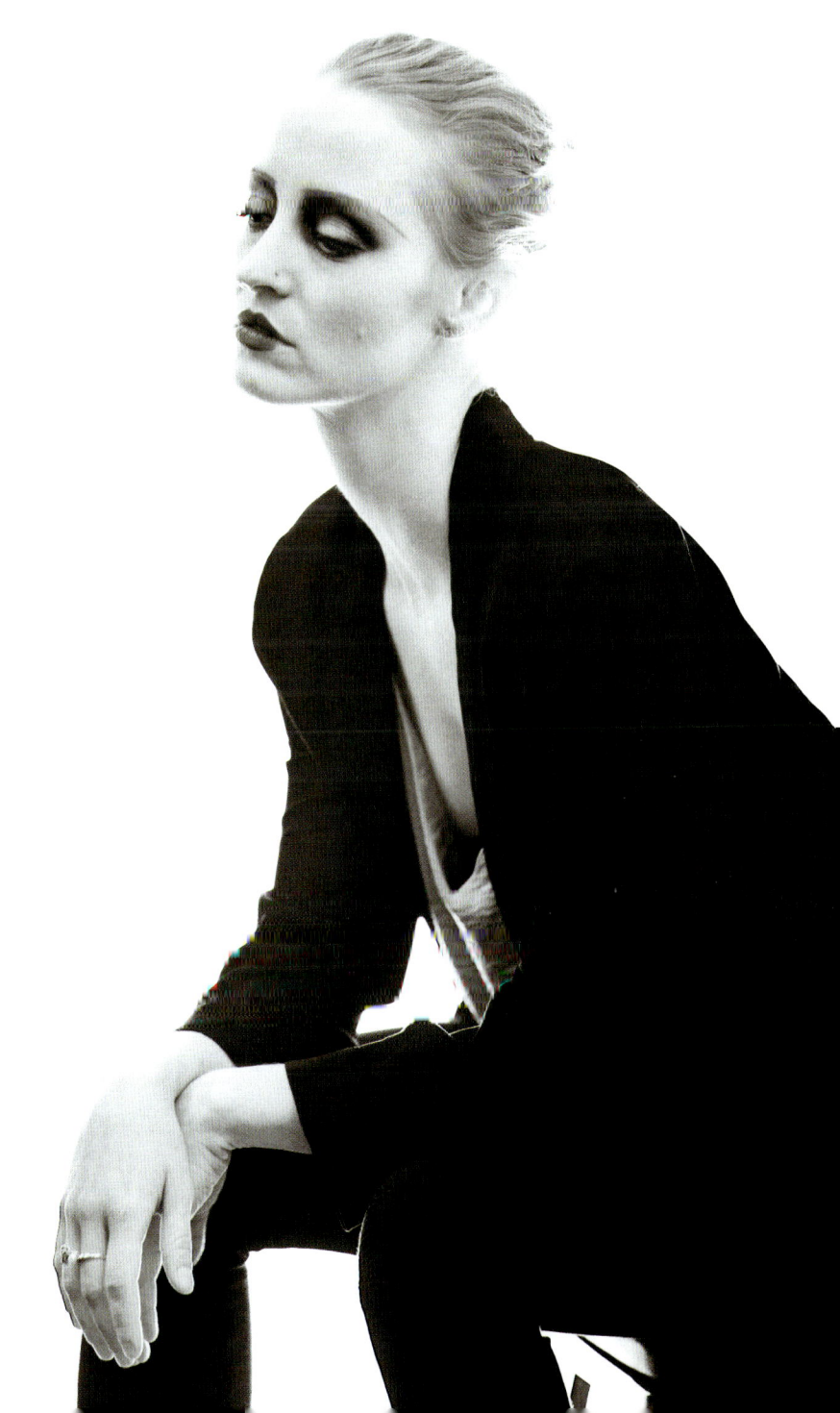

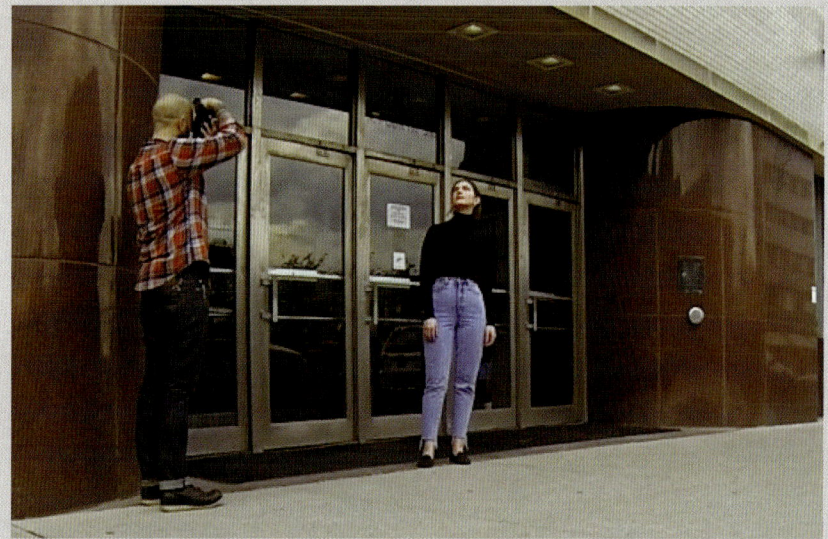

The setup for S.4

Just as you can get an available light portrait on a white background, you can also get an available light portrait on a black background fairly easily. You just need to reverse the setup from the second scenario (S.2) we discussed. Find a spot of shade on a sunny day and place your subject in the sun. As long as the sunny area is several stops brighter than the shaded area, the background should pretty easily go to black. Note that photographing a person who is lit by harsh sunlight can be unflattering if not done right. Rather than trying to eliminate shadow, try to place the shadow on your subject in a flattering way. Also, by converting your image to black and white in post, you can hide a multitude of sins.

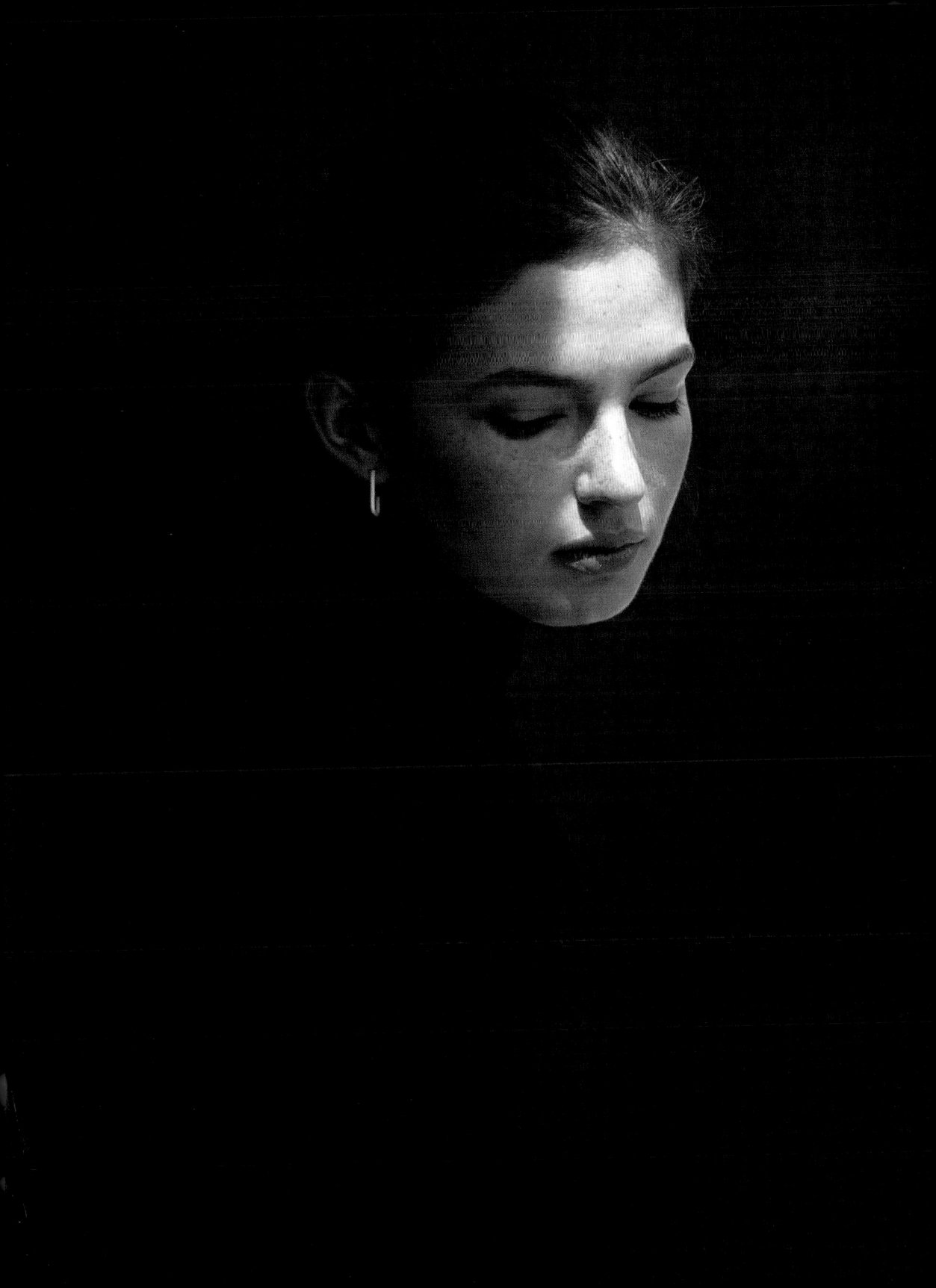

#studioanywhere

INDEX